Praise for Barbara Schenck

"Barbara Schenck's *Small Business Marketing For Dummies* threads the needle between sky-high strategy and ground-level tactics — the space every small business owner experiences daily and sometimes hourly. Most importantly, Barbara isn't afraid to drive stakes in the ground with business ratios, average costs, and response rates that deliver practical value at both levels. The book is organized and concise, allowing headstrong entrepreneurs to cheerfully ignore her "How to Use This Book" advice. For those venturing into e-commerce, Chapter 19 is worth the price of the book."

> — Gene Kincaid, Instructor, Department of Advertising, University of Texas at Austin

"Barbara's effervescent, can-do spirit permeates this book, which is like a 4-year degree in marketing packaged by a person who has been there, done that. Her understandable and realistically actionable advice gives you the street smart steps to do the right things."

> — Bob Boylan, Executive Presentation Consultant and Author, President/Owner of Successful Presentations

"Go ahead, clear your shelf of all other marketing books. From now on you only need one and this is it! The accuracy and detail of this concise volume is remarkable. This book reads like your getting the real scoop from a trusted friend only this friend is a knowledgeable marketing pro. Give it to your marketing people and ad agency; they could use it as well."

> — Robert L. Newhart II, CEO, Oregon Innovation Center

"It's fun to read Barbara Schenck. But more than fun, it's enlightening to read Barbara Schenck. It's profitable as well to read Barbara Schenck. That's a lot to pack into 384 pages. But it's all there; if you don't believe me, just read it!"

> — Dan Lufkin, Co-founder, Donaldson, Lufkin & Jenrette, Inc.

"Business is the war. The book gives entrepreneurs the ammunition they need to survive — and thrive."

> — Riva Lesonsky, *Entrepreneur Magazine*

™

BESTSELLING BOOK SERIES

References for the Rest of Us!®

Do you find that traditional reference books are overloaded with technical details and advice you'll never use? Do you postpone important life decisions because you just don't want to deal with them? Then our *For Dummies*® business and general reference book series is for you.

For Dummies business and general reference books are written for those frustrated and hard-working souls who know they aren't dumb, but find that the myriad of personal and business issues and the accompanying horror stories make them feel helpless. *For Dummies* books use a lighthearted approach, a down-to-earth style, and even cartoons and humorous icons to dispel fears and build confidence. Lighthearted but not lightweight, these books are perfect survival guides to solve your everyday personal and business problems.

> *"More than a publishing phenomenon, 'Dummies' is a sign of the times."*
>
> — The New York Times

> *"...you won't go wrong buying them."*
>
> — Walter Mossberg, Wall Street Journal, on For Dummies books

> *"A world of detailed and authoritative information is packed into them..."*
>
> — U.S. News and World Report

Already, millions of satisfied readers agree. They have made For Dummies the #1 introductory level computer book series and a best-selling business book series. They have written asking for more. So, if you're looking for the best and easiest way to learn about business and other general reference topics, look to For Dummies to give you a helping hand.

Hungry Minds™

Small Business Marketing

FOR DUMMIES®

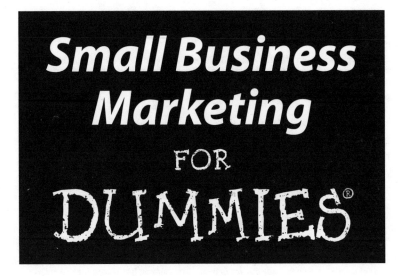

Small Business Marketing

FOR

DUMMIES®

by Barbara Findlay Schenck
with Linda English

Hungry Minds™

HUNGRY MINDS, INC.

New York, NY ◆ Cleveland, OH ◆ Indianapolis, IN

Small Business Marketing For Dummies®

Published by:
Hungry Minds, Inc.
909 Third Avenue
New York, NY 10022

Library of Congress Control Number: 00-111131

ISBN: 0-7645-5309-7

Printed in the United States of America

10 9 8 7 6 5 4 3 2 1

1O/QS/QU/QR/IN

Distributed in the United States by Hungry Minds, Inc.

Distributed by CDG Books Canada Inc. for Canada; by Transworld Publishers Limited in the United Kingdom; by IDG Norge Books for Norway; by IDG Sweden Books for Sweden; by IDG Books Australia Publishing Corporation Pty. Ltd. for Australia and New Zealand; by TransQuest Publishers Pte Ltd. for Singapore, Malaysia, Thailand, Indonesia, and Hong Kong; by Gotop Information Inc. for Taiwan; by ICG Muse, Inc. for Japan; by Intersoft for South Africa; by Eyrolles for France; by International Thomson Publishing for Germany, Austria and Switzerland; by Distribuidora Cuspide for Argentina; by LR International for Brazil; by Galileo Libros for Chile; by Ediciones ZETA S.C.R. Ltda. for Peru; by WS Computer Publishing Corporation, Inc., for the Philippines; by Contemporanea de Ediciones for Venezuela; by Express Computer Distributors for the Caribbean and West Indies; by Micronesia Media Distributor, Inc. for Micronesia; by Chips Computadoras S.A. de C.V. for Mexico; by Editorial Norma de Panama S.A. for Panama; by American Bookshops for Finland.

For general information on Hungry Minds' products and services please contact our Customer Care department; within the U.S. at 800-762-2974, outside the U.S. at 317-572-3993 or fax 317-572-4002.

For sales inquiries and resellers information, including discounts, premium and bulk quantity sales and foreign language translations please contact our Customer Care department at 800-434-3422, fax 317-572-4002 or write to Hungry Minds, Inc., Attn: Customer Care department, 10475 Crosspoint Boulevard, Indianapolis, IN 46256.

For information on licensing foreign or domestic rights, please contact our Sub-Rights Customer Care department at 212-884-5000.

For information on using Hungry Minds' products and services in the classroom or for ordering examination copies, please contact our Educational Sales department at 800-434-2086 or fax 317-572-4005.

Please contact our Public Relations department at 212-884-5163 for press review copies or 212-884-5000 for author interviews and other publicity information or fax 212-884-5400.

For authorization to photocopy items for corporate, personal, or educational use, please contact Copyright Clearance Center, 222 Rosewood Drive, Danvers, MA 01923, or fax 978-750-4470.

Hungry Minds˜ is a trademark of Hungry Minds, Inc.

About the Author

Barbara Findlay Schenck has marketed universities, international jewelers, high-tech manufacturers, major financial institutions, sole-proprietor retail shops, and every kind of business in between. For more than 20 years she's formed her thoughts into headlines, news releases, and marketing plans.

Her career started in the public relations office of the University of Oregon and then led to Honolulu where she became director of admissions and instructor of writing at what she calls the world's most scenic small college. Later she joined the staff of Hawaii's largest public relations firm.

In 1978, she and her husband, Peter, packed up their communications skills and left Hawaii for a village on the South China Sea where for two years they worked with the Peace Corps in Malaysia.

In 1980, they returned to their home state of Oregon and founded an advertising and marketing firm that grew to be one of the top agencies in the Pacific Northwest. With clients that included small businesses, ski and golf resorts, community banks, major apparel and equipment manufacturers, as well as the state's tourism division and lottery, the agency provided a wealth of hands-on experience profiled in this book.

Running the firm also provided a firsthand look at how quickly the marketing environment is changing and how important the online world is becoming to marketing success.

To provide this book with the necessary focus on the future of the Internet as a marketing tool, Barbara called on the talents of **Linda English** to contribute her unrivaled expertise for the online marketing chapters of this book. Linda is a Microsoft veteran whose career has taken her around the world with the Microsoft organization, earning titles that include International Program Manager, European Training Channel and Marketing Manager, and Managing Web Site Editor. Today she guides the online marketing efforts of businesses large and small through her company, Net Ingredients, www.netingredients.com.

Barbara also keeps her finger on today's business pulse by providing marketing consultation, seminars, and advice to entrepreneurs and small business marketers. For information, you can contact her at BFSchenck@aol.com.

Author's Acknowledgments

In order of their Herculean assistance, I thank:

My collaborator, editor, mentor, partner, friend, and husband Peter, and our son Matthew, whose computer expertise was invaluable to this effort and whose college updates and insights kept us laughing even when deadlines weren't very funny.

Linda English, for her second-to-none knowledge of online marketing, her interest in helping small businesses succeed, and her ability to reel in the talents of other online gurus, especially those of her business partner, Joel McNamara.

My longtime and treasured business associates and friends Kathy DeGree, who never saw a marketing book she didn't want to buy and whose library was a priceless and always-available resource; and Meaghan Ryan Houska, who never saw a marketing document she didn't choose to save and whose archives saved me more hours than I can begin to count.

I am indebted to the resources of our hometown newspaper, *The Bulletin,* and its editor-in-chief John Costa; to Bob Newhart of the Oregon Innovation Center, who served ably as the technical editor of this book; to Jeanne Boylan, who introduced me to the world of publishing when she invited me to co-write her book *Portraits of Guilt;* and to the experiences gained through professional associations with a lifetime's worth of the best clients and friends a marketer could wish for.

I am immeasurably grateful to Jim Schell, who introduced me to the blue-ribbon ...*For Dummies* author Eric Tyson, who introduced me to the team at Hungry Minds, Inc., beginning with Senior Acquisitions Editor Mark Butler, who introduced me to Vice President and Publisher Kathy Welton, through whom I was fortunate enough to meet Senior Acquisitions Editor Holly McGuire, Acquisitions Editor Jill Alexander, Acquisitions Coordinators Jennifer Emrich and Ann Wildman, and Editors Norm Crampton and Tina Sims — an editorial team that would make any author wish for an encore performance.

Finally, I thank my sisters and my parents, Walt and Julie Findlay, for their daily progress inquiries and never-failing support. Words are insufficient for the gratitude they deserve.

Publisher's Acknowledgments

We're proud of this book; please send us your comments through our Online Registration Form located at www.dummies.com.

Some of the people who helped bring this book to market include the following:

Acquisitions, Editorial, and Media Development

Project Editor: Norm Crampton

Acquisitions Editor: Holly McGuire

Copy Editor: Tina Sims

Acquisitions Coordinator: Ann Wildman

Technical Editor: Robert Newhart II

Editorial Manager: Pamela Mourouzis

Editorial Assistant: Carol Strickland

Cover Photos: © 1997 Telegraph Colour Library/ FPG International LLC

Production

Project Coordinators: Leslie Alvarez, Jennifer Bingham

Layout and Graphics: Amy Adrian, LeAndra Johnson, Jeremey Unger

Proofreaders: Andy Hollandbeck, Angel Perez, York Production Services, Inc.

Indexer: York Production Services, Inc.

General and Administrative

Hungry Minds, Inc.: John Kilcullen, CEO; Bill Barry, President and COO; John Ball, Executive VP, Operations & Administration; John Harris, CFO

Hungry Minds Consumer Reference Group

   Business: Kathleen A. Welton, Vice President and Publisher; Kevin Thornton, Acquisitions Manager

   Cooking/Gardening: Jennifer Feldman, Associate Vice President and Publisher

   Education/Reference: Diane Graves Steele, Vice President and Publisher; Greg Tubach, Publishing Director

   Lifestyles: Kathleen Nebenhaus, Vice President and Publisher; Tracy Boggier, Managing Editor

   Pets: Dominique De Vito, Associate Vice President and Publisher; Tracy Boggier, Managing Editor

   Travel: Michael Spring, Vice President and Publisher; Suzanne Jannetta, Editorial Director; Brice Gosnell, Managing Editor

Hungry Minds Consumer Editorial Services: Kathleen Nebenhaus, Vice President and Publisher; Kristin A. Cocks, Editorial Director; Cindy Kitchel, Editorial Director

Hungry Minds Consumer Production: Debbie Stailey, Production Director

◆

The publisher would like to give special thanks to Patrick J. McGovern, without whom this book would not have been possible.

◆

Contents at a Glance

Cartoons at a Glance

By Rich Tennant

"Okay, so maybe the Internet wasn't the best place to advertise a product that helped computer illiterate people."

page 315

"So-what the heck are you selling?"

page 5

"Right here...,crimeorg.com. It says the well run small criminal concern should have no more than nine goons, six henchmen and four stooges. Right now, I think we're goon heavy."

page 247

"Bad news- Buddy flipped the van spilling 8 crates of samples into rush hour traffic. Good news- the van flipped logo side up."

page 79

"Listen up- I brought in a consultant to help figure this thing out. Old MacDonald, these are the boys. Boys, say hello to Old MacDonald."

page 141

Cartoon Information:
Fax: 978-546-7747
E-Mail: richtennant@the5thwave.com
World Wide Web: www.the5thwave.com

Table of Contents

Introduction

As a small business today, you have lots of company — and *lots* of competition.

The 21st century presents a world where new businesses are sprouting up faster than new customers. According to U.S. Small Business Administration statistics, there are now well over five *million* small businesses with fewer than 20 employees in America, and by all indications the growth spurt is by no means over.

The success stories — and you must want to be among them or you wouldn't be holding this book — come from those businesses whose leaders know how to grab onto marketing as the lifeline to business success.

Whether you're running a single-person home office, a small firm, or even a local nonprofit organization, to succeed in today's changing and competitive marketplace, you *have* to know everything you possibly can about winning and keeping customers.

And that's exactly what *Small Business Marketing For Dummies* is all about.

How to Know That This Book Is for You

Do the words *marketing, advertising,* and *sales* seem interchangeable? Are the concepts of e-commerce and Web marketing foreign and confusing? Do you feel too busy running your small business to concentrate on marketing? Do you wish some marketing guru would step in and help you?

If you answered yes to any of these questions, then you're holding the right book. *Small Business Marketing For Dummies* is especially for businesses like yours that operate without the benefit — or the expense — of a high-powered marketing vice president, an award-winning ad agency, or even a staff person dedicated full-time to the task of managing the ad program.

Every example and every piece of advice is directed to the small businessperson who wears all the hats — and who markets in whatever time is left.

If that person sounds a lot like you, keep reading!

How to Use This Book

If you fit the small business leader mold, you're more than a little strapped for time. You have a company to manage, customers to serve, product issues to address, and a lineup of deadlines and decisions looming. You need quick answers, rapid-fire advice, and street-smart solutions that you can put to work immediately.

If you only have minutes to spare, hit the Table of Contents or Index and dart straight to the pages that hold the advice you need at the moment.

But if you can (please, allow a moment for lobbying here), your business will benefit if you read this book from cover to cover. If you start at Chapter 1 and end at Chapter 22, this book can walk with you through the full marketing process and help you tailor a complete marketing program for your own unique business.

By using the tables, charts, and examples, you can analyze your marketing needs and take all the steps involved to target your marketing, create your marketing messages, and produce and place your ads and other communications. For the cover price of this book, you can get what big businesses pay big dollars for: a self-tailored marketing "consultation."

How This Book Is Organized

Each section of *Small Business Marketing For Dummies* tackles a different aspect of your marketing program, helping you to brainstorm new possibilities as it assists you in making marketing decisions. From marketing terms to marketing plans to the nitty-gritty how-to's of putting your marketing message into ads and promotions — even getting your message onto the Internet — you find it all shoehorned into the pages of this book.

Part 1: Getting Started in Marketing

This first section begins with the obvious: a plain-language definition of the term "marketing" followed by explanations of the various marketing tools that you can use to get your message into exactly the right marketplace for your business. From there it goes through an assessment of your marketing situation to help you make decisions about your program, including how to analyze your product or service, your sales, your customers, and your competitors. Then it describes the differences between marketing goals and objectives before leading you step-by-step through the goal-setting process that can shape your business future.

Part II: Sharpening Your Marketing Focus

The second section helps you take an unbiased look at your company's marketing. It starts by guiding you through an "impression audit" to help uncover the gaps that may exist between what people believe about your business and what you think or wish they believed. Then it looks at what you've been saying (or not saying) to lead to misperceptions. With all that in mind, it steers you through the process of defining your company's position and brand — including explanations of what those terms mean. Finally, it offers advice on when and how to bring in advertising agencies and freelance professionals to help you implement your marketing programs.

Part III: Getting the Word Out

This part takes you on a guided tour of the advertising world, complete with a quick-reference guide to mass media and the language of advertising, how-to's for creating and evaluating ads and sales literature, and step-by-step instructions for establishing your advertising, direct mail, and publicity game plans.

Part IV: Marketing Online

This part is dedicated entirely to the newest and most mysterious component of small business marketing programs: the Internet. In four fact-packed chapters, you find information to help you decide whether you need a Web site, how to build a site, how to drive traffic to your site once it's up and running, and — most important — tips and advice for competing in the burgeoning new cyberworld.

If you're up against the clock or into shortcuts, you're going to want to race straight to Parts III and IV so you can start getting your marketing message out immediately. Your business will be on a stronger track, though, if you can first carve out some time to spend on Parts I and II, which focus on the make-it-or-break-it topics of what your ads should say — and to whom.

Part V: The Part of Tens

Each chapter in this final part contains our Top Ten thoughts on issues that you're bound to face in your marketing future. Chapter 20 leads you through the questions to ask yourself before coming up with a company name. Chapter 21 focuses on how to keep customers satisfied and devoted. And Chapter 22 gives you a ten-step plan for assembling a marketing plan.

Icons Used in This Book

Marketing is full of logos, seals of approval, and official stamps. So in keeping with marketing tradition, throughout this book you find symbols that spotlight important points, shortcuts, and warnings. As you use this book, watch for these icons:

The Golden Rules for small business marketing are highlighted by this icon. Write them down, etch them in your memory, frame them on your wall. Just try not to forget them.

Remember the line "don't tell me, show me"? When this icon pops up in the margin, you find an example that shows you what the surrounding text is talking about.

Not every idea is a good idea. This icon alerts you to situations that deserve your cautious evaluation. Consider it a flashing yellow light.

The bull's-eye marks tried and true approaches for stretching budgets, short-cutting processes, and seizing opportunities.

It's not all Greek, but marketing certainly has its own jargon. When things get a little technical, this icon appears to help you through the translation.

Ready, Set, Go!

The role of marketing is to attract and maintain enough satisfied customers to keep your business not just *in* business, but on an upward curve. And that's what this book is all about.

Part I
Getting Started in Marketing

In this part . . .

Whether you're running a multimillion-dollar enterprise, a do-it-yourself sole proprietorship, a professional practice, a retail establishment, or a nonprofit fundraising effort, Part I helps you focus on the plain-and-simple marketing issues that you need to address.

The chapters in this part don't just describe what is involved in the marketing process — by taking you on your own marketing-fact-finding mission and helping you analyze your customer, your product or service, and your competition, they show you why marketing is your make-it-or-break-it business linchpin. If you're in business, you're a marketer: Part I gets you directed so that you can do your job well!

Chapter 1

A Helicopter View of the Marketing Process

*Y*ou're by no means alone if you don't have a pat answer to the question "What is marketing, anyway?" If you pick up the phone and call any number of marketing professors, marketing vice presidents, or marketing experts and ask them to define "marketing," odds are you won't get the same answer twice.

In fact, if you look the word up in any number of different dictionaries, you'll find an equal number of different explanations. So it's time to settle the matter right now with some plain talk descriptions:

- ✔ Marketing is the process through which you create — and keep — customers.

- ✔ Marketing is the matchmaker between what your business is selling and what your customers are buying.

- ✔ Marketing covers all the steps that are involved to tailor your products, messages, distribution, customer service, and all other business actions to meet the desires of your most important business asset: your customer.

- ✔ Marketing is a win-win partnership between your business and its market.

Marketing isn't about talking *to* your customers; it's about talking *with* your customers. Marketing relies on two-way communication between a seller and a buyer.

Marketing and Sales Are Not Synonymous Terms

Many businesses, especially many small businesses, confuse the terms "marketing" and "sales." They think that "marketing" is a high-powered or dressed-up way to say "sales." Or you'll hear them mesh the two words together into a single solution that they call "marketing and sales." But selling is not a substitute for marketing, even though the sales function is one of the ways you communicate your marketing message.

Sales is the point at which the product is offered, the case is made, the purchasing decision occurs, and the business-to-customer exchange takes place. Selling is an important part of the marketing process — but it is not and never can be a replacement for the marketing process.

Getting the Big Picture

Marketing is a continuous cycle. It begins with customer knowledge and cycles round to customer service before it begins all over again. It involves product development, pricing, packaging, distribution, and communication of the marketing message, including the steps involved with making the sale.

If you could get an aerial view of the marketing process, it would look like Figure 1-1. Every successful marketing program — whether it is for a billion-dollar business or for a hardworking individual — follows this same marketing cycle. Follow this "wheel of fortune" to go around the cycle, starting at the top and circling clockwise.

As you loop around the marketing wheel, here are the steps you encounter:

1. **You get to know your target customer and your marketing environment.**

2. **You tailor your product, pricing, packaging, and distribution strategies to meet the customer, market, and competitive realities of your business.**

3. **You use your customer and product knowledge to create and project marketing messages that will grab attention, inspire interest, and move your customer to action.**

4. **You go for the sale — but still you're not done.**

5. **Once the sale is made, marketing moves into the customer service phase, where your business works to ensure customer satisfaction so that you can convert the sale into an opportunity for repeat business and word-of-mouth advertising for your business.**

And so the marketing process goes round and round.

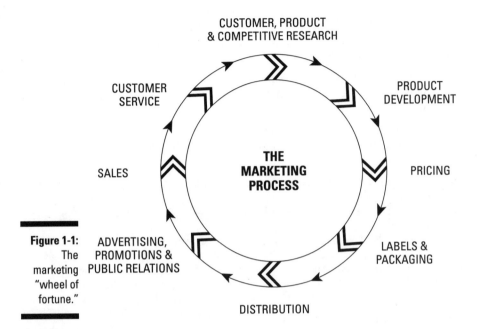

CUSTOMER, PRODUCT
& COMPETITIVE RESEARCH

CUSTOMER
SERVICE

PRODUCT
DEVELOPMENT

**THE
MARKETING
PROCESS**

SALES

PRICING

Figure 1-1:
The
marketing
"wheel of
fortune."

ADVERTISING,
PROMOTIONS &
PUBLIC RELATIONS

LABELS &
PACKAGING

DISTRIBUTION

In marketing, there are no shortcuts. To build a successful business, you can't just jump to the sale, or even to the advertising stage, of the marketing process.

The role of marketing

Without customers, a business is out of business. It sounds pretty obvious, doesn't it?

Yet how many times have you heard small business people say that they just don't have time to market? The follow-up to that statement is easy: Make time.

Think of it this way. If marketing is the process through which a business creates and keeps customers, then marketing is the difference between "business" and "out-of." Put in terms like that, marketing is the single most important process in any business — including yours.

Measuring your marketing strength

To determine whether your marketing is strong, quickly score yourself to see whether you think your business rates well in the following areas:

   ✔ You and those who help run your company have a complete understanding of the products and services that you offer.

- You have knowledge of the competition you face.

- You are aware of and responsive to the threats and opportunities that exist in your business world.

- You have a clear description of who your potential customer is, and what it will take to make that person — who can choose not to buy — willing to buy from you.

- You think not in terms of making the sale, but rather in terms of developing mutually beneficial long-term relationships with your customers.

Marketing: The whole is greater than the parts

Advertising. Marketing. Sales. Promotions. What are the differences? See if this memorable example that has circulated the marketing world for decades doesn't help draw some clearer lines:

- If the circus is coming to town and you paint a sign saying "Circus Coming to the Fairground Saturday," that's *advertising*.

- If you put the sign on the back of an elephant and walk it into town, that's *promotion*.

- If the elephant walks through the mayor's flower bed, that's *publicity*.

- And if you get the mayor to laugh about it, that's *public relations*.

- If the town's citizens go to the circus and you show them the many entertainment booths, explain how much fun they'll have spending money at the booths, and answer questions, and, ultimately, if they spend a lot of money at the circus, that's *sales*.

Add it up, and you have a memorable delineation of what's what in the field of marketing communications.

But because marketing includes communications and much more, we invented a finish to the circus story to show how sales, research, product development, and the rest of the components of the full marketing process might fit in. Here's how it goes:

- If, before painting the sign that says "Circus Coming to the Fairground Saturday," you check community calendars to see whether conflicting events are scheduled and you study who typically attends the circus and you figure out how much they're willing to pay and what kinds of services and activities they prefer, that's *market research*.

- If you invent elephant ears for people to eat while they're waiting for elephant rides, that's *product development*.

- If you create an offer that combines a circus ticket, an elephant ear, an elephant ride, and a memory-book elephant photo, that's *packaging*.

- If you get a local restaurant named Elephants to sell your elephant package, that's *distribution*.

- If you ask everyone who took an elephant ride to participate in a survey, that's *customer research*.

- If you follow up by sending each survey participant a thank-you note along with a two-for-one coupon to next year's circus, that's *customer service*.

- And if you use the survey responses to develop new products, revise pricing, and enhance distribution, then you've started the *marketing process* all over again.

Don't try to rate the success of your marketing based on your sales figures alone.

A business can rack up strong sales in a single quarter or year, but if it hasn't planned and priced its products correctly, or if it hasn't put in place ways to retain customers and to win their repeat purchases and word-of-mouth endorsements, then its marketing is weak even though the sales figures — at least for the time being — are strong.

Small Business Marketing Is Definitely Different

Not all marketing programs are created equal. All marketing programs need to follow the same marketing process, but the similarities between big business and small business marketing stop there. Budgets, staffing, approaches, and techniques vary hugely between an international mega-marketer like, say, Coca-Cola and a comparatively micro-budget marketer like, well, like you.

This book is for *you*. Here's why.

Dollar differences

As a small business, you already know one difference between your marketing program and those of the corporate behemoths that loom over you in all directions. The big guys have the big budgets. They talk about a couple hundred thousand dollars as a discretionary line item issue. You talk about a couple hundred dollars (forget the thousands in that figure) as a request worthy of careful consideration. The advice in this book is scaled to your budget, not to the million-dollar jackpots you see referenced in most other marketing books.

Staffing differences

Look at the organization chart for any major corporation. Nearly always you find a marketing vice president. Under that position you see a bank of professionals, including advertising directors, sales managers, online marketing managers, research directors, customer service specialists, and more. In contrast, strong small businesses blend marketing with the leadership function. The small business organization chart puts responsibility for marketing in the very top box, where the owner oversees the process as a hands-on task and essential role.

Creative differences

The top-name marketers routinely spend six figures to create ads with the primary goal of building name recognition and market preference for their brands — usually without a single word about a specific product or price. They spend their money projecting messages aimed at achieving market awareness, with the belief that sales will naturally follow.

Small businesses take a dramatically different approach. They strive for ads that can inspire measurable and immediate market action. They want the phone, the doorbell, or the cash register to ring — *now*. You know firsthand that every single small business advertisement has to do some pretty heavy lifting. Each effort has to stir enough purchasing action to offset the cost of the ad in the first place. The trick, discussed in Part III of this book, is to create consistency in your ads so that they inspire the necessary customer action while also advancing a clear brand message for your business.

Strategic differences

In big businesses, bound copies of business plans grace every bookshelf, whereas in many small businesses, the very term "marketing plan" provokes a guilt pang. If you just felt the typical reaction, turn to Chapter 22 for the antidote. It provides an outline for putting your plan in writing — without any mysterious jargon and with advice and examples scaled specifically to small businesses like yours.

Truth is, creating a marketing plan is pretty straightforward and a reasonably manageable process. It's one of those pay-a-little-now-or-pay-way-more-later propositions. If you invest a bit of time up front to plan your annual marketing program, then implementation of the plan becomes the easy part. But without a plan, you'll spend the year racing around in response to competitive actions, market conditions, and media opportunities that may or may not fit your business needs.

The small business marketing advantage

As a small business owner, you may envy the dollars, people, and organizations of your big-business counterparts, but you have some advantages they envy as well.

The heads of Fortune 500 firms allocate budgets equal to the gross national products of small third-world countries to fund research to get to know and understand their customers. Meanwhile, you can talk with your customers face to face, day after day, at virtually no additional cost at all.

Because the whole point of marketing is to build and maintain customer relationships, it stands to reason that no business is better configured to excel at the marketing task than the very small business. To take advantage of this small-business edge in the area of customer relations, see Chapter 2.

Realistic Talk about Small Business Marketing Budgets

You'll never hear successful companies say, "We'll see how much money is available, and then we'll spend it on advertising." They dedicate funds in advance because they know that without good marketing there won't be any money left over!

The most important commitment you can make to your marketing program is to establish a budget and then stick to it. What does "commitment" mean? In this case, it has four parts:

- ✔ Establishing a marketing budget
- ✔ Spending the funds on a planned marketing program
- ✔ Viewing the allocation as an important business investment
- ✔ Managing the program well

When a business cuts back on marketing, it puts itself on a dangerous downhill slide. Sure, you recoup some money at the time of the budget cut, but following that one-time savings, look at what happens. With less money for marketing, you can place fewer advertisements. With fewer advertisements, your sales decline. Declining sales reduce your overall revenues, which means you have even less money to allocate for future marketing.

Not spending your full marketing budget is every bit as dangerous to your business as spending way too much. Think long and hard before trimming costs out of your marketing budget, which is the one expense item designated specifically to the effort of attracting and keeping customers.

How much should you be spending?

You can follow a number of paths to arrive at your marketing budget. You can go with the flow and do what others do, using surveys as a guide. For example, one industry survey finds that businesses that market primarily to other businesses spend an average of 3.49 percent of their revenues on marketing. Other studies say that businesses that market to the general public tend to spend closer to 8 to 10 percent.

You also can choose from methods like these to find out how much to budget for marketing:

- ✔ **The arbitrary method:** Think of this as best-guess budgeting. The budget is based on intuition and experience, often using the past year's budget as a benchmark.

✔ **Competitive parity:** This could be called "budgeting to keep up with the Joneses." The budget is based on awareness of how much your competitors are spending and how your business compares in terms of size and strength. In other words, if your volume is even with that of a particular competitor, then your budget should be at least even as well.

✔ **Goal-oriented budgeting:** This is a "spend what's necessary" approach. It involves a serious look at what you expect your business to accomplish over the upcoming year and what level of marketing is necessary to accomplish the task. It is based on a calculation of the costs involved to implement a marketing program capable of achieving your business goals.

✔ **Percentage of sales budgeting:** Another name for this could be "name the magic number." Under this model, a business forecasts its next year's sales and allocates a percentage of those sales to marketing. Though this is the most frequently cited means of establishing a budget, it is problematic because the percentages that businesses allocate to marketing vary from 1 percent to, believe it or not, 50 percent — depending on the industry, the product or service, the competitive arena, and the cost of media in the particular market area.

There is no one-size-fits-all formula for setting your marketing budget. To demonstrate the far-flung range of amounts that companies spend on their marketing budgets, look at Table 1-1, which presents findings compiled by *Inc.* magazine following a survey of 346 companies.

Table 1-1	Marketing Expenditures
Percentage of Sales Spent on Marketing	*Percentage of Responses by 346 of the "Inc. 500" Companies*
Less than 1%	3%
1–5%	43%
6–10%	25%
11–20%	18%
21–50%	9%
More than 50%	1%

Budgeting considerations

As you consider how much your business should allocate for marketing, consider the following:

✔ **The nature of your business and your market:** Businesses that market to other businesses — such as attorneys and accountants — tend to allocate a lower percentage of sales to marketing than businesses that market to the public-at-large. It's the proverbial rifle versus shotgun difference. The business-to-business marketer can set its site and reach its customers through direct sales efforts, while the business-to-consumer marketer must cover a wider range, usually involving more costly investments in mass media advertising.

✔ **The size of your market area:** A business that serves customers who are primarily located within a short drive or walk from the business location — a neighborhood coffee shop or a locals-only fitness center, for example — can target all of its marketing into a concise market area. As a result, it can probably allocate a lower percentage of its sales to marketing than would be the case if the business had to purchase ads in statewide, national, or even international media to reach its market.

✔ **Your competition:** Another important budgeting consideration has to do with your competitive situation. If you've been the only game in town and you find out that several competitors are about to open their doors, you have to invest in a ramped-up marketing program if you intend to defend your business. Or if you've been the underdog and you want to take on the leaders, you have to spend accordingly.

✔ **Your objective and task:** The most important consideration in setting your budget is to understand what you want to accomplish with your marketing. Look at your sales and profit goals. The more aggressive they are, the more you need to budget. For example, if you're planning to launch a new product or open a new location, you need to increase your marketing efforts to gain the awareness, interest, and action, and to fund the training, marketing support, and additional advertising required to meet your business objective.

Can you afford to hire professional help?

When advertising agencies first came into being, they sold their services in return for 15 percent of a company's advertising budget. The 15 percent figure happened to be the amount that newspapers, magazines, and broadcast media offered as a commission to agencies that provided the media with ready-to-use ad materials. As an example, if an agency placed a $1,000 ad for a company, the media let the agency keep $150 — or 15% — as the agency commission. The agency then used the $150 to cover the cost of its effort on behalf of the client.

Today businesses communicate their marketing messages in so many forms in addition to media advertising that agencies can't perform under such a set formula. And especially for businesses with small ad budgets, the 15 percent doesn't amount to enough to attract the attention of outside professionals.

Still, 15 percent of your marketing budget is a good place to start as you try to decide whether your budget is big enough to cover the cost of outside professional assistance. Table 1-2 lists businesses with sales ranging from $100,000 to $2 million. The middle column shows what the marketing budget would be if the business allocated 5 to 10 percent of sales to the marketing process. The third column shows how much would be available to hire outside help if the business limited the expense to 15 percent of the marketing budget.

Table 1-2	Should You Bring in Marketing Pros?	
Sales	*Marketing Allocation (5–10% of Sales)*	*Professional Services Allocation (15% of Marketing Allocation)*
$100,000	$5,000–$10,000	$750–$1,500
$200,000	$10,000–$20,000	$1,500–$3,000
$500,000	$25,000–$50,000	$3,750–$47,500
$1,000,000	$50,000–$100,000	$7,500–$15,000
$1,500,000	$75,000–$150,000	$11,250–$22,500
$2,000,000	$100,000–$200,000	$15,000–$30,000

Before you bring in the pros, be sure that you can afford the service. Professionals charge upwards from $50 an hour, depending on whether you are hiring freelance design services or marketing consultation and advice. Here are a few more practical guidelines on the marketing budget:

- ✔ Companies with billings under $500,000 should probably limit their purchase of outside talent to on-call copywriting and design services.

- ✔ Companies with sales of over a million dollars may be wise to invest in an annual consultation by a marketing professional.

- ✔ As the marketing budget nears the $100,000 to $200,000 levels, consider retaining a small advertising agency — large enough to offer the quality services you need but small enough to consider your business important — to help leverage the dollars through strong creative messages and targeted media purchases.

Chapter 9 can help you when you're ready to consider an advertising agency or consultant. In the meantime, let the information in the following chapters guide your thinking as you plan, implement, and manage a marketing program that can move your business to the next level.

Chapter 2

All about Customers: Your Reason for Being

*E*very small business owner mulls the same questions: Who are my customers? How did they hear about me? Why do they buy from me? How can I find more customers just like them?

Successful businesses use the answers to these questions to influence every product design, pricing, distribution, and communication decision they make.

✔ If your business is going great guns, use this chapter to create a profile of your best customers so that you can attract more just like them.

✔ If your business feels busy but your sales and profits are weak, this chapter can help you differentiate between the customers who are costing you time and money and the customers who are making you money. Once you know the difference between the two, you can direct your marketing efforts toward getting more of the moneymakers.

✔ If your business is loping along — or worse, sliding downhill — you need to get and keep more customers, period. That means knowing everything you can about who is buying products or services like the ones you're selling and what it will take to make those people buy from you.

Business owners don't work for themselves; they work for their customers.

This chapter places your perspective on the only boss that really matters in business: that person over there with an open billfold.

Looking at the Anatomy of a Customer

An important part of knowing your customer is differentiating who's who among your clientele. It's called *market segmentation* — the process of breaking your customers down into segments that share distinct similarities.

First, you need to understand the lingo. Here are some common market segmentation terms and what they mean:

- **Geographics:** Segmenting customers by regions, counties, states, countries, zip codes, and census tracts.

- **Demographics:** Segmenting customers into groups based on such aspects as age, sex, race, religion, education, marital status, income, and household size.

- **Psychographics:** Segmenting customers by lifestyle characteristics, behavioral patterns, beliefs and values, and attitudes about themselves, their families, and society.

- **Geodemographics:** Also called *cluster marketing* or *lifestyle marketing*. Geodemographics is based on the age-old idea that birds of a feather flock together — that people who live in the same area tend to have similar backgrounds and consuming patterns. Geodemographics describes the most prevalent kind of consumer in certain geographic areas by combining demographic information such as age and income; life stage information such as whether the residents of the area are young and single, married with kids, early retirees, and so forth; and customer buying behaviors. It is considered the holistic approach to market segmentation in that it combines geographic, demographic, and psychographic information to identify groups of potential consumers.

Collecting information about your customer

Target marketing starts with customer knowledge. Learn everything you possibly can about the person who currently buys from you; then you can direct your marketing efforts toward others who match the same profile. People with the profile of your customer are apt to become customers as well.

Do-it-yourself fact-finding

You can get a good start on conducting customer research without ever walking out the front door of your business.

✔ **Review addresses from shipping labels and invoices and group them into areas of geographic concentration.** For example, you can group customers into those living within a certain number of miles of your business, customers living within various regions of your state and within neighboring states, and so on.

✔ **Follow the data trail from credit card transactions to see where customers live.**

✔ **Request zip code information at the beginning of cash register transactions.**

✔ **Survey customers.** If your business generates substantial foot traffic, find places where customers naturally pause and be there to conduct formal or informal research — depending on your business environment. Whether you survey all customers or limit your effort to every *n*th customer (every tenth customer, for example), keep the question period short and keep a log of the answers. Spread your interviews over a span of time so that your findings reflect responses from customers during various days and weeks. (Obviously, you don't want to end up with results based only on customers who visit your business at noon on Thursdays!)

A cardinal sin in small business is to treat a long-standing customer like a stranger to your business. As you interview customers, instead of asking "Is this your first visit?" try to get at the answer indirectly, as shown in these examples:

- The front desk staff can ask, "Have you been here since we moved the reception area?"

- Hotel clerks can ask, "Have you stayed with us since we started our evening wine reception?"

- Savvy restaurateurs don't have to ask at all. They know that if a customer asks for directions to the restroom, that person is likely to be a first-time patron. On the other hand, a waiter who over-hears a customer recommending a certain menu item to a table-mate can assume that the patron is a repeat guest.

The important thing is to find ways to treat your loyalists like the very important business insiders they are.

✔ **Observe your customers.** What kinds of cars do they drive? How long do they spend during each visit to your business? Do they arrive by themselves or with friends or family members? Do those who arrive alone account for more sales or fewer sales than those who arrive accompanied by others? Where do they pause or stop in your business? Your observations may lead to product decisions, as shown in these examples:

- A small theme park may find that most visitors stay for two hours and 15 minutes, which is long enough to want something to eat or drink. This could lead to the decision to open a park café or restaurant.

- A retailer may realize that women who shop with other women spend more time and money in the store, which may lead to a promotion offering a special lunch for two on certain days of the week.

- A motel may decide to post a restaurant display at a hallway entry where guests consistently pause.

✔ **Use contests to collect information.** Create a postcard-sized survey and use it as a contest entry form. For the cost of a nice prize, you'll collect information that will help you develop your customer profile.

✔ **Monitor the origin of incoming phone calls.** When prospects call for information about your business, find out where they're from and how they found you.

Callers will tolerate only a certain number of questions. Remember that they're calling to *receive* information, not to become research subjects.

- If you use a caller identification phone feature, use it to collect the incoming phone number prefix and area code, which will enable you to create an incoming call geographic origin report.

- Many phone service providers can provide lists of incoming phone area codes or dialing prefixes for your reference.

✔ **Track response to ads and direct mailers.** Include an offer for a brochure, a product sample, or some other incentive to inspire a reaction to your ads. As prospects respond, collect their addresses and other information to build an inquiry profile.

Be sure to deliver the promised item promptly upon request so that the value of your research effort isn't offset by a bad impression generated by slow follow-through.

✔ **Study Web reports to learn about prospects who visit you online.** See Chapter 19 for information on how to mine this information.

Research methods

Consider the information in Table 2-1 as you make research decisions:

Table 2-1	Research Approaches		
Method	*Purpose*	*Advantages*	*Challenges*
Questionnaires and surveys	Obtain general information	Anonymous. Inexpensive. Easy to analyze. Easy to format and conduct.	Impersonal. Feedback may not be accurate. Wording can skew results.

Method	Purpose	Advantages	Challenges
Interviews	Obtain information and probe answers	Develops customer relationships. Adaptable to each situation. Accesses fuller range of information.	Time consuming. Reliant on good viewers. Difficult intern to analyze.
Observation	Document actual buyer behavior	Anonymous. Immediate findings. Relatively easy to implement.	Can be difficult to interpret findings. Can be difficult to target which behaviors to monitor. Can be expensive.
Documentation review	Study factual history of clients and transactions	Readily available. Not disruptive to operations. Not subject to interpretation.	Time-consuming. May be incomplete. Research is limited to previously collected data.
Focus groups	Learn about and compare customer experiences and reactions	Convey information to customers. Collect customer impressions.	Requires expert facilitation. Requires advance scheduling. Difficult to analyze findings.

When to call in the pros

Doing it yourself doesn't mean doing it all on your own. Here are places where a little bit of money invested in professional advice pays off:

- **Questionnaires:** Figure out what you want to learn and create a list of questions. Retain a trained marketer or market researcher to review the wording, sequence, and format for you. Then have an on-staff or freelance designer prepare the handout or mailer so that it makes a good visual impression on your business's behalf. Include a letter or introductory paragraph explaining why you're conducting research and presenting your business as a strong, forward-thinking organization that cares about its customers' opinions and experiences.

- **Phone or in-person surveys:** Employ an outside group to do the questioning on your behalf. When you ask the questions yourself, it's easy to let your biases, preconceptions, and business pressures leak through and sway your customers. Posing questions so that you don't skew the results is a real art. Plus, customers are more apt to be candid with third parties. (If you need proof, think of all the things people are willing to say behind someone's back that they'd never say to the person's face. The same premise applies in customer research.)

✔ **Focus groups:** If you're assembling a group of favorite clients to talk casually about a new product idea, you're fine to go it alone. But if you're trying to reveal helpful information from outsiders, or if you want to learn opinions about such delicate areas as customer service or pricing, use a professional facilitator who is experienced in managing group dynamics so that a single dominant participant doesn't steer the group outcome.

For outside help, contact research firms, advertising agencies, marketing firms, and public relations companies. Tell them what you're trying to accomplish and see whether they can either do the research for you or direct you toward the right resources.

Another great starting point is the business department of the nearest university or community college. Or see whether your region has a small-business development center, which is often part of your state's higher education system.

Geographics: Locating your market areas

The fact that you can be located in Rome, Georgia, and serve customers in Rome, Italy, doesn't necessarily make the Eternal City a target market for your business. To target your market geographically, you need to ask, "Where am I most likely to find potential customers, and where am I most apt to inspire enough sales to offset my marketing investment?" To help you answer these questions, here's some advice:

✔ **Start with the addresses of your existing customers.** Where you have a concentration of existing customers, you also have a concentration of *potential* customers. Those are the areas where you should direct your advertising efforts and money.

✔ **Follow your inquiries.** Inquiries are customers waiting to happen. They are consumers whose interest you've aroused and whose radar screens you have managed to pop onto, even though they haven't yet made the decision to purchase your product or service. The addresses of your inquiries will lead you to geographic areas where there is interest in the products and services you offer. Your first objective should be to convert that interest into a consumer action (see Chapter 10 for the process involved in converting consumer interest into consumer purchases). Even if you can't achieve an inquiry-to-customer conversion, follow up with the inquiries anyway. You may be able to find out why they *didn't* buy, and that information may help you retool your product, pricing, distribution, or communications for the future.

✔ **Locate your non-customers.** Identify people who have the attributes of your current customers but who don't yet buy from you. These are non-customers who are also *potential* customers. Here are some ways to find geographic areas where concentrations of these potential customers reside so you can target those places for market development:

- Start with a call to an advertising representative for one of the leading publications or broadcast outlets that serve your business. They conduct and purchase volumes of research, and often they will share information as a way to convince you of their ability to carry your marketing message to the right people. Ask them which areas have a concentration of people who fit your customer profile.

- Talk with your industry association representatives. Ask whether they can share copies of consumer profile reports compiled for your industry.

- Visit your college library reference desk. Study the *SRDS Lifestyle Market Analyst,* a rich source of market-by-market demographic and lifestyle information; and the *CACI Sourcebook of ZIP Code Demographics,* which details the population profiles of 150 U.S. zip codes and county areas. Through these resources, you can find and target the areas that have a concentration of customers with lifestyle interests ranging from sewing to golfing to crossword puzzles — and everything in between. Just ask and you'll be surprised how much good information is available about the geographic markets you serve. (See Appendix A for additional information about these and other resources.)

Each time you discover a geographic area with easy access to your business and with a concentration of residents who fit your buyer profile, you've uncovered an area that should be on your list of geographic target markets.

After you know where your markets are located, try to determine the kind of products that are of greatest interest in each market area. This information can help you target your product promotions.

A hotel owner may find that customers from a particular market area stay predominantly at the hotel for only one night at a time and usually only over weekends, while guests from another area tend to stay three nights and usually arrive mid-week.

Knowing this, the hotel may promote quick getaway offers, perhaps offering incentives to get guests to stay a second night. But the hotel wouldn't likely promote three-night stays, as that offer wouldn't fit the proven interests of the target market. Similarly, the hotel would be wasting money if it marketed one-night offers in the three-night market, because customers in that area are interested in booking longer stays.

Table 2-2 shows how a motel might categorize its market geographically so that it can learn the travel tendencies of each area and respond with appropriate promotional offers.

Table 2-2	Geographic Market Distribution Analysis: Mountain Valley Motel			
	Hometown	*Rest of Home State*	*Neighboring States*	*Other Natl./ Internatl.*
Total Sales				
$712,000	$56,960	$462,800	$128,160	$6,080
	8%	65%	18%	9%
Sales by Length of Stay				
1-night stay	$48,416	$83,304	$19,224	$3,204
2-night stay	$2,848	$231,400	$70,488	$32,448
3–5 night stay	none	$101,816	$32,040	$28,428
6+ night stay	$5,696	$46,280	$6,408	none
Sales by Season				
Summer	$5,696	$277,680	$96,120	$54,468
Fall	$11,962	$55,536	$12,816	$6,408
Winter	$4,557	$37,024	$6,408	none
Holiday	$22,783	$23,140	none	none
Spring	$11,962	$69,420	$12,816	$3,204

With detailed market knowledge, a business can make market-sensitive decisions that lead to promotions tailored specifically to consumer patterns and demands. The following examples show how the motel featured in Table 2-2 might use its findings to make future marketing decisions:

✔ **Local market** guests primarily stay for a single night, and mostly during the holiday season. This tendency provides some great local packaging opportunities. Additionally, 10 percent of local guests stay for six nights or longer, likely while they are going through household renovations or lifestyle changes. This long-stay business tends to occur during non-summer periods when the motel occupancy is low, so the motel may want to consider special rates to attract more of this off-season business.

✔ **Within the home-state market area,** half of the guests spend two nights per stay, although nearly a third spend three to six nights, which proves that the area is capable of drawing statewide guests for longer stays. This provides a good promotional opportunity. Three-quarters of home state guests visit during the peak-season summer. The motel would be wise to offer special incentives to encourage guests to return in the spring and fall to try to spread out this business.

✔ **National and international guests** account for approximately one-quarter of the motel's guest stays. The motel can't afford to reach this far-flung group with advertising, so it needs to research how these guests found out about the motel in the first place — from travel agents, tour group operators, referrals, and so on, — and then cultivate those sources for more bookings.

Demographics: Collecting data to define your market

After you've determined *where* your customers are, the next step is to define *who* they are so that you can target your marketing decisions directly at people who fit your customer profile.

Small-business owners come face-to-face with their markets day in and day out, yet when it comes time to define their customers in demographic terms, the silence can be deafening. Sometimes business owners want to think that their products have such wide appeal that everyone is part of their market. That's a costly mistake, though, because if you try to market to *everyone,* you'll have to place ads *everywhere,* which is a budget-breaking proposition. The answer is to narrow your customer definition by using demographic facts to zero in on exactly whom you serve. Follow these steps:

1. **Start with your own general impressions to define your customers in broad terms based on age, education level, ethnic background, income, marital status, profession, sex, and household size. Ask these questions about your customers:**

   • Are they mostly male or female?

   • Are they mostly children, teens, young adults, early retirees, or senior citizens?

   • Are they students, college grads, or PhDs?

   • What do they do — are they homemakers, teachers, young professionals, or doctors?

   • Are they mostly single, young childless couples, heads of families, grandparents, or recent empty nesters?

2. **Break your market into subgroups, perhaps categorized by the kinds of products purchased or the time of year they do business with you.**

A restaurant might analyze its weekday lunchtime clientele and its summer dinner business and learn that the two market subgroups have dramatically different demographic profiles. As a result, the restaurant may realize that its weekday lunch hour clientele is comprised mostly of businesspeople from the nearby area, whereas the summer dinner traffic is comprised largely of tourist families. This may lead to development of two very different and highly targeted promotions: a "50 minutes or it's free" lunchtime offer aimed at the nearby business community and promoted through the chamber of commerce newsletter or some other low-cost local business publication, and a "kids under 7 eat free" offer aimed at tourists and promoted through hotel desk clerks and local visitor publications.

3. **Verify your answers by asking your customers.**

You can do so informally by incorporating questions into conversations you have during inquiry and sales contacts. Table 2-1 in this chapter outlines a list of information-collection options.

Psychographics: Customer buying behaviors

Knowing *where* your customer is and the statistical facts about *who* your customer is gives you the information that you need to select the right media to carry your advertising messages. As you decide *what* to say and *how* to present your message, you also want to know as much as you can about the attitudes, beliefs, purchasing patterns, and behaviors of your customers. This information helps you form advertising messages that interest your prospects and motivate them to buy from you.

Start by defining who your customer isn't

Sometimes the easiest way to start your customer profiling is to think about who your customer *isn't*.

✔ A manufacturer of swingsets knows that its customers aren't young professional couples living in urban loft apartments. It needs to talk to families whose homes have backyards.

✔ A landscape and nursery business knows that it won't find many customers in downtown high-rise apartments.

✔ A manufacturer of architectural siding may decide that its customer isn't the end user at all, but rather the architect who specifies the product in the first place.

✔ A homebuilder specializing in custom-built family houses with price tags starting at $275,000 can be pretty certain that its customers aren't young families getting ready to dive into home ownership for the first time, nor are they families currently living in neighborhoods full of half-million-dollar homes. Instead, the builder might narrow its focus to 30- to 40-year-old individuals or couples with at least one child, who currently live in homes they own but who are seeking to move to nicer residences in areas with higher prestige than those provided by their current addresses.

Look at what your customers have in common

Particularly study the tendencies of your best customers — the ones who account for the fewest service problems and the greatest profits. Make a list of their comment traits by answering the following questions:

✔ Do they buy on impulse or after careful consideration?

✔ Are they cost-conscious, or are they more interested in quality and prestige of the purchase?

✔ Are they loyal shoppers who buy from you on a frequent basis, or are they one-time buyers?

✔ Do they buy from your business exclusively, or do they also patronize your competitors?

✔ Do they reach you through a certain channel — for instance, do they use your satellite office, do they shop via your Web site, or do they reach you via referrals from other businesses or professionals?

For example, a retailer in a vacation destination area might categorize its customers into the following subgroups:

✔ **Geographic origin:** Local residents, in-state visitors, out-of-state visitors, international visitors

✔ **Activity preference:** Golfers, skiers, campers, business travelers/ convention guests

By creating customer subgroups, the retailer can begin to chart which kinds of guests purchase which kinds of products or respond to which kinds of offers.

You'll see patterns emerge. Certain customer groups account for higher sales volume or more frequent purchases. Or perhaps some market groups purchase certain types of products from you. Once you know the tendencies of your various market segments, you know what to say to each target group.

Using customer profiles to guide marketing decisions

Customer knowledge leads to strong marketing decisions, including decisions that affect product development, media selections, and the creation of advertising and promotional messages. The following two examples show how businesses use customer knowledge to steer their marketing efforts.

- ✔ A downtown dry cleaning and laundry business determines that its market is primarily affluent professionals who live and work in the nearby area. Knowing this, the business decides to remain open from 6:30 a.m. until 7:00 p.m. so that its customers, who work full-time during the day, can drop in before and after work. Additionally, when placing ads, the business avoids airing broadcast messages during daytime hours when its prospects are at work. Instead, it schedules ads during evening and weekend financial, news, and sports programs.

- ✔ A life insurance representative finds that her clients are primarily young, newly married couples. Knowing this, she rejects a half-price offer to run an ad in an upcoming special section of the local newspaper focusing on senior citizens. Instead, she approves a schedule that includes ads in the newspaper's entertainment section, where her prospects may be looking for information about things to do over the weekend. And she asks the media advertising representatives to let her know when they're publishing special sections on home improvements or do-it-yourself money-saving remodeling — or any other ideas that would correlate with the lifestyle and interests of her market.

For more information about how to use your customer profile to plan your marketing strategy, see Chapter 8.

Determining Which Customers Buy What

Especially for small businesses, marketing is a matter of resource allocation. It's about figuring out who's buying what and then weighting your marketing efforts behind the products and markets apt to give you the best return on your marketing investment.

No budget — not even that of General Motors or McDonald's or any other mega-brand — is big enough to do it all. At some point, every marketer has to decide to throw its dollars into the markets and products that have the best chance of achieving the highest return on marketing investment.

Viewing your sales by market segment

Break your sales down by product categories to determine what kind of buyers your products attract. Then define the customer for each line.

✔ A furniture manufacturer might divide its products into office, dining, and children's lines — each meeting the demands of a different market segment and even employing a different distribution and retailing strategy. In creating and placing ads, the manufacturer follows three separate strategies, placing primary emphasis (and budget allocation) on the line that research shows is most apt to deliver increased sales over the upcoming period.

✔ An accounting firm might sort its clientele both by type of service purchased and by client profile. It might target individual clients for tax return business during the first quarter of the year, high-net worth clients for estate- and tax-planning right after the shell-shock of the April 15 tax filing deadline, and business clients for strategic planning services in early fall, when those customers are thinking about their business plans for the upcoming year.

Conduct a similar analysis for your own business:

✔ How do your products break down into product lines? (See Chapter 3 for more information about this important topic.)

✔ What kind of customer is the most prevalent buyer for each line?

If you determine that one of your product lines attracts customers who are highly discerning and prestige-oriented, you probably won't want to employ a strategy that relies on coupons, for example. Likewise, if you know that a certain product line appeals to a particularly athletic or health-conscious group, you can forget about trying to prompt purchases by offering such things as all-you-can-eat dinners.

Tracing your distribution channels

Distribution is the means by which you get your product to the end user. A good distribution system blends knowledge of *who* your end user is (after going through the first half of this chapter, that part should be clear) with knowledge of *how* that person ended up with your product (that's what distribution is about). It's often a surprisingly roundabout route.

To demonstrate, take a look at how visitors might arrive at a regional museum.

Say that 250,000 visitors walk through the museum turnstiles every year. Suppose that 50,000 of those visitors are schoolchildren who arrive on school buses; 25,000 arriveas part of tour groups; 25,000 buy tickets through local motels or hotels; 50,000 attend as museum annual members who are entitled to free entrance; 75,000 are independent visitors who just wander in on their own; and 25,000 attend in response to special promotional events.

Based on these facts, the museum's distribution channels include the following:

- ✔ Educators (teachers, possibly influenced by curriculum directors)
- ✔ Tour companies (possibly influenced by state or local travel bureaus)
- ✔ Motels and hotels (probably through their sales and marketing departments)
- ✔ The museum's own entrance gate (that is, museum direct sales and promotions)

The museum's channels of distribution are shown in Table 2-3.

Table 2-3	Channel Distribution Analysis		
Distribution Channel	Ticket Price	# of Guests/ % Of Total	Sales Revenue/ % of Total
Schools/teachers	$5	50,000/20%	$250,000/18%
Tour companies	$6	25,000/10%	$150,000/11%
Motels/hotels	$6.50	25,000/10%	$162,500/12%
Museum members	$3*	50,000/20%	$150,000/11%
Independent visitors	$8	75,000/30%	$600,000/42%
Promotion visitors	$4	25,000/10%	$100,000/7%

Member ticket price based on membership dues divided by average visits/year

Study how your business generates customers and the levels of business that come through each distribution channel.

1. Track changes by distribution channel.

If you start to see one distribution channel decline radically, either you need to give that channel more marketing attention or you need to enhance another channel to replace the distribution loss.

2. **Compare percentage of sales to percentage of revenue from each channel.**

   You can see which channels deliver higher-than and lower-than income per unit sold. Channels that deliver lower-than-average income per unit either require lower-than-average marketing investment or should be targeted to develop an alternative benefit to your business. For example, in the case of the museum in Table 2-3, the promotional events deliver lower-than-average revenue and likely demand a substantial marketing investment. Yet they introduce people to the museum and therefore cultivate memberships, donations, and word-of-mouth support.

3. **Communicate with the decision makers in each distribution channel.**

   If the school groups arrive because your museum is on an approved list at the state's educational curriculum office, that office is the decision point, and that's where you want to direct your marketing efforts. Or if they arrive because art or history teachers make the choice, you need to get information to art or history teachers. Once you know your channels and who influences their decisions, you know exactly whom to contact with special promotional offers or marketing information.

Winning at Customer Economics

Every customer who approaches your business for the first time represents a major marketing investment. Your business invested time and effort to build awareness of your name in the person's mind, to develop the person's interest in your offerings, and, finally, to put forth messages that motivated the person to take buying action — and to convert from a prospect to a customer of your business. Whether a customer buys from you once or a hundred times, your initial marketing investment is the same. The only thing that changes is your return on investment — which goes up dramatically when the consumer becomes a loyal and repeat customer instead of a one-time buyer at your business.

Customer interactions follow one of two routes:

- Prospect Development⇨Sale
- Prospect Development⇨Sale⇨Customer Service⇨Sale⇨Customer Service⇨Sale⇨Customer Service⇨Sale⇨and on and on and on

In other words, you're fostering either one-time sales or repeat business. And anyone who can balance a checkbook will agree that the repeat-sales scenario is vastly better for your business because it enables you to offset the cost of prospect development with multiple sales rather than with the revenue from a single sale.

The cost of getting a customer

Imagine for a second that each of your customers arrived wearing a price tag reading "Replacement Cost: $1,500." Imagine that even your inquiries, or your responses to ads, came equipped with signs reading "I cost $75" or some other amount. Don't you think that everyone in your company would handle each inquiry and customer contact with greater care if they realized what it cost to bring that person into your business — and what it will cost if you lose that person and have to recruit a replacement?

Here's how you can estimate what it costs your business to bring in a new customer:

1. **Start with the total cost of last year's marketing program.**

2. **Back out costs that you know were directed toward repeat or loyal customer marketing programs.**

3. **Project how many new customers you think you attracted last year.**

4. **Divide the number of new customers into the amount you spent trying to get new customers.**

The result gives you a rough approximation of the price of developing a single new customer for your business. The formula relies on a fair amount of guesswork, but even if you base your math on nothing but ballpark estimates, the final number will provide a good — and eye-opening — indication of the value of every new customer. Share the figure with others in your company so that they are aware of the valuable commodity with which they are dealing each time they have customer contact.

Leveraging your customer development investment

Every time a first-time customer becomes a repeat buyer or a repeat buyer becomes a loyal and committed customer, your business puts money on the bottom line by getting more value out of its initial marketing investment.

Making customers for life

Small businesses are fortunate because they automatically think in terms of making customers for life because they aren't hindered by rigid departments and responsibility-limiting job descriptions. Instead, in most small businesses, the person who facilitates the sale almost always continues to have customer contact after the fact. As a result, the style and service mode that attracted the customer to your business continues unaltered, and the customer's decision to do business with you is reaffirmed during every contact with your business.

On the contrary, large businesses are usually organized in departments: The marketing group is usually in charge of getting customers. Then, once the customer is on board, customer contacts switch to people in the purchasing, distribution, delivery, and other departments. The "marketing" mind-set changes to an "operational" mind-set, and too often the customer gets lost in the shuffle.

As small businesses begin to get larger (which is the whole point of marketing!), they sometimes begin to adopt structures that resemble those of their big-business role models — and suddenly their customer focus begins to change. Don't let this happen to you. Manage your business so that every person in your organization realizes the value of every customer — not only to your sales today, but also to your sales tomorrow and well into the future, when the customer's positive comments will lead others to your business. (See Chapter 21 for ideas on how to coddle, cultivate, and win more business from your most frequent and loyal customers.)

Why customers leave and what it takes to keep them

Once you know the cost of getting a customer, you know exactly how much you can afford to spend to keep that customer on board and still come out ahead.

In other words, if your calculations determine that getting a new customer costs you $300, you know not to risk losing that person's business over a $50 dispute. Whether it means accepting a questionable return or writing off a contested charge or — on the positive side — indulging your customer in a complimentary service or form of entertainment, the investment will cost less than replacing that customer with a new recruit.

What's worse, if you let the current customer go away unhappy, that person may tell up to hundreds of people (sometimes many more now that the Internet allows international laundry-airing) about his or her dissatisfaction with your business.

Get your staff together to brainstorm answers to two questions:

- ✔ Why do our customers leave?
- ✔ What would it take to get them to stay?

Throw out the names of a couple recent departees to help focus the discussion. Write down every reason you can come up with for why they moved their business elsewhere. What will emerge is information that will help as you analyze your competitive arena, your pricing policies, your customer service, and your product offerings.

Be prepared for your first response to be "We're too expensive," but don't allow your thinking to stop there. Price alone is rarely the reason that customers move their business.

Customers "quit" for four reasons:

- ✔ They die, move away, or are no longer in the buying category.
- ✔ They are unhappy with the price.
- ✔ They are unhappy with the product.
- ✔ And the number one reason cited by nearly three-quarters of departed customers: They felt that the business owner or employees treated them with indifference.

Try to see your business from your customer's viewpoint and look for five inexpensive things you could do to make your customers feel more appreciated by your business. Table 2-4 helps you analyze areas where customers might praise or fault your operation.

Table 2-4	Customer Satisfaction Analysis
Customer Satisfaction Factor	*How We Rate (1 to 10)*
Responsive to the customer's wants/needs	
Competent in the customer's field of interest	
Experienced with the customer's problems	
Meets deadlines/keeps promises	
Delivers quality products/merchandise	
Stays within estimated costs/budgets	
Attention by owners/principals	
Is highly recommended/good references	
Competitively priced	
Good value for the price	
Good location/easy to do business with	
Enjoyable atmosphere	
Good follow-up after the sale	
Prestigious company	

Measuring customer satisfaction

Customers vote with their billfolds, and your cash register is their ballot box. If your sales-per-customer and repeat business rates are both increasing, you're doing something right. If they're declining, it's time to go into repair mode.

✔ **Monitor your transactions.** One quick way to see how well your business is serving your customers' needs is to monitor the size of customer transactions. What is your average sale, and is that number going up or down? If you're a retailer, you can get this data from the cash register tape. If you're a service business, your invoices will tell the story. Keep in mind that marketing-oriented companies consider the customer the boss. Ask yourself, "Is my boss giving me a raise?"

✔ **Treat sales records as a customer-satisfaction barometer.** Your marketing can be considered successful only if it results in

- A greater number of customers coming in the front door

- A lower number of customers slipping out the back door

- A growing number of dollars passing hands in between

See Chapter 21 for tips on keeping customers satisfied for life.

Playing the 80/20 customer odds

You may have heard of the 80/20 rule that applies to business, and especially to marketing. It is the premise that 80 percent of your efforts relate to only 20 percent of your business. The concept actually has a name. It's called Pareto's Law, named after the economist who developed the theory, which is formally known as the *law of maldistribution.* By Pareto's Law, 20 percent of your consumers will account for 80 percent of your sales. Conversely, 80 percent of your problems will come from 20 percent of your customers.

It stands to reason that you want more customers like those in the trouble-free, highly profitable 20 percent market group. But if you're not careful, the problematic 20 percent will consume your time instead.

Sure, you need to listen to your discontents and do what you can to right the wrongs they cite. But don't allow all your energy to be consumed by those who may never be entirely happy with you or your business — or any other business, for that matter.

Create a profile of your *best* customers. Focus on what those customers like about your business and telegraph those satisfactions to your market. You'll tip the marketing odds in favor of your business by focusing on your most content and profitable customers and planning your marketing program to work like a magnet to attract more people just like them.

Chapter 3

Your Product: Seeing It through Your Customers' Eyes

The best products aren't *sold* — they're *bought*.

You'll never hear customers say they *bought* a lemon. Nope, that lemon was *sold* to them — but hopefully not by you or your business. Because if you're a good marketer, when it comes time for the purchase, you aren't *selling* anyone anything. Instead, you're helping customers to select the right products to solve their problems, address their needs, or fulfill their desires. You're helping them to *buy*.

As a result, you devote the bulk of your marketing efforts to the steps that take place long before money changes hands. These efforts involve targeting customers, designing the right product line, and communicating your offerings in terms that address your customer's wants and needs. Then when the customer is ready to make the purchase, all you have to do is facilitate a pleasant exchange and make sure that your customer feels good about trading his or her money for the right product.

Chapter 2 focuses on your customers — who they are, where they are, and what needs they are seeking to fill. The purpose of this chapter is to figure out everything there is to know about the products you offer and, even more so, all the reasons why your customers would want to buy those products from you.

In a Service Business, Service is the Product

In case you're among the great number of small businesses that sell services rather than three-dimensional or packaged goods, we want to get one thing clear right up front: Services are products, too.

By 2005, nearly 80 percent of all Americans will work in service companies. The only difference between services and tangible products is that you can see and touch the tangible product *before* you buy it, whereas with services you commit to the purchase before you see the outcome of your decision. Services — such as preparing tax returns and wills, creating radio ads, unclogging kitchen drains, and designing house plans — aren't things that you can hold in your hands before buying them.

The 14-year-old kid who babysits for the neighbors has a product. For that matter, even nonprofit organizations have products. Look at a local Boys and Girls Club. One of its products is the service it provides to young people. Another is the recognition and satisfaction it provides to the benefactors who contribute the funds to keep the club in business. If it rents the club facility out to other groups to use during off-hours, that's yet a third "product."

If you generate revenue, then you're selling *something,* and that something is your product.

Telling "Just the Facts" about What You Sell

Freeze-frame your business for a minute to study the products you offer your customers.

To get started, look at the products of a lakeside resort as an example. The owners would list the number of cabins, seats in the restaurant, and rowboats for rent and even include the shopping opportunities provided by the resort's Barefoot Bait Shop. The list would also include summer youth camps, winter cross-country ski packages, and all-inclusive corporate retreats.

A small law office may tell you the number of wills, estate plans, incorporations, bankruptcies, divorces, adoptions, and lawsuits it handles annually. And if it's well managed, the lawyers will know which of those product lines are profitable and which services are performed at a loss in return for the promise of future business or a larger customer relationship.

What about your business?

- ✔ What do you sell? How much? How many? What times of year or week or day do your products sell best?
- ✔ What does your product or service do for your customers? How do they use it? How does it make them feel?
- ✔ How is your offering different and better than your competitors' offerings?
- ✔ How is it better than it was even a year ago?
- ✔ What does it cost?
- ✔ What do customers do if they're displeased or if something goes wrong?

The faster you can answer these questions, the better you understand your business. And the better you understand your business, the more able you are to steer its future.

Tallying your sales by product line

Make a list of every kind of product you offer to your customers, along with the revenue generated by each offering. Concentrate only on the end products you deliver. For example, an attorney offers clerical services, but those services are part of other products and not the reason why a person would seek to do business with the attorney in the first place, so they shouldn't show up on the attorney's product list.

To get you started, here are examples for two businesses:

Table 3-1	Advertising Agency Product Analysis	
Product	**Product Revenue**	**Percentage of Revenue**
Advertising creation, production, placement	$1,770,000	39%
Brochure creation, production, printing	$900,000	20%
Direct mail creation, production, implementation	$720,000	16%
Display and signage creation, production	$225,000	5%
Packaging creation, production	$175,000	4%
Marketing and advertising planning services	$160,000	4%

(continued)

Table 3-1 *(continued)*

Product	Product Revenue	Percentage of Revenue
Speech writing	$50,000	1%
Publicity generation	$225,000	5%
Special events planning	$150,000	3%
Computer graphics services	$125,000	3%

Table 3-2   **Independent Bookstore Product Analysis**

Product	Product Revenue	Percentage of Revenue
Books	$250,000	44%
Books-on-tape	$45,000	8%
Book and tape rentals	$18,500	3%
Greeting cards and stationery	$55,000	9%
Pens and writing supplies	$18,000	3%
Magazines	$95,000	16%
Coffee and pastries	$95,000	16%

Using the cash register to steer your business

Your revenue analysis will detail exactly what products your customers are buying. You can put this information to work as you prioritize and manage your product line.

> ✔ **Sell what people want to buy.** Study your list for surprises. You may find products that are performing much better than you imagined. This knowledge may alert you to a change in customer interests that you can ride to higher revenues. As an example, the ad agency in Table 3-1 didn't realize until it scoured its revenue analysis that nearly a tenth of its business was coming from public relations activities like speechwriting, publicity generation, and special events — an area of expertise the agency hadn't even been promoting. This finding led to the decision to build agency business by emphasizing this service among current and potential clients.

✔ **Promote the products that you've hidden from your customers.** You may find that you have a product line that is lagging simply because your customers aren't aware that they can buy the offering from you. Our hypothetical ad agency couldn't figure out why its computer graphics services were being underused at a time when so many clients needed help designing their Web sites. A bit of customer research proved that the term "computer graphics" didn't translate to "Web site design" in the minds of the agency's clients, who were going elsewhere for the service. The agency decided that it could double or even triple sales in this category simply by a quick relabeling and some promotion among existing clients of the agency's proven expertise in the Web site design arena.

✔ **Back your winners.** Your revenue analysis will also let you track which product lines are increasing or decreasing in sales so you can respond accordingly. The bookstore's revenue analysis (Table 3-2) documented that its café and magazine business was growing while its book sales were ebbing, probably due to erosion by online booksellers. This led to the decision to increase the size and offerings of the in-store restaurant and to add a new product line to offset the declining book sale revenues. Customer research led to the decision to add an array of reading accessories to the store's inventory, including reading lamps, bookshelves, and the town's best assortment of over-the-counter reading glasses.

✔ **Bet on the products with adequate growth potential.** Before committing marketing dollars to any product line, use your revenue analysis to project your potential return on investment. For instance, a glance over the bookstore revenues shows that only 3 percent of sales result from book and tape rentals. If the store could *double* this business, it would increase annual revenues by only $18,000. Realizing this, the owners need to ask themselves: What is the likelihood that we're going to double this business — and at what cost? On the other hand, if the bookstore could increase café sales by just 20 percent, it would realize $19,000 of additional revenue, which the owners decide is a safer marketing bet and a stronger strategic move.

Illogical, Irrational, and Real Reasons People Buy What You Sell

When you can buy bread at two loaves for a dollar at the grocery store, why would anyone pay nearly $4 to pick up a loaf at the out-of-the-way Italian bakery?

Why pay nearly double to buy a Lexus instead of a Toyota, when some models of both brands are built on the same chassis with many of the same components?

For that matter, why would clients seek cost estimates from three different service providers, and then go with the most expensive one when all three offer nearly the same proposed solution?

Why? Because people rarely buy what you think you are selling.

People don't buy your *product*. They buy the promises, the hopes, or the satisfactions that they believe your product will deliver.

They buy the $4 loaf of salt-crusted rosemary bread because it satisfies their sense of worldliness and self indulgence. They opt for the high-end sedan for the feeling of prestige and luxury it delivers. They pay top price for legal, advertising, or even accounting services because they like having their name on a prestigious client roster, or maybe because they simply like or trust the attorneys, advertisers, or CPAs more than the people who provided the lower cost estimates.

People may choose to buy from your business over another simply because you make them feel more important, or successful, or satisfied when they walk through your door.

Don't fool yourself into thinking that you can win your competitor's customers simply by matching features or price.

People decide to buy based on all kinds of illogical reasons, and then they justify and rationalize their purchase by pointing out product features, services, or even the price tag. They buy because they see some intangible and often impossible to define value that makes them believe the product is a fair trade for the asking price. Often that value has to do with the fact that they like the people they're dealing with. Never underestimate the power of a personal relationship.

Buying Decisions Are Rarely about Price, but They're Always about Value

Whatever price you charge for your product, that price must accurately reflect the way your customer values your offering.

For example, if your customer thinks your price is too high:

- The customer won't buy.
- The customer *will* buy but won't feel satisfied that he or she received adequate value, which means that you'll win the transaction but sacrifice the customer's goodwill and possibly the opportunity for repeat business.
- The customer will tell others that your products are overpriced.

Before you panic over being called high-priced by a customer, remember that it is only bad news if others respect this particular person's opinions regarding price and value. It's often better to let a cherry-picking bargain hunter go than to sacrifice your profit margins trying to price to that person's demanding standards. More importantly, be certain that if your prices are on the high end, the prestige — and *value* — that you offer must be commensurate with your pricing.

On the other hand, if your customer thinks that your product is worth more than its price tag:

- ✔ You may sacrifice the sale if your customer interprets the low price as a reflection of a second-rate offering.

- ✔ You may make the sale, but at a lower price (and lower profit margin) than the customer was willing to pay — therefore leaving money in your customer's billfold and possibly a question mark in your customer's mind. The customer may leave with the impression that you are a discounter. That perception will steer the kinds of purchases that person chooses to make from you in the future.

People interpret lower prices to mean lower quality. And even if you have the lowest cost, someone can always beat you by a penny. Unless you really want to try to own the bargain basement position in your market, aim for good value and set your prices accordingly.

The value formula

During the split second that customers rate the value on your product, they weigh a range of attributes (see Figure 3-1):

- ✔ What does it cost?
- ✔ What is the quality?
- ✔ What features are included?
- ✔ Is it convenient?
- ✔ Is it reliable?
- ✔ Can they trust your expertise?
- ✔ How is the product supported?
- ✔ What is the guarantee, promise, or ongoing relationship they can count on?

These considerations start an invisible juggling act to determine what, in the customer's mind, is the value of your offering.

The Value Formula

How Customers Compute Value

Price
Quality
Features
Convenience
Reliability
Expertise
+   Support
─────────────────
V A L U E

If your product's quality and features are only average, then they'll expect a low price to tip the deal in your favor.

On the other hand, if customers value your promise of product reliability (think of Federal Express as an example), they'll likely cut you some slack when it comes to other attributes like low price or convenience.

Remember the signs you've seen that list the terms "Price, Quality, and Speed" followed by the recommendation that you "choose any two"?

Well, for successful small businesses, those days are gone. Your customer expects you to be competitive in all *three* areas. But — and here is the good news — they don't expect you to be the *best* in all three areas. Just competitive.

To be a leader in your field, your business has to have the best cost, the best product, *or* the best total solution. You can't be best on all fronts, and no one expects you to be. What customers do expect, though, is for you to be competitive all across the board, and *best* at something.

Look at these well-known examples:

- ✔ Costco = Best price
- ✔ Nordstrom = Best service
- ✔ Starbucks = Best quality and convenience
- ✔ Federal Express = Best reliability
- ✔ BMW = Best performance
- ✔ Rolex = Best quality

Riding the price/value teeter-totter

REMEMBER

Price emphasizes the dollars spent. Value emphasizes what is received in exchange for the dollars spent.

Pricing truths

When sales are down or customers seem dissatisfied, small businesses turn too quickly to their pricing in their search for a quick-fix solution. Before you reduce your prices in an effort to increase sales or satisfaction levels, think first about other ways to increase the value you deliver. Consider the following points:

- Your customer has to perceive the value of your product to be greater than the asking price. If you charge 99 cents, deliver at least a dollar's worth of value.

- The less value customers equate with your product, the more emphasis they'll put on low price.

- The lower the price, the lower the perceived value.

- Customers like price reductions way better than they like price increases, but be sure when you reduce prices that you can live with the change, because reversing your decision — and upping your prices again later — may not settle well.

- Products that are desperately needed, rarely available, or one-of-a-kind are almost never price-sensitive.

The difference between penny-pinching and shooting the moon

People pay for what they value.

So what makes a product price-sensitive?

Tell a person he needs angioplasty surgery, and he'll pay whatever the cardiac surgeon charges — no questions asked. But tell that same person he's out of dishwasher detergent, and he'll likely perform some price-comparison shopping. Why? Because one is more essential, harder to substitute, harder to evaluate, and needed far, far less often than the other. One is a matter of life and death, and the other is mundane and ordinary.

See where your product fits by checking out Table 3-3.

Table 3-3	Price Sensitivity Factors
Price Matters Less if Products Are:	*Price Matters More if Products Are:*
Hard to come by	Readily available
Purchased rarely	Purchased frequently
Essential	Non-essential
Hard to substitute	Easy to substitute
Hard to evaluate and compare	Easy to evaluate and compare
Emotionally sensitive	Emotion-free
One-of-a-kind	A dime a dozen

Pricing considerations

Give your prices an annual check-up. Here are the factors to consider and the corresponding questions to ask.

- ✔ **Your price level:** What is the perceived value of this product compared with its price? What is the price of competitive products? How easy is it for the customer to find a substitute for this product, or to choose not to buy at all? (See Chapter 4.)

- ✔ **Your pricing structure:** How do you price for extra features/benefits? What features/benefits do you include at no extra charge? What promotions, discounts, rebates, or incentives do you offer? Do you offer quantity discounts?

- ✔ **Pricing timetable:** How often do you change your pricing? How often do your competitors change their pricing? Do you anticipate competitive actions or market shifts that will affect your pricing? Do you expect your costs to affect your prices in the near future? Are there looming market changes or buyer taste changes you need to consider?

The Care and Feeding of Your Product Line

There are two ways to increase sales:

1. Increase business from existing customers.

2. Attract new customers.

Figure 3-2 demonstrates the opportunities to build business from new and existing customers through new and existing products.

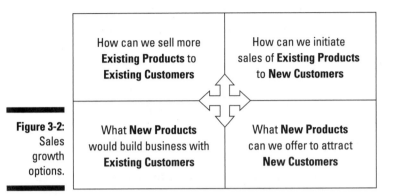

Figure 3-2:
Sales
growth
options.

How can we sell more **Existing Products** to **Existing Customers**	How can we initiate sales of **Existing Products** to **New Customers**
What **New Products** would build business with **Existing Customers**	What **New Products** can we offer to attract **New Customers**

Enhancing the appeal of existing products

At least annually, small businesses need to assess whether their products still appeal to customers, or whether it's time to adjust features, services, pricing, and product packaging or to make other changes that may sustain or reignite buyer interest. Here are some of your options:

✔ **Same product, new use:** Start by looking for ways you can re-present your offerings.

One of the best historic examples of re-presenting a product comes from Arm & Hammer baking soda. When people reduced the amount of baking they did, the amount of baking soda they needed tumbled into the basement. So rather than stand by and watch sales slide, Arm & Hammer responded by reintroducing baking soda — this time not as a recipe ingredient but rather as a refrigerator deodorizer.

✔ **Same product, new promotional offer:** Examine ways to update the way you offer your product to customers, including new customer-responsive pricing, new packages that combine top-selling products with other offerings your customers may not yet have tried, or other ways to help your customers see your offerings with a new appeal.

Be sure your new offerings are true improvements that address customer wants and needs. Don't substitute quick-fix discounts just to lure people back in, and don't try to slap together some combination of new promotional offerings, revised terms, or special offers that only confuse the market. Before you offer a new "deal," be sure that you can say yes to the following question: Does this provide customers with a better, higher-value way to buy our products?

A Web site designer may increase sales of consulting services by bundling quarterly site traffic reporting and analysis with its Web site design, thereby delivering consulting services to customers who otherwise would have purchased only design expertise.

A landscape/nursery business may decide to offer half-price terra cotta pots with all perennial purchases over $50 — thereby giving customers an incentive to buy higher volumes of flowers *and* increasing interest in the nursery's line of pottery.

Chapter 4 includes more information on winning a greater share of your customer's buying decisions and, as a result, increasing your sales to existing customers.

✔ **Same product, new customer:** As you're devising ways to refresh your product for your existing customer group, remember that there is a whole market full of strangers to whom your product could appeal as an entirely new offering. The trick with new customers is to grab their attention and then to invite them into your business with a fairly risk-free offer. Try presenting your existing products through introductory or trial offers, or find ways that new prospects can sample your offerings. Issue invitations to free seminars or guest lectures, or even serve as the host of a community fundraiser that attracts the kinds of people you serve. For more information on how to build interest among new prospects, see Chapter 10.

Remember, even products have life cycles

Products get old, too! They follow a life cycle (shown in Figure 3-3) that begins with product development and proceeds until the product reaches the point where it is old hat, at which time its growth rate grinds to a halt and profits decrease.

Raising a healthy product

Product sales follow a predictable pattern as a product moves through the life cycle illustrated in Figure 3-3. The following descriptions explain the marketing steps and sales expectations that accompany each phase of the product's life:

✔ **Introductory phase:** Build awareness, interest, and market acceptance while working to change existing market tendencies. Use introductory offers to motivate customers to try the product and also to drive sales to speed up your cost/investment recovery.

Though it is tempting to drive early sales through low pricing, be careful because that first impression will stick and will limit your ability to increase pricing later. Set your price where it belongs in relation to your product value and gain your sales through introductory offers and heavier start-up advertising.

✔ **Growth phase:** The product enters its growth phase once it has been adopted by the first 10 to 20 percent of the market, often known as the market "innovators" or "early adopters." The masses follow this pace-setting group, and once the masses start buying, growth takes off. At this point, competitors enter, and the business launches promotions to protect and build market share.

✔ **Maturity:** When the product reaches maturity, its sales are at their peak level, and sales growth starts to wind down.

✔ **Saturation phase:** The market is now flooded with options. The business has to rely largely on replacement purchases and has to offer pricing and other incentives to recruit new customers by winning them away them from competitors.

✔ **Declining phase:** When the product reaches the depth of its sales decline, a business has several choices. One is to abandon the product in favor of new opportunities, perhaps introducing phase-out pricing to hasten the cycle closure. Another is to leave the product to exist on its own with minor marketing support and, as a result, minor sales expectations. Yet a third option is to reinvent the product's usage, application, distribution, or other marketing strategy to appeal to a new market.

Figure 3-3: Product life cycle.

Developing new products

Whether it is to seize a new market opportunity or to offset shrinking sales with replacement products, one of the most exhilarating aspects of small business is that of creating and introducing new products. It's also one of the most treacherous, because it involves betting your business resources on a new idea. Figure 3-4 shows the product development process. Follow it, without jumping over the important middle step, to minimize your business risk.

The Chinese character for "crisis" combines the characters for "danger" and "opportunity." Proceed with caution to avert danger while you seize opportunity by adding new products to your line.

Figure 3-4:
The product development sequence: Don't try to leapfrog over the essential middle step that involves evaluation, research, and testing.

IDEA

EVALUATION, RESEARCH, TESTING

LAUNCH

As you pursue a new product idea, push yourself by asking these questions:

- ✔ What current product can we significantly update or enhance?
- ✔ What altogether new idea will satisfy the known wants and needs of our customers and prospective customers?
- ✔ What market trend can we ride via a new product?

Many new products are developed to address a hot new market trend. Before you consider riding a market trend, though, be sure that you aren't entering the product category too late. Take a second to review Figure 3-3, the product life cycle. You see that if you enter when a product is already in the saturation phase, you have to offer pricing and other incentives to win business from the line-up of competitors already in the field. If you're going to offer a product responsive to a market trend, have a marketing plan that allows you to get in and get out fast, so that you've realized success and moved on before the product idea reaches the end of its life span.

New product evaluation

If you have an innovative product with a sales history of less than six months, the Wal-Mart Innovation Network (WIN) will evaluate your idea for commercial strengths and areas that would benefit from improvement.

To request an evaluation form, go to www.walmartstores.com/win/what.html and click on the How To Apply button. You'll receive a Confidential Registration and Disclosure Document. Once you complete the form, the Innovation Institute at Southwest Missouri State University will conduct an evaluation covering everything from market potential to environmental impact. The process takes approximately six weeks and currently costs $175. (Wal-Mart receives no portion of the fee, just FYI.)

Here are some questions to ask yourself during the research stage of your product development:

- ✔ Is it unique? Is the idea already being produced or offered by another business, and, if so, how will your product be different — and better?

- ✔ Does it deliver customer value? If this is an upgrade of existing products, how is it different in a way that will matter to your customer?

- ✔ Does it have market potential? Will it appeal to a growing market? What is its custom profile? What do potential customers say about it?

- ✔ Is it feasible? What will it cost to produce or deliver, and how much can you charge for it?

- ✔ Is it credible? Does this new product fit with your company image? Is it consistent with what people already believe about you, or does it require a leap of faith?

- ✔ Is it legal and safe? Does it conform to all laws? Does it infringe on any patents? Does it have safety concerns?

- ✔ Can you make and market it? Do you have the people and cash resources to back this product? Can you get it to market? Is it easily marketable and feasible for success?

- ✔ Can you find a unique niche in the marketplace for it? The topic of positioning and branding products is a chapter unto itself, so turn to Chapter 7 for more information.

As you study new product ideas, beware of the following:

- ✔ Features that don't inspire your customer

- ✔ Variety without clear customer benefit

- ✔ Product enhancements that don't add significant product value

- ✔ "New" products that are really old products disguised with some new-fangled guise that means nothing to customers
- ✔ Products that don't fit within your expertise and reputation
- ✔ Products that address fads or trends that are already starting to wane

Product line management isn't about what you're selling; it's about what the market is buying. Keep your focus on your customers, on what they value not just today — but what they will value *tomorrow*.

Chapter 4

Sizing Up Competitors and Growing Your Share of the Market

*N*o matter how unique your offering, no matter how much you think you play on a "field of one," even if you're the only hitching post in a one-horse town, you have competition.

Every business has competition.

When Alexander Graham Bell called to Mr. Watson through his newfangled invention in 1876, even he already had competition. He held in his hand the one-and-only such device in the whole wide world, yet from its very moment of inception, the idea of the brand-new telephone had to fight for "market share." It had to compete with all the existing and familiar means of message delivery, plus it was certain to spawn a crop of copycat products to vie for message delivery in the future.

Competition may not be obvious. It may not even be direct. But it is always there. The sooner you face it and plan for it, the better. This chapter shows you how.

Playing the Competitive Field

Competition is at the heart of all sports, and it is also the core of the free enterprise system and business as we're lucky to know it.

Competition is the contest between businesses for customers and sales.

The opposite of competition is a *monopoly,* where a single company has complete control of an industry or service offering.

Thanks to the forces of competition, the free enterprise system is undergoing constant improvement. Here are a few examples:

- Competition prompts product upgrades and innovations.
- Competition leads to higher quality and lower prices.
- Competition enhances selection.
- Competition inspires business efficiencies.

The terminology of competition

Your sales figures provide your first indication of how you're doing in your competitive arena. If they are strong and growing, your business is on the right track. If they're sliding downhill, you have your work cut out for you. Either way, you can take control of your sales — and therefore of your business success — by using the information in this chapter to gauge and grow your "share" of business, as defined by the following three terms:

Market share is your slice of the market pie — or your portion of all of the sales of products like yours that are taking place in your market area. Say that you manage a movie theatre in a market with a dozen other movie theatres within a reasonable driving distance. Your market share would be the percentage that your theatre sells of all the movie tickets sold by all 13 movie theatres. See the section "Calculating Your Market Share," later in this chapter, for tips on how to determine and grow your market share.

Share of customer is the percentage that you capture of all the possible purchases that your customer *could* make at your business. Continuing with the movie theatre example for a minute longer, in addition to tickets, the theatre sells popcorn, soda, candy, movie posters, "movie money" gift certificates, and who knows what else. Every customer who purchases only a movie ticket — nothing else — represents lots of room for growth in terms of "share of customer," also known as "share of billfold." For tips on calculating and growing your share of customer, see the section titled "Expanding Your Share of Your Customer's Billfold," later in this chapter.

When you increase your market share, you grow your business by luring customers away from your competitors. When you increase your customer share, you grow your business by winning more sales from existing customers. But when you increase your *share of opportunity,* you find ways to get more people to decide to turn to your products to solve their needs, even if they aren't currently buying products like yours at all. In other words, share of opportunity forces you to look beyond proven customers and competitors and to look into who is *not* buying products like yours, and what it might take to let those people see your product as a solution to their needs.

Not long ago, Coca-Cola released research documenting that 5.7 billion people in the world consume, on average, 64 ounces of fluid a day, and of that total intake, only 2 percent of the liquid consumed was in the form of Coca-Cola. Coca-Cola officials used this information as the basis of an effort to increase what they termed their 2 percent "share of stomach."

This kind of planning goes beyond market share (how much of all soft-drink purchases are captured by Coke), and even beyond customer share (how much of each Coke drinker's total soft drink purchases are captured by Coke). It moves into the arena of market development by seeking to capture sales by *likely* customers who are currently opting for substitutes or alternatives rather than purchasing soft drinks at all.

Find a "stomach share" analogy for your business. What greater opportunity or satisfaction does your product address? What greater solution does your business provide? Then think about how you can present your products to grab a greater share of that total opportunity. Here are a couple examples:

- ✔ A roller skating rink sells skating, of course, but it also provides a solution for youth and teen recreation. Its opportunity comes from all those kids who spend money to fill out-of-school hours. It might think in terms of "birthday party share" or "youth leisure time share."

- ✔ An insurance brokerage sells life insurance, which provides a solution for peace of mind. Its competition comes not only from competing insurers but from all the other ways people could seek to address their long-term needs — which may include everything from investing in stocks to stashing money under the mattress to buying lottery tickets. The insurance brokerage might think in terms of its "nest egg share."

Knowing what you're up against

Your business faces three kinds of competition, as illustrated in Table 4-1.

Direct competitors

These businesses offer the same kinds of products or services you do and appeal to customers in the same geographic markets where you do business. When you think of increasing your market share, you're thinking about how you can woo business away from your direct competitors and over to your business.

Indirect competitors

You're either losing sales to or splitting sales with these businesses. For instance, if you're selling paint and your customer is buying the paintbrush somewhere else, that brush seller is an indirect competitor of your paint store, because it is capturing the secondary sale. When you think of increasing your share of customer, look at the business going to your indirect competitors. See whether you can find a way to increase your ability to serve as a one-stop solution for your customers by offering not only your primary product but also the secondary, complementary, or add-on products that your customers currently leave your business to obtain elsewhere.

Phantom competitors

No one *has* to buy what you're selling, and in fact one of the biggest obstacles to the purchase — and therefore the biggest phantom competition — is your customer's inclination to do nothing at all or to find some alternative or do-it-yourself solution instead of buying what you're selling. Taking the paint store example a step further, if you're offering the choice between enamel and latex paint and your customer is opting for never-need-paint vinyl siding, that siding outlet is a phantom competitor capable of roadblocking your business. For that matter, if your customers decide that their houses can go another year or two without a paint job, the option to do nothing is your phantom competitor. When you think of increasing your share of opportunity, think long and hard about where your phantom competitors are hiding. Then find ways to make your product the easier, more gratifying, more satisfying, and more valuable alternative.

Table 4-1	Examples of Competition		
The Product	*Direct Competitors*	*Indirect Competitors*	*Phantom Competitors*
Log home construction	Other log home builders	Traditional housing contractors, kit homes, manufactured housing	Remodeling, motor coaches, time share offers, doing nothing
Movie theatre	Other movie theatres	Video rental shops, cable TV, satellite services	Other leisure activities such as attending sporting events, listening to live music, bowling, watching TV, doing nothing

The Product	Direct Competitors	Indirect Competitors	Phantom Competitors
Life insurance	Other life insurance brokers	Savings accounts, savings bonds, investment accounts, IRAs	Paying bills, paying tuition, buying lottery tickets, gambling, stashing money under the mattress, doing nothing

No matter what you're selling, you face one common competitor with all other businesses, and that is the customer's ability to choose to do or buy nothing.

Your phantom competitor is your hardest competition of all.

To win more business, look beyond strategies for besting your direct and indirect competitors. Think also of ways to package, present, and promote your offerings to make them a far better, easier, and more rewarding choice than your phantom alternative — which is for your customer to pocket the money, find some do-it-yourself solution, or opt to do nothing at all.

How businesses compete

When everything else is equal, most customers opt for the product that is offered at the lowest price. If you want to charge more, make sure that everything else *isn't* equal between you and your competitor. Most competitors fall into one of the following two categories:

- ✔ **Price competitors:** These businesses emphasize price as their competitive advantage. They must be prepared to offset lower profit margins with higher sales volume. They also have to be prepared for someone to always beat their price.

- ✔ **Non-price competitors:** These businesses charge a higher price than their competitors. They must be prepared to compete and win based on superior quality, prestige, service, location, reputation, uniqueness of offering, and customer convenience. In other words, they must offer value.

Winning Your Share of the Market

You win market share by taking business from your direct competitors, therefore reducing their slice of the market pie while increasing your own. To advance in the market share game, here's what you must do:

1. **Figure out who your direct competitors are — which businesses you're actually losing sales *to*.**

2. **Learn why your customers are choosing those competing businesses over yours.**

3. **Analyze how you can vacuum off your customer red carpet and beef up the value that the market equates with your business and product so that buyers will opt for your offerings rather than the competing alternatives available to them.**

Defining your direct competition

On an annual or regular basis, ask yourself these questions:

✔ **Who does our business really compete with?**

When your prospect considers buying your product or services, what other businesses does that person think of at the same time?

Be realistic as you answer this question. Just because a retailer sells jewelry in New York City, that business doesn't necessarily compete with Tiffany's. List the businesses that actually swipe your customers' business away from you.

If you have a service business, list the competitors against whom you regularly have to go head-to-head to win the contract or job. If you're a retailer, list the businesses whose shopping bags your customers tote into your store, or the business names you overhear while they deliberate whether to buy your product or some other alternative. Investigate further by conducting customer research (see Chapter 2).

✔ **How does our business rate among the businesses that our prospects also consider when they consider our offerings?**

It's worth it to create a list with the name of every business with which you regularly and actually compete. For each competing business, assess the following three factors:

- What are this competitor's strengths when compared to our business?

- What are this competitor's weaknesses when compared to our business?

- What could our business do differently to draw this competitor's customers over to our business?

To help as you evaluate your business in comparison with your competitors, see the Customer Satisfaction Analysis in Chapter 2. It presents a list of the attributes and values that prospects consider when choosing between competing businesses.

✔ **How does our business *rank* among our competitors?**

Avis knew where it fit in the rental car competitive hierarchy back when it began advertising that Avis was #2 and trying harder. The company built a success strategy and marketing plan around an honest assessment of how it ranked competitively. What about your business?

- Evaluate your sales revenues in comparison to those of your competitors to get a feel for how you rank by size alone.

- Estimate your market share compared to that of your competitors. (See the following section for market share calculation advice.)

- Evaluate your "top of mind" rating — sometimes called your "mind share." When prospects are asked to name three to five businesses in your field, does the name of your business consistently pop up as one of their answers? If so, listen to the other names as well — and you'll have a great indication of what businesses you're up against at that dominant top-tier competitive level. And if you don't hear your business name, listen anyway, because once you know which businesses *are* in the top-of-mind category, you can begin to analyze what they're doing differently than you to achieve the prominence you seek.

✔ **How can we move up the competitive ladder?**

One of the most certain truths about small business competition is that most businesses misdirect their time and energy by tackling the wrong competitors. They shoot too high — taking on the biggest names in their market area rather than the biggest threats to their business. As you develop your competitive plan of attack, follow these steps:

- Start by winning market share from the businesses you're actually losing customers to *today* — even if that involves facing the harsh reality that your customers consider your business among a less prestigious group than you wish they did.

- Make a list of the companies you *wish* you were running with. Evaluate why you're not in that group. Is it because the nature of your customers "marks" you as a lower-level player? Or is it the physical look or location of your business? Or maybe the kind of products and prices you present?

- Assess whether your business is more apt to be successful at its current competitive level (think of the big-fish-in-a-small-pond concept) or at the next competitive level (where perhaps you can compete for bigger and more lucrative business).

- *If* you decide that your business would be better off competing with the more visible, larger, and prestigious businesses in your arena, then commit to making the business changes necessary to get the market to see you through new eyes. See Chapter 7 for information on how to influence market perceptions and win your chosen place in your marketplace.

Calculating Your Market Share

Having a sense of your market share gives you a good indication of your competitive rank. It also provides a way to monitor the growth of your business within your target market.

Sizing up your target market

Before you can calculate your share of the market, you need to determine the size of the market in which you compete.

The *total* market includes the entire nation or world — a market area that matters enormously to such major advertisers as Nike, Levi's, General Motors, Citibank, or other internationally known brand names.

But to a small business like yours, what matters far more than the total market is the *target* market — the market that is within the sphere of your business's influence.

You can assess the size of your target market by using one or several of the following criteria:

- **Geographic targeting:** Where are your customers? Begin by defining the physical boundaries of your business area. For example, a retailer may determine that its geographic target market consists primarily of people who live or vacation within a two-hour drive of the retailer's place of business. An accountant may determine that her business is concentrated within the city limits.

- **Customer targeting:** Few businesses are designed to appeal to the entire population within a geographic market area, so customer targeting is essential. This is especially true for businesses that market via the Web, which makes the whole world an accessible market. So rather than consider the full market (or world) population as your potential market, determine the number of people who actually fit your customer profile. (See Chapter 2 for profiling information.) A golf course community developer, for instance, may determine that its target market includes only high-income golfers aged 50 and over who live in the surrounding three-state region. An office furniture manufacturer may target all of the nation's office furnishing retail establishments, along with architects and interior designers who specify furnishings. An online florist may focus exclusively on wedding planners and brides-to-be. (See Chapter 17 for tips on defining Web customers and why they come to your site.)

✔ **Product-oriented targeting:** Sometimes the most effective way to measure the size of the target market is by unit sales of a particular type of product. For instance, a microbrewery would measure its share of the market as a percentage of all premium beer sold in its geographic target area. By segmenting the target from *all* beer sales to the premium beer segment, the microbrewery can accurately measure its performance within the sphere of its business influence. Likewise, an attorney who specializes in land-use planning would assess the number of land-use cases in his statewide area before trying to calculate market share.

Doing the math

Once you have a good sense of the size of your total target market, you can use several approaches to calculate your share.

✔ **Unit sales:** Some businesses can easily figure out the total number of products like theirs that are sold each year. A motel manager, for instance, would calculate the number of motel rooms and the approximate occupancy rates in the local market to arrive at an estimate of how many motel rooms are rented in the area annually. Based on this calculation, the motel manager can figure out the percentage of rooms being rented by guests of her motel. That percentage is the motel's market share based on unit sales.

A real estate agent may do a similar calculation, checking assessor office records to determine the total number of residential house sales over the previous year and comparing that total figure with the number of houses the agent sold personally.

✔ **The number of potential customers:** If you know that there are 30,000 adults in your target market area, and if you can make an educated guess that one in ten of those adults — or 10 percent of the total — is a consumer of services like yours, you can assume that your business has a total potential market of 3,000 adults.

To aid in your guesswork, obtain size-of-market estimates based on statistics available from your industry association. Or see whether your library has a copy of the Standard Rate and Data Service (SRDS) *Lifestyle Market Analyst*. Find the section that profiles participants in the industry you serve.

For instance, the owners of a fabric and sewing supply store in Albany, Georgia could turn to the "Sewing" profile, and scan to the Albany, Georgia market area statistics. Here the owners would learn that 18.5 percent of the households in the Albany area participate in home sewing. Perhaps the store owners realistically think that their business serves only the 7,000 households in the area nearest to their store.

Therefore, they could do the math and know that they have 1,295 potential customers (18.5 percent of their 7,000-household market area). Knowing this total market figure, the owners need to count up the number of residents they serve and divide that number into the 1,295 total to arrive at their current market share — the percentage of all potential customers being served by the store.

✔ **Based on total sales volume:** Another way to estimate market share is to estimate the sales revenue of all of your direct competitors. Then add those figures to your own annual sales to arrive at a total estimate of how much people are spending at businesses like yours each year. For example, if you determine that you have six direct competitors which together account for $5 million in annual revenues, and if your business does $550,000 in annual sales, you can assume that your business has 10 percent market share ($550,000 divided by $5,550,000 total market sales).

Many businesses can obtain competitive sales figures by working back from publicly available tax figures. For instance, most lodging establishments pay a transient room tax, and those payments can serve as the basis for a motel owner to project total revenue of a competitor.

Also, many businesses submit their revenues (often slightly inflated, so read them with a realistic eye) as a basis for being ranked by industry and business publications. Watch your industry publications and regional business newspapers for lists of the top 25 businesses in various industries from architecture to Web site design. Within these lists, you'll find a clue to sales revenues.

Market share: Sample calculation

Say that a residential landscaping business, Green Gardens, serves a market area that includes 20,000 houses, of which approximately 10 percent use landscape services. This creates a total potential residential landscape service market of 2,000 homes. If Green Gardens has a client roster that includes 250 homes, then Green Gardens has a 12.5 percent market share based on the total number of potential customers in the area (250 divided by 2,000).

Another way to look at market share is by dollar volume. Green Gardens could calculate the revenues of each of its competitors and then add those figures to the Green Gardens revenue figure. That would produce an estimate of the total amount being spent on residential landscape services in the given market area annually. If the total dollar volume is 4 million dollars, and if Green Gardens has an annual revenue of $600,000, then Green Gardens has a 15 percent market share ($600,000 divided by $4 million).

If Green Gardens analyzed its market share based on unit sales (number of houses served) *and* based on dollar volume, the owners could conclude that although they have only a 12.5 percent share of the houses served, they have 15 percent of the total dollar volume. This finding could lead them to conclude that they are serving larger-sized accounts than some of their competitors. And based on that, they should have a small celebration!

Increasing Your Market Share

As you work to increase market share, don't get intimidated by the refrain that "no one has ever heard of us." The comment usually follows on the heels of an encounter with a new prospect who has admitted to having no knowledge of your business.

Rest assured, if you are in business and ringing up sales, then you enjoy at least *some* level of market awareness. But you can be equally certain that not *everyone* knows about your business. And that shouldn't be a great surprise.

In 1997, McDonald's spent more than $575 million on advertising. Coca-Cola spent more than $250 million. And Home Depot rang in at $180 million. And yet not one of those brands — in fact no brand in the world — has 100% brand awareness, let alone market share.

Coke Classic enjoys approximately 21 percent share of the carbonated soft drink market. General Motors captures 30 percent of the vehicle market, and according to the US Business Reporter, Nike has 47 percent of the athletic footwear market. And those successes follow hundreds of millions of dollars spent on market communications.

The moral of the story is: Be reasonable as you set your market share goals and growth expectations.

Also be careful as you seek to increase market share to steer clear of a couple common landmines:

- ✔ **Avoid "buying" market share through price reductions.** Keep an eye on your profitability. Don't sacrifice your bottom line as you prepare to welcome new customers through the door. Before you go the price-slashing route, glance through the pricing advice in Chapter 3.

- ✔ **Be ready before issuing an invitation to new customers.** Don't procrastinate, but at the same time, give yourself the time you need to be sure you're ready to make a great first impression. Run through the following checklist before launching your next ad campaign:

  - **Current customer satisfaction levels:** Are your current customers happy with the product you're advertising? Are they happy with your business in general? Do they return to your business again and again, or do you have a high turnover rate? Do customers speak well on your behalf? Do you rank well on the customer satisfaction attributes detailed in Chapter 2?

  - **Customer service adjustments:** Before you advertise to draw in more customers, can you make changes that will enhance your customer satisfaction levels? Do you need to fine-tune your product offering — how you price it, how you package and present it, even how you guarantee it? Do you need to dust off your environment? This could include everything from enhancing the appearance of your office space to revising the on-hold message to improving speed and accuracy of the Web site. And definitely review your customer conveniences — ranging from public restrooms to payment policies. Have you received legitimate customer complaints about your product or service, and have you done all that you can to address them positively and effectively?

- **Business readiness:** Are you ready to issue this invitation for new customers to try your business out? Do you have the inventory (or in the case of a service business, the staff and talent and capacity) to deliver what you're offering? Is your staff fully informed of the offer and ready to help prospects to become buyers once they respond to the ad? (How many times have you called in response to an ad only to have a sales associate say, "What? I don't know about that offer. Let me ask my supervisor." And how many times have you hung up after being placed on hold? *That's* wasted advertising!)

When market share means market saturation

The common rule is that 25 percent market share is considered a dominant market position. As you calculate your share within your target market area, watch closely as it reaches a dominant position. When it gets there, take time to celebrate, for sure, but then be aware that as your share edges upward, it will near a level that is called market saturation.

Market saturation occurs when a business captures the sales of close to a majority of the potential customers within the target market. Usually that figure is pegged at about 40 percent.

Once a business is doing that well, one of several things tends to happen:

- Competition enters the market area. Take a second to review the Product Life Cycle (Figure 3-3 in Chapter 3). Saturation happens sometime after your product has reached its maturity in the marketplace. By then others have seen the market as a good one for products like yours, which brings on a line-up of Johnny-come-lately competitors.

- Your business gets complacent, and quality gets lax. As a result, customers begin to stray.

- Your customers have bought the products they need from you. Other than replacements, their purchases are few and far between.

- It's time for change. Look for new markets to open, and ways to offer new products within your current market. And most of all, it's time to restore emphasis on customer service and satisfaction — the very thing that made the business a success in the first place.

Market dominance is the dream of every business, and there are worse fates than to experience the victory of actually achieving market saturation. But keep your eye on the road in front of you, so that should you near saturation, you have a plan for where you'll go next to build your business. Don't abandon a growing market too soon, and don't cling exclusively to a saturated market too long. Use your market share as your navigating device.

Expanding Your Share of Your Customer's Billfold

The fastest way to put money on your bottom line is to make existing customers want to increase the business they do with you. Here's how to reach that goal:

- ✔ Think of the sale as the starting point in your customer relationship. Consider the sale as progress *toward* the goal, but remember that the goal is to win the customer as a customer for life — or at least for as long as that person remains in the market for the kinds of product you offer.

- ✔ Develop relationships with your customers.

- ✔ Listen. Let your customers tell you what they want. Let them do most of the talking and work hard not to jump in with why their ideas won't work. Realize that if you can't address the customers' needs, someone else will. Hear what they're saying. Remember that their words are the path to their billfolds — and to your success.

- ✔ Help customers to see your full product range. Use customer communications, promotions, and product packaging to make it easy for customers to make additional purchases from your business.

- ✔ Increase the relationship between your business and your customers by developing ways to reward customers for their increased business.

Make a list of all the products and services your business offers, and use it to analyze how much of your full product line your customers currently buy.

If you run a service business with a fairly short client list, keep a chart such as the one illustrated in Table 4-2 on each client. If your customer list is very long, just choose a handful of representative clients to start with.

Table 4-2   Sample Chart: Analyzing Customer Share Levels

Customer Name: _____

List every product your business offers	*✔ if customer buys this product from you*	*✔ if customer buys this product from a competitor*	*✔ if customer does not buy this product at all*	*Note how customer might be enticed to buy this product or to buy it more often*
Product A				
Product B				

(continued)

List every product your business offers	✔ if customer buys this product from you	✔ if customer buys this product from a competitor	✔ if customer does not buy this product at all	Note how customer might be enticed to buy this product or to buy it more often

Table 4-2 (continued)

| Product C | | | | |
| Product D | | | | |

The information you compile helps you to see what share of your customers' business you are capturing. It also helps you to learn about customer buying tendencies. As you analyze your customer activity, consider the following points:

- ✔ **Find out which of your products your customers are buying from your competitors rather than from your business.** This finding will help you to evaluate the reasons for this loss of business. Does your customer not know that you offer this product? Does your customer believe that your competitor offers better value for this product? Would this product gain appeal if it were packaged with a primary product that your customer *is* buying from your business?

- ✔ **Discover which products your customers aren't buying from you *or* anyone else.** This information may help you decide whether to drop certain products from your line or whether these products merit reintroduction via a new marketing investment. You may choose to let a lagging product fade out on its own, but only if it isn't costing you an unwarranted investment in space or staff attention.

- ✔ **Learn what combinations of products your customers tend to buy.** If your best customers consistently purchase a certain combination of products from you, use this information to create added-value single-purchase packages that bundle the offerings with a bonus product or a beneficial price. By doing so, you will be giving your best customers a slight discount (or bonus), but you'll also be using the purchasing patterns of your loyalists to attract others like them.

- ✔ **Capitalize on products that your customers buy on a regular basis.** When customers make regular purchases of a certain product from your business, try to make those buyers "customers for life" by seeking to automate the purchases that they make from you on a frequent basis.

  - Offer an annual contract at a preferred rate. Your customer will benefit from preferential pricing while you benefit from assured business.

- Sell a service contract at the time of equipment purchase, or bundle the price of the contract right into the purchase price. Doing so helps ensure that your customer's purchase gets consistent service while also tying the customer to your business through a positive relationship.

- Set up the next appointment before the customer leaves the current appointment. Promise a reminder 48 hours before the next meeting and ensure your own repeat business.

- See whether there is an equivalent to the good old milk delivery service for your business. Can you think of some way to automate delivery of your product so that you aren't asking for each sale, but rather delivering on a standing agreement?

- Think of ways that you can establish an "on approval" agreement with your best customers — where you deliver new offerings to your customers on the condition that they can return them (or you will pick them up) if they aren't wanted or needed. Interior designers are perfect "on agreement" suppliers. They can charge a set fee for decorating services, bringing in all their recommendations — with price tags intact. The clients then keep the whole works or call for pickup of the items that they don't want.

Sell what people are buying, provide it in the way that they want to receive it, emphasize the value rather than the price, and convert each customer into a friend. *That's* how to beat your competitors and win in business.

Chapter 5

Setting Goals, Objectives, and Strategies

. . . .

In This Chapter

▶ Defining your business mission and vision

▶ Setting goals and objectives — and knowing the difference between the two

▶ Fueling your marketing program

. . . .

Small business owners who know where they want to go nearly always get there. In huge companies, the process of getting all the departments focused on the same end point can be akin to herding cats. But in small businesses, the task is easier — there are fewer people to orchestrate, and the will of the owner can more clearly impact the actions of the full business team. To borrow the old Volkswagen advertising theme: Small *is* beautiful.

As a small business marketer, if you establish a goal, a plan, and a reasonable budget for achieving your desired outcome, chances are better than good that you'll succeed at getting where you want to go. But that success comes only *if you establish a goal, a plan, and a reasonable budget.* This chapter shows you how.

Where Are You Going, Anyway?

Mission. Vision. Goals. Objectives. What's what?

Some consultants do nothing other than lead corporations and major organizations through the "visioning" process, helping them to clarify why they exist, what they hope to achieve, and how they intend to get from where they are to where they want to be.

Small companies rarely have the funds to dedicate to this kind of a strategic process. For that matter, they rarely have the time to stop and think about what they're really trying to accomplish beyond the survival objective of bringing in enough revenue to cover the expenses. But your marketing — and your business — will have a far greater chance for success if you devote some time up front to setting your sights and aiming yourself and your business team.

The "vision" thing

Successful businesses set annual goals that are supported by the foundation of a business vision and mission. The terms mission and vision are often used interchangeably, but there is a fine-line difference.

Your *vision* is a statement of what your company *strives to be*. It defines your desired future. Your *mission* is a statement of how you will create your vision. It defines the *core purpose* of your business and the approach you will take to achieve your objectives.

Your company vision is the big picture of where you're going, while your mission is the path you plan to follow to achieve success.

One hallmark example of a clearly stated purpose comes from the unparalleled 19th-century trek that started in Missouri and ended in Oregon: the Oregon Trail. If ever an organization needed a vision to overshadow the rigor of the mission and to guide all goals and objectives, it was this 2,200-mile journey across America.

Oregon Trail Vision: To find a better life

Oregon Trail Mission: To travel by wagon to Oregon

Even if your own challenges pale in comparison to that of America's pioneers (and with any dose of luck, they do!), your organization will still benefit from a clear statement of purpose defining your direction, focusing your organization, and rallying your employees, associates, and customers behind a common purpose.

A more modern example of vision and mission comes from the Habitat for Humanity program, which now reaches around the globe to provide housing for people in lower-income groups.

Habitat for Humanity Vision: To eliminate poverty housing and homelessness from the world and to make decent shelter a matter of conscience and action

Habitat for Humanity Mission: To build and rehabilitate simple, decent homes with the help of the homeowner (partner) family

Developing a statement of purpose for your business

Some companies choose to combine the concepts of mission and vision into a single purpose statement that defines the organization's purpose, long-range goals, and core values.

It's totally up to you whether you choose to create statements of mission and vision, or an overall statement of purpose, but one way or another you need to put into writing the ultimate reason that you come to work every day. Consider these questions as you work on your reason for being.

- Why did you get into this business in the first place?

- What need did you see that you felt you could fulfill better than anyone else could?

- What makes your business different from other options?

- What commitment do you make to those you deal with — from employees to suppliers to customers?

- What is the ultimate reason for your work?

Don't let the bottom line *become* your purpose. Although turning a profit should be the result of your success, be sure that you can articulate what positive change you are trying to create through your business. After you can put this purpose into a sentence, you will have defined the heart and soul of your company and the driving force behind all the decisions that you make. From there, success — and profits — should flow naturally.

Success stories

Most successful companies display their statements of purpose throughout their workplaces and in their written communications. Check annual reports and Web sites to find out the statements of purpose from the business world's success stories. Here are some examples:

- **Intel:** To be the preeminent building block supplier to the worldwide Internet economy.

- **3M:** To solve unsolved problems innovatively.

- **Disney:** To make people happy.

- **Microsoft:** To empower people through great software — any time, any place, and on any device.

Now it's your turn: Use the formula in Figure 5-1 to create a single sentence that serves as the beacon to which your business navigates. As you work on your statement, think in terms of your vision (what positive change you are working to achieve) and your mission (what you will do to make your vision real).

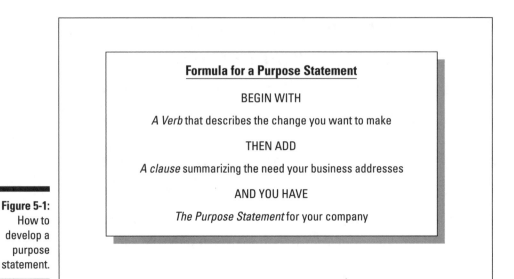

Formula for a Purpose Statement

BEGIN WITH

A *Verb* that describes the change you want to make

THEN ADD

A *clause* summarizing the need your business addresses

AND YOU HAVE

The Purpose Statement for your company

Figure 5-1:
How to
develop a
purpose
statement.

Explaining Goals and Objectives in People Language

The terms "goal" and "objective" stump even accomplished marketers. Following are definitions for the terms goal, objective, strategy, and tactic. For an illustration of how the terms fit together with your core purpose to form a planning pyramid, see Figure 5-2.

- ✔ **Goal:** The overall sales or professional target that your marketing program seeks to achieve. Your goal is an expression of a realistic and clearly defined target, usually accompanied by a timeframe.

- ✔ **Objective:** The measurable result that will be necessary to achieve the goal. A plan usually has several objectives that define the major means by which the goal will be met.

- ✔ **Strategy:** The plan of action for achieving each measurable objective.

- ✔ **Tactic:** An action you will take to enact your strategy.

Setting goals and objectives

The line between goals and objectives is razor thin, and many marketers spend undue time trying to differentiate between the two. The truth is that you can run a perfectly successful company without drowning in goal-versus-objective details. Yet sure enough, the minute you decide to skip the whole drill, some banker or venture capitalist or major partner will ask you to define how you've set some of each, and you'll be left tongue-tied in the meeting. If that happens, the following descriptions will bail you out:

✔ **Your goal** defines what you want to achieve in broad terms. It clarifies what you want to achieve during the upcoming marketing period to achieve the vision of your company.

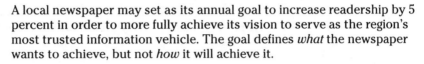

A local newspaper may set as its annual goal to increase readership by 5 percent in order to more fully achieve its vision to serve as the region's most trusted information vehicle. The goal defines *what* the newspaper wants to achieve, but not *how* it will achieve it.

✔ **Your objectives** define how your business will achieve its goals over the upcoming year. In Table 5-1, you see what amounts to an X-ray of a sentence describing the objectives a newspaper might set in order to meet its goal of increasing subscriptions by 5 percent.

Figure 5-2:
The planning pyramid.

THE ACTIONS WE WILL TAKE — Strategy

HOW WE WILL ACHIEVE IT — Objectives

WHAT WE WANT — Goals

WHY WE DO THIS — Vision, Mission and Core Values/Purpose

Table 5-1	Anatomy of an Objective	
A Verb	*A Noun*	*A Precise Description of the Desired Change*
To introduce	a new section	aimed at young, affluent urban professionals
To gain	5 percent	market share from Competitor X
To improve	delivery time	by 1 hour daily

Notice that the goal is a broad definition of what the newspaper aims to achieve (5 percent increase in readership), while the objectives are the specific actions that the newspaper will take to make the 5 percent readership increase possible.

Setting strategies

Strategies are the action plans for achieving business objectives. Strategies are practical, achievable, and action-oriented, leading to marketing actions. Strategies are also flexible so that a business can remain responsive to changes in economic conditions and market opportunities.

Strategies generally detail changes that a business plans to make to its pricing, its product, its promotion, or its distribution in order to achieve its goals and objectives. These four functions are the variables in every marketing plan, and a couple key terms describe them.

Marketing mix refers to the combination of marketing actions that businesses employ to meet their goals and objectives. The mix includes strategic use of the four marketing functions of product, place, price, and promotion. They are easily remembered as *The Four Ps*.

- ✔ **Product:** What will you sell? How will you alter you offering?
- ✔ **Place:** Where will you make your product available to your customers? How will it be distributed?
- ✔ **Pricing:** How will you set your pricing? What will you charge?
- ✔ **Promotion:** What will you say in your advertising and promotions? How will you communicate your product benefits?

Cast your goals and objectives in cement when you create your marketing plan each year. But your strategies must remain flexible. They may change depending on competitive forces, economic realities, and even opportunities that arise over the course of the year. As you alter your strategies, though, remember that the only strategy that is worth pursuing is one that directly supports your goals and objectives.

An example of goals, objectives, and strategies in action

After your business purpose is clear to you, setting your annual goals becomes a progressive effort toward achieving your ideal vision. And after you're clear about your annual goals, then every action becomes a building block toward achieving that ultimate desired end.

Too many small businesses falter when asked to state their goals. Instead they tell you that they're going to open a new office, begin selling a new product, or increase prices in June. But those aren't goals — those are strategies. Knowing your strategies without being clear on your goals is like wandering in the woods wearing a blindfold.

Figure 5-3 shows an example of a well-directed business program for an urban housing developer.

In Figure 5-3, you can see how all parts of the business program fit together:

- The *goal* is the overall target that supports the *purpose* of the business.
- The *objectives* are the major ways the goal will be reached.
- The *strategies* are the how-tos for achieving the objectives.

    The marketing *tactics* are selected after the strategies are established. Tactics include new brochures, a new ad campaign, special event planning, e-mail marketing, Web site redesign, and other communication efforts that support the strategies outlined in the annual plan.

Tactics *follow* strategies — not vice versa.

The failproof planning sequence

Successful business marketers all follow the same lock-step marketing scenario:

1. **Conduct market research.**

    Doing so ensures that you know everything you can about your customer, your product, your competition, and your business environment. In other words, do the work outlined in Chapters 2, 3, and 4.

2. **Establish marketing goals and objectives.**

    The previous portion of this chapter is full of instructions on this step.

3. **Set the marketing strategies and determine the marketing mix that you will employ to achieve your objectives.**

4. **Choose your marketing tools and tactics.**

    That's what the rest of this book is about.

Never, ever, ever start with Step 4. In other words, never decide on your tactic — whether to run an ad or hire a new distributor or take on a new partner — until you know your strategies. Because when you know your strategies, you know your objectives, which means that you know your goals, which means that you know where your business is going.

To start with Step 4 would be like choosing which highway to take when you have no idea to which state you're driving.

Purpose: To create a vibrant urban core community featuring quality housing opportunities for a wide range of residents.

Annual Goal:
Increase gross revenues by 10%.

Objectives:
Increase prospect generation by 20%.
Achieve prospect-to-sale conversion rate of 5%, an 8% increase over current rate.
Increase number of units sold by 8%.
Increase revenue from ancillary services by 20%

Strategies:

Place or Distribution Strategy

- Redesign, reintroduce and increase visits to the development sales office.
- Establish an exclusive designated real estate broker relationship.
- Revise commission schedule to enhance incentive for regional realtor referrals.

Pricing Strategy

- Increase prices by 3-15%, depending on residential product, to adjust for inflation and enhanced appeal.
- Establish a 90% developer financing option.
- Add buyer incentive by offering a lifetime health club membership for second-quarter closings on new unit sales.

Product Strategy

- Announce and break ground on a 24-hour health club with swimming, tennis, exercise and social facilities.
- Announce and break ground on a new building featuring view units, private courtyards, garages, and other high-value attributes.
- Plan and open a design division to guide new owners through the selection of unit finishes and appliances, and to provide fee-based design consultation services.

Promotion Strategy

- Host and promote special events including urban-garden tours, a variety of classes and seminars, and Thursday night events featuring live music and cultural tie-ins to draw the target audience to the sales office arena.
- Include sales center travel directions, invitations and special event announcements in all advertisements and promotional material.
- Include call-to-action in all marketing communications and collect names into a data base.
- Institute a data base communication program that ensures meaningful and progressive prospect contact every two weeks

Figure 5-3:
An urban housing developer's business program.

Investing to Reach Your Goals

To reach your goals and achieve your objectives, be prepared to fuel your strategies with a marketing investment appropriate to the size of the task at hand.

Why a static budget is headed downhill

Every year the cost of media, personnel, consultants, and virtually every other element of marketing go up by at least the cost of inflation. So if your budget remains static from year to year, your ability to market isn't just capped. Rather, it is cut back by whatever percentage the rest of the business world moved forward.

Chapter 1 includes advice about small business marketing budgets. Refer to it as you set a budget capable of meeting your goals and objectives, rather than one that establishes parity with your previous investment.

You can cut your marketing budget, and the decision will put an extra $100, $1,000, $10,000, or even $100,000 onto your bottom line. But you'll realize that savings once and only once.

But if you leave your wisely aimed marketing budget intact, it can positively impact your bottom line not only this year but well into the future. Marketing investments keep delivering even after the ad is no longer running or the sales call has long since ended. If you wonder about the truth of that statement, finish this sentence:

"Where's the —?"

Wendy's hasn't run that campaign for years. But the company's investment in the slogan "Where's the beef?" still pays off all these years later.

Supporting your goals with your budget and your calendar

Let's use the travel analogy one last time. Obviously you can't get from California to New York unless you know where you want to go and you're willing to invest a whole lot of money in gasoline or in a train, bus, or plane ticket — or a big chunk of time so that you can pop out a thumb and try hitchhiking your way cross-country.

The essential truth in marketing is exactly the same.

You *must* dedicate either time or money, or both, if you want to market your business from where it is to where you want it to be.

There is no single answer to the question "How much should we be spending?" Successful businesses budget anywhere from 1 to 50 percent of their revenues on marketing, depending on such variables as the nature of the business, the size of the market area, the competitive environment, and the aggressiveness of the company's goals and objectives.

Budgeting all comes back to knowing your goal, establishing a plan to meet it, investing appropriately — through some combination of time and money — and then sticking with your decision unless economic or competitive changes require a fine-tuning of your strategy.

Your money or your time? How companies decide

Some businesses rightly decide *not* to invest significant dollars in marketing programs. Instead, they may determine that they can best meet their goals by dedicating time to charitable and social events where they come face-to-face with prospects, instead of trying to reach the same people through promotions and media investments. That doesn't mean, though, that those businesses aren't investing in marketing. The difference is that they are investing time (and entertainment, charitable contributions, and related investments) rather than dollars spent directly on traditional media channels. Following are examples of businesses that invest time, instead of money, in their marketing programs:

✔ **An advertising agency** may set as its goal to add one prestigious account to its roster. It may decide that the best way to do this is by handling the campaign of a high-profile charity on a pro bono or volunteer basis. Subsequently it invests heavily in industry creative contests to showcase its pro bono creative work in an effort to win industry accolades and, ultimately, the attention of high-profile accounts. In this case, the agency's marketing investment involves a donation of time (for the pro bono account) and a few checks to the creativity competitions.

✔ **A motel** may have a goal to increase bookings, but instead of tackling the goals through an advertising strategy, it may decide to affiliate with a motel chain — a Best Western, for instance. This decision would shift the motel's self-generated prospect development and promotional costs into the cost of membership in the chain, which would include the motel in its nationwide marketing program.

Part II
Sharpening Your Marketing Focus

The 5th Wave   By Rich Tennant

MARKETING

"Bad news - Buddy flipped the van spilling 8 crates of samples into rush hour traffic. Good news - the van flipped logo side up."

In this part . . .

First impressions are indelible, and every business encounter can determine whether your prospect decides to buy or to take his business elsewhere. Each impression you make is a priceless moment to convince — and amaze — those who deal with your business.

Part II helps you fine-tune every contact point to your advantage — and it helps you ensure that your every marketing act is capable of moving your business in the direction that you want it to go.

Chapter 6

Taking a Business Impression Inventory

. . . .

In This Chapter

▶ Identifying the ways you project your business image to the market

▶ Taking an inventory of your communications

▶ Evaluating your marketing communications

. . . .

*R*ight now, your business is making an impression somewhere. Some prospect is encountering your ad, seeing your logo, placing a first-time call to your business, or walking through your door for the first time. Maybe someone is driving by the backlit sign on your locked-up shop at night. Or perhaps someone's eyes land on your listing when the Yellow Pages fall open.

If the impression is a first impression, it will determine how the prospect categorizes where you fit in the business pecking order. Do you look like a top-tier player, an economical alternative, or a struggling start-up? It really doesn't matter how *you* might answer that question, because your prospect is answering it for you, based on an impression that you may not have been aware you were making.

No matter whether the impression is the second, third, fourth, or hundredth time that your business has made contact with this prospect or customer, at this moment you are either reinforcing or revising a previously formed opinion about your business — for better or for worse.

This chapter is about where and when you make impressions and how you can align your communications so that people will form the opinion of your business that *you* want them to have.

Making First Impressions

You've heard the saying a thousand times: "You never get a second chance to make a first impression." The advice is self-evident, and it sounds easy enough to follow until you realize that your business most often makes its first impressions when you're nowhere to be found. In your stead is your ad, your voice mail message, your direct mailing, your business sign, your employee, or maybe your logo on the back of some Little League player's uniform.

Most of the time, your marketing communications make your first impressions for you. Ask yourself these questions as you assess whether your materials are representing you well:

- Seeing is believing. When people receive multiple impressions of your business, do they see evidence of a consistent, reliable, well-managed, successful enterprise?

- Do your communications look like they all represent the same company?

- Does your logo always look the same? What about your use of type styles and color selections?

- If you use a tagline or slogan, is it always the same, or does it change from one presentation to the next?

Ads, publicity, direct mailings, personal contacts, referrals from mutual friends, building signage — these are all make-it-or-break-it impression points.

To evaluate what kinds of messages you're sending — and what kinds of impressions you're making — begin by tracking the ways that customers initially approach your business. Then work backward to determine what marketing efforts led to their phone calls or visits. Work forward to determine what kinds of impressions they form once they actually "meet" your business, whether that first contact is made in person, over the phone, by an ad, or online.

Arriving by telephone

Usually with no prompting at all, callers tell you how they found your number. "John Jones suggested I call" or "I'm curious about the new whatchamacallits I see in your ad" or "I was on your Web site, but I couldn't tell whether or not your business is open Sundays." If the conversation doesn't naturally uncover how the person obtained your phone number, take a few seconds (but only a few seconds) to ask. "I'm glad you called us. We're always working to improve our communications, and I'd love to note how you got our phone number."

The responses help you see what is and isn't working to generate phone calls. They also help you determine which first impression points are bringing you qualified prospects who are likely to convert to customers for your business, and which ones are reeling in people who are "just looking." When the latter is the case, realize that the problem isn't with the caller; the problem is with the impression point.

For instance, suppose that a real estate brokerage specializing in high-end residential properties continuously fielded calls from shoppers trying to buy homes in a much lower price tier than those listed by the realty company. Upon questioning, the real estate agents learned that most of the dissatisfied callers found the phone number in the Yellow Pages, where the company's ad reads, "We have your dream home." Although the agents thought that their tagline appropriately reflected the caliber of the brokerage offerings, upon study they realized that it appealed to the wrong target market. As a result, they amended their ad to include a discreet line reading "Specialists in fine properties and estate homes."

If you want people to call your business, help them understand what you offer, make your phone number appropriately large and bold, give them a reason to dial it, and then be ready to treat every call as a very valuable contact — which it is.

The cost of phone book listings, Web sites, advertising placements, and the other efforts that prompt a first-time phone call mounts higher and faster than most small businesses realize. Then when the hard-won call comes, too often the phone rings and rings, or an outdated message clicks on. Just as bad, sometimes a coveted contact gets dropped into a costly phone silence after a harried person answers the phone with "Could you hold please?"

Here are some tips to make sure that your phone calls don't get fumbled:

- **Answer calls promptly.** Try to pick up after the first or second ring whenever possible. Even if you have a receptionist, train others to serve as automatic back-ups, picking up calls if they reach a third ring. When a phone rings on and on, it sends a silent message: "We're too busy to talk to you right now."

- **Transfer calls as quickly as you answer them.** Be just as prompt about getting the caller to the appropriate person in your business. If that person isn't available, say so immediately. Offer to take a message, put the caller through to voice mail, or find someone else to help. On-hold is a dangerous and costly place to leave valuable prospects.

- **Get everyone in your company to answer the phone in a consistent, professional manner — always starting with the business name.** In this age of personal lines on every desk, people too often answer all calls as if they were personal calls. "Hello, this is John" is not an appropriate business greeting unless you're a one-person business that receives calls only from people who know they want to talk with John.

- **Keep voice mail messages brief and friendly.** Use wording that conveys your business purpose and personality. Avoid long, overly programmed greetings. Offer a very limited number of menu choices (try to limit it to three — otherwise you'll lose callers in the confusion) that invite callers to jump quickly to the option they seek. "Thank you for calling 20/20 Vision. We're focusing on eye exams and frame selections right now, but please press 1 for our hours and location, or press 2 to leave a message. We promise to call you back within the hour."

✔ **Ask your phone company to monitor and report on your hang-up rate.** Multiple rings, lengthy hold times, and endless voice mail messages are all reasons for hang-ups and indications of faulty customer service.

Consider placing mirrors near the phones if your business relies heavily on telephone contact. The theory is that people instinctively smile at themselves in mirrors, simply because it makes them look more attractive. Beyond that, a smile also makes a voice more attractive — and more natural, friendly, and enthusiastic. You'll be able to hear the difference — and so will the person on the other end of the line.

Approaching your business in person

To walk through your front door, a prospect had to have been attracted by some other first impression, most likely your business or building signage, your window displays, your advertising and publicity, or the recommendation of a friend or business referral.

Making your voice mail more personal

A personal greeting, a meaningful message, and a commitment to prompt follow-up are all it takes to turn voice mail from a personality-free automated and sometimes annoying fact of life to a pleasant and efficient means to present yourself and your message when you're otherwise unavailable. Follow these tips:

✔ Record a personal greeting that accurately reflects the image of your business, update it regularly, and check for messages faithfully.

✔ Make sure that your greeting tells your company name (or your own name if it is a desk line), gives an indication of when the call will be returned, and invites the caller to leave a message.

✔ Encourage detailed messages. "Please leave a message of up to three minutes, and we will get back to you by day's end." If you encourage a lengthy message, the caller is more likely to convey complete information, reducing the need for telephone tag after the call.

✔ If at all possible, include in your message the option of pressing 0 (zero) to speak to a real, live person.

✔ If you can't get back to the caller within the specified time period, call with a polite explanation and tell when you will have a response.

✔ Voice mailboxes have limited storage capacity. Delete messages regularly to ensure that new messages can be stored.

✔ Call your own voice mail on a regular basis to be sure that it's working and that the message is current.

If a visitor walks into your business, looks around puzzled, and asks, "What kind of a business is this?" you can make an educated guess that the drop-in was unplanned, triggered only by signage or displays. (Given the question, you may want to think about how to improve these impression points to better address this obvious question.)

On the other hand, if the visitor refers to an ad offer or to the name of a business associate or employee, you can assume that you made an impression long before the person wandered up to your front door.

Many businesses boast that their signage is their most effective means of attracting first-time visitors. But before banking on your sign to reel people in, realize that when people respond only to your signage, they're making spur-of-the-moment, drop-in visits — perhaps at a time when they're short of both time and money. Instead, work to achieve "destination visits" by making impressions and cultivating interest well in advance of the time that prospects notice your sign and walk up to your front door.

Leading people to your business

If you have a retail or hospitality business, convey directions in ads, mailings, or advance contacts, or invest in road signs, outdoor billboards, or other directional signage to lead people to your business. If you are a service establishment, be sure that your building signage includes your name — spelled correctly and in your established type font if possible. Don't expect people to find your business on their own. Lead them to your door.

Parking

If people have to drive to your business, is it clear where they should park? If a parking fee is involved, do you have a validation program that customers know of in advance? Is the parking area clean, well marked, and capable of making a good impression? Have you saved the nearest spots for customers, rather than for your own car or for those of your employees? (How many times have you driven up to a parking space only to see the spot nearest to the door marked "Reserved for Manager"? And what do those three simple words tell you about your standing as a customer?)

Nearing your front door

As a prospect approaches your entrance, does your business look open and inviting? Here's a list of questions to consider:

- ✔ Is your signage visible and professional?
- ✔ Do your signs and a look into your windows clearly indicate what your business does?
- ✔ Is the front door easy to find?

✔ Is your entry signage welcoming — or is it papered with negatives such as "No UPS," "No Smoking," "Deliveries Use Back Door," or "No Outside Food or Beverages"? You need to add only a few words to set your rules in a positive way. "Let us hold your umbrella and packages while you shop" sure beats "No backpacks."

✔ If your business success relies on foot traffic, do your window displays have show-stopping capacity? Stand back and look hard. If necessary, adjust the lighting to cut glare. Replace small objects with big, bold displays that are magnets for attention. Remember that mirrors slow people down *and* cause them to adjust their dispositions, both of which are likely to benefit your business.

The moment of arrival

Walk step-by-step through the process of approaching and entering your business for the first time. Forget for a minute that this is *your* business. Imagine how it feels to a stranger — compared to how you want it to feel. If you're striving for the feel of a private, invitation-only club, you want first-timers to literally feel the exclusivity. But if you want to broaden your appeal, your goal is to eliminate all barriers while increasing the sense of warmth and welcome. Consider the following:

✔ Is your entry area impeccably clean?

✔ Is it decorated to make a strong statement about the nature of your business, its customers, and its products?

✔ Look around. Do your surroundings present and promote *your* business, or is the first impression a statement for other businesses whose logos happen to appear on calendars, posters, coffee cups, and other items that sneak their way into your environment? Instead, feature beautiful photos of your products, your clients, or your staff, depending upon the statement you want to make about your business. If you want customers to be proud to associate with your business, showcase and spotlight *your* offerings.

✔ Is there a clear "landing area" — a place where a visitor can pause and receive a good first impression?

✔ Does your business offer an obvious greeting — either by a person or by a welcoming display?

✔ If you have a customer waiting area, do people head straight for it, or do they pause, looking for an invitation before entering? In some businesses, a thermos of fresh coffee, a stack of logo ID cups, and a welcoming sign are all it takes to break the ice. Other times, you may need to remodel or at least redecorate to break down obstacles and enhance the sense of welcome.

✔ If customers consistently stop in a certain area or study a particular display, consider that area prime marketing real estate, and think of ways that you can enhance the area to deliver the strongest possible statement on behalf of your business.

What it's like to be a customer in your business

Pretend that you're a first-time customer and experiencing your business from a stranger's point of view. Take some time to role-play, following the path that customers take through your business by following this scenario:

✔ **Stop where they stop.** Stand in an inconspicuous spot and watch what people do when they enter your business.

- How long do they wait until someone greets them?

- Do they look around for a clue regarding what to do next?

- If you're a retailer, do they see a bottleneck at the cash register as their first impression? If so, how often do they make a U-turn and leave before they get all the way into your shop?

✔ **Shop like they shop.** Study what it's like to purchase your product. Note the impressions you make as customers encounter your business at different phases. Where do points of concern or resistance arise? How can you alleviate obstacles that hinder the decision to buy or the ability to enjoy dealing with your business?

- If you have a service business and customers want to know how your charges add up, create a brochure that explains your service offering and fee structure.

- If they want to touch the merchandise, build appropriate displays.

- If they need to try before they buy, offer samples.

✔ **Wait where and for as long as they wait.** Test your customer service from a customer's viewpoint. Look at how they react to the way they are treated by your business.

- Have you provided chairs in areas where they end up waiting?

- In areas where customers pause, have you placed displays that move them toward buying decisions?

- If spouses, children, or friends accompany customers, have you created entertainment areas and appropriate diversions?

- If their visits consistently last longer than an hour, do you provide some form of refreshment?

- Do customers offer nonverbal complaints about a lack of attentiveness by glancing at their watches or fidgeting while watching employees handle phone calls or desk work? Keep in mind that waiting time is the single most important factor in how a customer gauges a business for customer service, so plan accordingly.

Marketing is about creating — and keeping — customers. In designing your business environment, be sure that it not only supports your operations and internal needs but also caters to the wants and needs of your customers.

Online encounters

Increasingly, prospects "meet" your business online when they encounter your Web site on their computer screens.

In cyberspace, your Web site *is* your business. You can't be there to welcome visitors and right wrongs should something go awry. Instead, as you build your online presence, you must be vigilant about adhering to your company's image and creating a site that works as flawlessly and efficiently as you would expect your physical environment to work.

For advice on advancing your business image and achieving your marketing objectives online, see Chapters 18 and 19. Both provide information on building a visually strong site that is easy to navigate, fulfills its marketing purpose, and is well linked within the Internet to optimize the number of people who reach you online.

Here are some things to keep in mind as you develop your online presence:

- ✔ **Your Web site will rarely — if ever — make a first impression for your business.** With billions of pages out there, chances of randomly wandering onto your site are remote at best. Instead, your first impression will come via some other marketing effort that includes your Web site address, or through a search engine or Internet link that leads people to your site.

- ✔ **Your Web site can also make a *final* impression for your business.** If it crashes, is slow to load, has "fatal errors," or is too confusing to navigate, visitors won't return. Chapter 18 is full of advice regarding what to do and not to do to build a site that works.

- ✔ **Be aware that people arriving at your site may not know where they are.** They may be coming from search engines, referrals, or links, so they may not know that they've arrived in your Web space. Be sure that your name or logo come up quickly; that your site presents your standard colors, look, and message; and that it accurately reflects the nature of your business.

- ✔ **Remember that online customers are like any other customers.** They are not of another world; they are not isolated to online encounters. They are the same people who see your magazine ads, walk by your display windows, find you in the Yellow Pages, and meet you at dinner parties. If you want your Web site to work for your business, make it *part* of your business. Integrate its look, its content, and its offerings with the rest of your marketing program, right down to the style of type you use, the kinds of messages you present, and the way you display your business name and logo. For more information, turn to the advice on establishing and maintaining a consistent image in Chapter 7.

Managing a few trillion e-mail impressions

Sometime in the late 1990s (sounds like ancient history, doesn't it?), the number of e-mail messages eclipsed the volume of traditional letters sent by businesses. Yet while traditional correspondence was routinely formatted, proofread, printed, and filed, e-mail messages were sent spontaneously, often with no standard policy and rarely with a company record for future referral.

Such an informal approach to e-mail is fine as long as your staff member is simply sending a thank-you note or quick update to a customer. But what if the message includes a fee estimate? Or a notice that the requested changes will result in an additional thousand dollars of expense? And what if the staff member is no longer with your company when the customer questions the bill?

For the sake of your business, set a few e-mail guidelines:

- ✔ **Unify all company e-mails by use of a common signature.** A "sig file" consists of a few lines of text that show up at the end of every e-mail message. Usually they include the name of the person sending the message, a tagline that tells what you do, your Web site address, your street address, and phone number. You can create a signature in almost any e-mail program. Go to the help function for instructions.

- ✔ **Set a tone and style for e-mail messages.** In well-managed businesses, all traditional letters go out on letterhead, are printed in a consistent typeface, and use a consistent style and clear, professional language. Consider e-mail a dressed-down version of your formal correspondence. It can be more relaxed and more spontaneous, and it can (and should) be more to the point — but it can't be impolite or unprofessional.

- ✔ **Respond to e-mail within 24 hours.** People expect a different level of response to e-mail than to other forms of correspondence. An e-mail that isn't answered promptly falls into the category of phone calls that are placed on endless hold or customers who wait in three-minute lines. The customer service impact is devastating. Answer e-mails quickly, even if you only send a one-line note offering a complete answer within a week.

- ✔ **Establish a system to print and file e-mails** that contain any form of pricing or delivery promise.

Before you hit the send button

Measure your e-mail policies against these standards:

- ✔ **Keep messages short.** Also use paragraph breaks to avoid the visual dread of a long block of type.

- ✔ **Add punctuation, but add it sparingly.** E-mail messages seem to come in two types: the kind that include no punctuation or the kind that sprinkle punctuation like salt. Sentences that begin with capital letters and end with periods are good. Strings of five exclamation marks are bad. When in doubt, revert to what you learned in English 101.

✔ **Keep "emoticons" out of business correspondence.** The alias for emoticons is "smilies," though not all convey happiness. You'll encounter emoticons to convey a smile :-), a frown :-(, or even a grin :-D. While they're clever and capable of showing what you mean, they are about as out of place in the business environment as a swimsuit.

✔ **Limit your use of abbreviations to those in common use.** E-mail is peppered with terms such as LOL (laughing out loud), BTW (by the way), and IMHO (in my humble opinion). Advice: Stick to abbreviations that almost everyone will know, like ASAP, FYI, or OK, and leave things like TNSTAAFL (there's no such thing as a free lunch) on the cutting room floor.

✔ **Use uppercase and lowercase.** Typing in all uppercase, using all capital letters, means one thing in cyberspace: You're screaming.

Creating an Impression Inventory

The only way you can be sure that you're making a consistent impression in your marketplace is to take inventory of and study every single communication you have with prospects, customers, and others who deal with your business. You can take an impression inventory by constructing a simple form tailored to your communications activities.

Across the top of the form, label five columns with the words listed in bold and described here:

✔ **Impression points:** No item is too small to include on this list. If your ad is a work of art but your proposal cover is ratty, the negative impact of one will cancel out the positive impact of the other. List every item that carries your name or logo into the marketplace, using the list as a means to trigger your thoughts.

✔ **Target market:** Determine the purpose of each communication. Is it to develop a new prospect or to service an existing customer — or maybe a little bit of both? If your business has a number of customer types or product lines, you may want to get even more specific. For instance, one ad for an insurance agency may target property insurance prospects, while another may target life insurance prospects. By knowing the different purposes, the agency could gauge how much it is investing in the development of each area. By defining the target of each communication, and then the cost, your small business can steer its marketing expenditures straight toward your objectives.

✔ **Who's in charge** of each impression point? Many impressions that impact a company's image are made by those who don't think of themselves as marketers. Nine times out of ten, no one is thinking about the marketing impact when an estimate is presented, a bill is sent, or a purchase order is issued. The secret is to think about the marketing impact way in advance and to create materials and usage systems that conform to a single image for your company.

✔ **Costs involved:** Do your best to include the cost of media or materials and the costs involved to develop the marketing effort. Then break the total down into what percentage should be allocated to prospect development and what percentage should go to customer relations. Again, if you have a number of market segments, estimate what percentage backs each area. The purpose of this exercise is to give you the information you need to determine whether you're dedicating enough effort to various purposes — including business development, customer retention, and marketing of each product line.

✔ **Evaluation:** Jump to the following section, "Rating Your Marketing Communications," for tips on how to evaluate your communications.

With the headers in place, your next step is to list down the left side all the "impression points" that apply to your business. To speed the process, you can add to or subtract from my list:

Impression Points

Advertising

Newspaper ads	Other ads
Magazine ads	Sales materials
Television ads	Brochures
Radio ads	Printed materials (menus, rate cards, instruction sheets, and so on)
Phone book ads	
Other directory ads	Videos
Community publication ads	Presentation supports (slides, overheads, PowerPoint presentations, and so on)
Internet banners or other ads	
Transit ads and outdoor boards	Presentation materials (proposal covers and so on)
Direct mailers	

Signage

Building signage	Event signs
Entry door sign	Posters
Department signs	Office displays
Trade show signs	

(continued)

Impression Points *(continued)*

Correspondence

Letters	Invoices/statements
Memos	Business cards
E-mail	Envelopes
Estimates	Package labels
Purchase orders	

Publicity

News release stationery	Press kit folders

Logo items

T-shirts	Specialty items (pens, coffee cups, paperweights, gift items, and so on)
Baseball caps	
Shopping bags	

As you "take inventory," fill in the blanks under the first column heading ("Impression Points") with every single communication that you send into the marketplace. Use the items shown in the preceding list to guide your thinking.

Then for each entry, go across the chart and fill out your description of the target market the communication vehicle reaches, who's in charge of the communication, what it costs, and how you rate the communication vehicle for clarity and consistency.

When you're done, ask yourself the following questions:

- ✔ Are we allocating our efforts well? Are we spending enough on reinforcing the decisions of our current customers, or are our efforts too heavily weighted toward getting new people through the door — or vice versa?

- ✔ Are we spending money on communications that fit our image and objectives? Especially study your specialty items and advertising inventory as you answer this question. Be sure that they contribute to the message you're trying to send into the marketplace, rather than to some decision made long ago based on the powerful presentation by a sales representative.

- ✔ Is our image consistent, professional, and well suited to the audiences that matter most to our business?

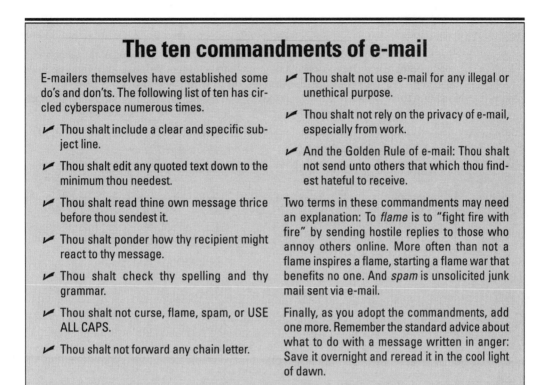

The ten commandments of e-mail

E-mailers themselves have established some do's and don'ts. The following list of ten has circled cyberspace numerous times.

✔ Thou shalt include a clear and specific subject line.

✔ Thou shalt edit any quoted text down to the minimum thou needest.

✔ Thou shalt read thine own message thrice before thou sendest it.

✔ Thou shalt ponder how thy recipient might react to thy message.

✔ Thou shalt check thy spelling and thy grammar.

✔ Thou shalt not curse, flame, spam, or USE ALL CAPS.

✔ Thou shalt not forward any chain letter.

✔ Thou shalt not use e-mail for any illegal or unethical purpose.

✔ Thou shalt not rely on the privacy of e-mail, especially from work.

✔ And the Golden Rule of e-mail: Thou shalt not send unto others that which thou findest hateful to receive.

Two terms in these commandments may need an explanation: To *flame* is to "fight fire with fire" by sending hostile replies to those who annoy others online. More often than not a flame inspires a flame, starting a flame war that benefits no one. And *spam* is unsolicited junk mail sent via e-mail.

Finally, as you adopt the commandments, add one more. Remember the standard advice about what to do with a message written in anger: Save it overnight and reread it in the cool light of dawn.

Use your inventory ratings as the basis for fine-tuning your communications, and then file it in a safe place. If you ever decide to change your name, your logo, or your overall look, this list will remind you of all the items that you need to update.

Rating Your Marketing Communications

Pull samples of stationery, ads, signs, brochures, coffee cups, and T-shirts that carry your company name or logo. Line them all up and put them through this test:

✔ Do your business name and logo look the same every time you make an impression?

✔ Do you consistently use the same colors?

✔ Do you consistently use the same typestyle?

✔ Do your marketing materials present a consistent image — in terms of look, quality, and message?

Get selective.

Study your samples and pull out the ones that don't fit. Perhaps some present outdated or inaccurate versions of your name or logo. Perhaps others look far too professional or unprofessional to fit in with the rest of your program. Perhaps the colors are wrong, or maybe the tone is wrong. Perhaps the message is flip or silly when the rest of your communications are fact-filled and serious.

Now, look at what's left.

- ✔ Does the consistent portion of your communications effort accurately reflect your business?

- ✔ Does it adequately appeal to your target market? Flip back to Chapter 3. Look over the attributes that customers weigh when choosing a product or service, and then determine whether your marketing communications are putting forth the right message.

- ✔ If your customers value top quality, study your marketing materials to see whether they accurately reflect the caliber of company that your market is seeking. Do your ads convey quality? Do you apply your logo only to prestigious items? If you're a retailer, are your shopping bags the finest you can afford? If you're a service company, do you hand over your proposals in folders that your customers will be proud to show to their associates and friends?

- ✔ If your customers value economy above all else, do your materials look too upscale?

- ✔ If your customers choose you primarily for convenience, do your materials put forth that assurance? If you believe that your highest virtue is your reliability, do you convey that attribute through a flawless commitment to a reliably consistent projection of your identity?

Your image is determined by your market, and your market relies on your communications to make an indelible impression, so watch what you project.

Use your impression inventory as the basis for rating your marketing communications. As you get ready to adjust and improve the quality of your communications, turn to Chapter 7 for everything you need to know about managing your image, setting a creative strategy to guide your communications, and writing an image style guide to cast your image rules in cement.

Chapter 7

Establishing Your Position and Brand

"*W*e're just a small business," you're probably thinking. "We aren't Nabisco or Nike or one of the powerful big guys, with some bazillion-dollar ad budget and the world for our market. We're just a 12-person firm trying to build a half million dollars in sales. We hardly need a brand."

Guess what? You *need* a brand.

A brand isn't some mysterious, expensive treasure available only to the rich and famous. And it isn't just for mega-marketers, though most certainly they all have one.

Branding simply (well, maybe not all *that* simply) involves developing and consistently communicating a group of positive characteristics that consumers can identify with and relate to your name. If those characteristics happen to fill a meaningful and available position in their minds — a need they've been wanting and trying to fill — then you just scored a marketing touchdown, and that half-million dollar sales goal will be way easier to reach.

This chapter is about paving the road for marketing success by building a brand, focusing on a market position, and aligning all your communications under a creative strategy that leads to a single image that customers can trust and rely upon. *That's* how small businesses become larger businesses, and that's what marketing is all about.

The ABCs of Branding

Your name is your brand. When people hear your name, they conjure up a set of impressions and characteristics that influence how they think and buy. Those thoughts define your brand.

Your brand resides in the consumer's mind.

You build your brand as a result of all the impressions made by encounters with your name, your logo, your marketing messages, and everything else that people see and hear about your business.

Something as basic as your business address contributes to how your brand is perceived. For that matter, every time that someone walks into your business and looks around, lands on your Web site, glances at your ad, or meets an employee, that person forms an impression that leads to a mind-set about your business.

If a person knows your name, you have a brand in that person's mind. It may not be the brand you want, and it may not be known as well as you wish it was, but you *have* a brand.

You can have a powerful brand without having a power brand

Levi's is a power brand. It's a more powerful brand than Wrangler, Lee, or Guess. All are brands. All convey an identity and a promise. But one is known internationally and by all age and demographic groups; the others have a more narrow influence and, therefore, less marketing power. The power of your brand comes from the degree to which it is known.

Your small business probably will never have a globally recognized "power brand" simply because you don't have (and for that matter you don't need) the marketing horsepower that would fuel that level of awareness.

But you *can* be the most powerful brand within your target market area. All it takes is the following:

  ✔ Knowing the brand image that you want to project

  ✔ Having the commitment and discipline required to project your brand well

  ✔ Spending the money necessary to get your message to your target market

  ✔ Managing your brand so that it makes a consistent impression capable of etching your desired brand image into the mind of your target prospect

Consistency builds brands

Your brand is the market's overall impression about your business. It is what people remember and trust to be true about what you offer, your values, and your company personality. If your marketing communications groove a single impression for your business, then you're building a strong brand. If, however, you put out conflicting messages or messages that present your business with an ever-changing look and feel, you can't expect the market to respond with a single, clear impression about your business. Be consistent in your marketing by following this advice:

✔ Project a consistent look.

✔ Project a consistent tone in your communications.

✔ Project a consistent level of quality, demonstrated by consistent communications, consistent products, and consistent services.

If you notice a word used *consistently* (hint, hint) in the above instructions, write it down and remember it! Be consistent.

Stick with your brand. Don't try to change your look or brand image unless you're certain that it's no longer appropriate for the market. (And if that's the case, you'd better be prepared to change your business — because your brand is the public representation of your business.)

Imagine how tired the people at Campbell's Soup must be of their label, but imagine what would happen to their sales if they abandoned it simply because a fickle marketing manager said, "Let's try something new."

Consistency builds brands. And brands build business.

The case for branding

If you need a motivating fact to boot you into branding action, here it is: Branding makes selling easier, and here's why. People want to buy from companies they know and like, companies they trust will be there well into the future. A brand puts forth that promise.

With a well-managed brand, your company hardly needs to introduce itself. Within your target market, people will already know you, your business personality, and your promise based on what they've seen and heard through your marketing communications.

Without a well-managed brand, you'll have to spend up to half of every consumer contact trying to introduce yourself and make your case, while some well-known Brand X down the street can spend that time making the sale.

Branding: An essential online ingredient

Without a brand, you have to build the case for your business before every sale. Doing that is tough work in person and even tougher work online, where you can't be there to make introductions, counter resistance, or break down barriers.

People are buying everything online — from contact lenses to cars — without the benefit of demonstrations or test-drives. Why? Because customers arrive at the e-business with confidence in the brands they are buying. If they don't see a brand they know, the odds of the purchase occurring plummet. But if they do see the brand they know, then they'll check the price and terms, make their selection, and purchase the product.

Branding facilitates sales and spurs business success all the way from Main Street to the cyberhighway.

Six steps to brand management

Good brand management follows certain steps.

1. **Define why you're in business.**

   What does your business do? How do you do it better than anyone else does?

   Refer to Chapter 5, which can help you put into writing the reason that your business exists and the positive change you aim to achieve.

2. **Consider what you want people to think when they hear your name.**

   What do you want current and prospective employees to think about your business? What do you want customers, suppliers, associates, competitors, and friends to think?

   You can't be different things to each of these different groups and still have a well-managed brand. The brand image held by each of these groups has to synch into one identity — one *brand* — that people will trust and believe.

   For example, if you want employees to think that you pay the very best salaries in your competitive arena, you can't also expect customers to think that you provide the most bare-boned and low-cost market options. Likewise, you can't have an internal company mind-set that says "economy at any price" and expect people to think that no one cares more about product quality and customer service than you do.

   Figure out what you want people to think when they hear your name. Then ask yourself whether that brand image is believable to each of your "stakeholder" groups. If it isn't, decide how you need to alter your business to make achieving your brand image possible.

3. Think about the words you want people to use when defining your business.

Ask your employees, close associates, and customers this question: When people hear your name, what images do you think come into their minds?

If everyone is saying the same thing — and if those words are the words you *want* associated with your name — you have a well-managed brand. But if gaps occur, you have your brand management work cut out for you.

List words that you want people to link to your business, and be certain that you live up to that desired image. Then lead people to the right conclusions by presenting those characteristics — that brand image — consistently and repeatedly in your marketing communications.

4. Pinpoint the *advantages* you want people to associate with your business.

Figuring out these benefits leads you to the definition of your position in the consumer's mind (there's way more on this topic in the section "Finding and Filling a Meaningful Market Position," later in this chapter). Doing so also leads you to the promise that you'll want all of your marketing communications to advance.

5. Define your brand.

Use the information from Steps 1 through 4 to develop a statement about what you offer, your company values, your business personality, and the promise you convey to those who deal with your business.

Try to look at your business through a customer's or prospect's eyes as you define your brand. What do people say — and think — about your business? Why do they choose your business and prefer to buy from you again and again? How would they define your brand?

Boil your findings down to one concept — one brand definition — that you honestly believe you can own in the minds of those who deal with your business. Following are examples of four widely known brands and how they're generally perceived by the public:

- Volvo is the safest car.
- CNN is the all-news channel.
- Pebble Beach is the most majestic and daunting golf challenge.
- Disneyland is the happiest place on earth.

6. Build your brand through every impression that you make.

Flip back to the Impression Inventory in Chapter 6. Every item on that list is either a brand-builder or a brand-detractor, depending upon how well you know your brand and are devoted to projecting it with clarity and consistency.

A well-managed brand creates a strong market impression, and a strong market impression fosters loyal customer behavior. Protect and project your brand through every representation of your business in the marketplace.

Finding and Filling a Meaningful Market Position

Positioning involves figuring out what meaningful and available niche in the market your business is designed to fill, filling it, and performing so well that your customers have no reason to allow anyone else into your market position.

The tricky thing about positioning is that it's not something *you* do to your business; it's something the market does for you. Customers position your company in their own minds. Your job is to lead them to their positioning conclusions through your branding and marketing communications efforts.

How positioning happens

When people learn about your business, subconsciously they slot you into a business hierarchy that includes the following:

- **Me-too businesses (also known as DOA contenders):** If the mind slot — or position — for your business is already taken, consumers do the equivalent of filing your message into the trash bin. If your offering simply duplicates what's already out there, you're DOA — dead on arrival, or at least close to it. The only hope for resuscitation is to find and promote a meaningful point of difference. It better be a pretty compelling distinction though, because you're going to have to convince people that 1) your difference is worth hearing about and 2) your difference is worth changing for.

- **Similar but different businesses (also known as successful end runs):** If your town already has three accounting firms but you open the first one that caters specifically to small businesses, you have a meaningful point of distinction. If you communicate that distinction well, you're apt to win a clear position in the minds of entrepreneurs and CEOs. Depending on the nature of your business, your positioning difference may be based on pricing, inventory, target market, service structure, or company personality. Be sure, though, that the difference is one that matters to your target market. Then clearly communicate your unique story to build appeal for your brand position.

✔ **Brand-new offerings (also known as positioning touchdowns):** If you can be the first to fill a market's needs, you have the easiest positioning task of all. But you must jump into the market skillfully and forcefully enough to win your way into the consumer's mind before anyone else can get there.

First-in-a-market businesses and first-of-a-kind products have to market fast and fastidiously because, in the end, being first isn't as important as being first into the consumer's mind.

Determining your positioning strategy

The easiest way to figure out what position you hold is to determine what hole would be left in the market if your company closed tomorrow. In other words, what does your business offer that your customers would have a hard or impossible time finding elsewhere? Other questions that will lead to your positioning statement include the following:

✔ How is your offering unique or at least difficult to copy?

✔ Is your unique offering something that consumers really want?

✔ Is your offering compatible with the trends of the economy and the market?

✔ Who do you compete with and how are you different — and better?

✔ Is your claim believable?

Don't aim for a position that requires the market to make a leap of faith on your behalf. If a restaurant is known for the best burgers in town, it can't suddenly decide to try to jump into the position of "the finest steakhouse in the state." Leapfrog doesn't work well when the game is positioning.

Remember what has built your success to date and develop your position around that distinct attribute. Here are several examples of positioning statements:

✔ Skyliner is a residential development offering neighborhoods with the finest view in Pleasantville.

✔ Treetops is an alpine inn hosting the most pampered ski vacationers in the East.

✔ *Small Business Marketing For Dummies* is a survival guide featuring easy-to-apply streetwise advice for solving small business marketing challenges.

See how it works? A positioning statement is easy to construct. Just apply the formula you see in Figure 7-1.

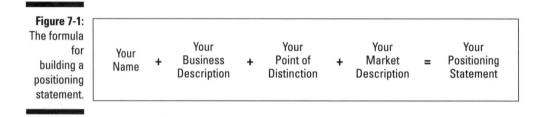

Figure 7-1:
The formula for building a positioning statement.

Your desired position must be

✔ Available

✔ Consistent with the character and offerings of your business

✔ Believable and desirable to the target market

As you write your statement, avoid these traps:

✔ Don't try to position yourself in an already overly crowded category or a category that has already hit its peak and is in decline.

✔ Don't base your distinction on a pricing or quality difference that a competitor can take from you. For instance, you're only egging your competitors on if you position yourself as "the lowest priced" or "the most creative." With a little effort, a competitor can beat you on either front.

✔ Don't hang your hat on a factor you can't control. For example, too many resorts have ended up red-faced after positioning themselves as "the region's only five-star resort," only to lose a star or have a competitor gain one.

Delivering Your Brand Message through Tag Lines

Your *tag line* is the phrase that helps consumers link your name to your brand message. Tag lines (also called slogans) provide customers with an indication of your brand message. Businesses often confuse tag lines with positioning statements. The following table helps sort out the differences.

Positioning Statement	*Tag Line*
Defines how your business wants to be perceived by the market.	Translates your positioning statement into a marketing statement meant to serve as a customer magnet.
Talks to *you*.	Talks to your market.
Small Business Marketing For Dummies is a survival guide featuring easy-to-apply streetwise advice for solving small business marketing challenges.	A Reference for the Rest of Us!

Good tag lines have the following attributes:

- They're memorable.
- They convey your brand image.
- They present key customer benefits.
- They differentiate your business from its competitors.
- They evoke a positive feeling.
- They're unique. For example, they won't work when linked to a competitor's name.
- They fit your branding strategy.
- They don't trigger sarcastic retorts.
- They don't sound like they were written by a corporate committee.

If you adopt a tag line, make it an official element in your marketing communications and use it with your logo on all printed materials. Here are some tips on using your tag line:

- Treat the tag line as part of your logo. Specify the type style and the relationship between the size of the tagline and the size of the logo, so that the slogan doesn't overpower your symbol.
- Insist that the tag line appear with your logo in all printed presentations except e-mail, where your tag line will stand alone as the representative of your brand and position. (Add your tag line to your e-mail signature as a way to advance your brand message through what has become the most common form of business correspondence. See Chapter 6 for more advice.)
- Occasionally (and with great care) change your tag line to support your marketing program. Although your brand strategy shouldn't change, your tag line can — so long as it continues to advance your brand message.

Advancing Your Brand through a Creative Strategy

A *creative strategy* is the plan that directs the development of all your marketing materials. Be aware as you write your strategy statement that you aren't trying to create advertising copy. You don't have to be witty or clever, but you *do* have to be concise and clear about the following:

- Whom you are talking to
- The believable and meaningful benefit you offer to that person, audience, or market
- How you will present your personality in your communications

Writing your creative strategy

One easy-to-follow formula for writing a strategy involves the development of three sentences that define the purpose, approach, and personality that guide the creation of your advertising and other marketing communications. Follow these steps to write your own creative strategy:

1. Sentence #1: "The purpose of our advertising and marketing communications is to convince [insert a brief description of your target market] that our product is the most [describe the primary benefit you provide to customers]."

2. Sentence #2: "We will prove our claim by [insert a description of why your distinct benefit is believable and how you will prove it in your marketing]."

3. Sentence #3: "The mood and tone of our communications will be [insert a description of the personality that all your communications will convey]."

Following are sample strategies for two fictitious businesses.

- **Glass Houses, a window washing service:** The purpose of our advertising is to convince affluent homeowners in our hometown that our service is the easiest and most immediately gratifying way to beautify their homes. We will prove our claim by guaranteeing same-week and streak-free service, by promising four-month call-back reminders, and by offering special three-times-a-year contract rates so that homeowners will never have to think about window cleaning after their first call to our business. The mood and tone of our communications will be straightforward and clean — just like our service.

✔ **Bookworms, an independent book shop:** The purpose of our advertising is to convince hometowners and visitors that our bookstore is the most friendly, welcoming, and informative place to browse and discover great reading material. We will prove our claim by extending invitations to enjoy free staff recommendations, hot drinks, and reading areas in our store and by including reading choices and staff reviews in all our ads. The mood and tone of our communications will be friendly and intelligent, conveying the kind of casual confidence and enthusiasm that members in a book club express to one another.

Using your creative strategy

Every time you create an ad, a direct mailer, a voice-mail recording, or even a business letter or a new employee uniform, think of your creative strategy and be 100 percent certain that your communication is consistent with the strategic message, mood, and tone that you've established to guide your business personality. Here are some ways to do so:

✔ **Begin every new marketing communications effort with a review of your creative strategy.** Whether you're developing a new building sign, a Web site, or a big splashy ad in an expensive magazine, hand the creators your strategy in advance and insist that the final product talk to the right market, advance the right benefit statement, and carry the right look and tone. Think of Nike as a sterling example of a company that has held fast to its creative strategy while creating some of the world's most recognized and creative advertising.

✔ **Use your creative strategy to guide every single representation of your business — and your brand.** Look around your business and at your employees. Do they project the mood and tone you want for your business? For example, if your creative strategy stipulates a discreet tone for your business, you won't want ad respondents to encounter a lively atmosphere with rock music playing in the background when they walk into your business. Work to be sure that the impression made by your marketing materials is in alignment with the experience your customers have walking through your door or meeting you over the phone or online. If it isn't, you won't be able to build a strong brand.

✔ **Fine-tune your creative strategy annually.** Each year as you update your marketing plan (see Chapter 22), you'll likely update your creative strategy as well. You may decide to reach out to a different target market, or you may decide to present a different marketing message, based on your assessment of market opportunities. But don't change your definition of the mood and tone of your communications without great reason and care, and then do so only slightly. (Flip back a few pages to the section "Consistency builds brands" for a reminder on why your look and tone need to be reliable indicators of your brand image.)

Writing Your Image Style Guide

The most well-branded companies and organizations have firm rules about how their logos may appear in printed materials, what type styles and colors must be used in marketing communications, how words are used, and when and how tag lines, copyrights, and trademark lines apply. These are called graphic and style guidelines, and together they protect the face of your business in the marketplace.

Before you let your business entrust its image into the hands of a small print shop, a specialty-advertising producer, or an in-house computer expert, set some rules that direct the outcome.

Your logo presentation

Your logo is the face of your business on marketing materials. To ensure that it is presented cleanly and without unnecessary alteration, ask and answer the following questions in your style guide:

- When your logo appears in black ink, what color backgrounds may be used?

- When your logo appears in white ink (called a *reverse*), what color backgrounds may be used?

- When your logo appears in color, what ink color or colors may be used? The person who designed your logo should specify the ink numbers from the Pantone Matching System used by nearly all printers. Do not allow variations from this color in any professionally produced piece.

- What is the smallest size that can be used for your logo?

Also indicate in your guidelines that the logo must be reproduced from original artwork or a camera-ready reproduction. It may not be reproduced from a photocopy or previously printed piece, because the quality will be inferior.

The type style used in your materials

Determine the type fonts you want to use consistently in your marketing communications. Choose a font (also called a typeface) for use in headlines and also one for use in ad copy. If your company also prints technical materials (such as instruction guides, warrantees, operating or assembly instructions, or other copy-intensive pieces), you may want to designate a third type font that lends itself to small print and heavy copy applications.

Serif type is type with short decorative lines at the start or finish of the letters, while *sans serif* (literally *without serif*) type features letters with no adornments. The serifs help guide the eye from letter to letter and are particularly useful when printing long paragraphs or pages of information.

This is an example of serif type.

This is an example of sans serif type.

The type font you choose for your marketing materials should reflect the personality of your company. If your materials are to convey an old-fashioned or traditional tone, you probably need a serif type. But if you want to have materials that appear very clean and straightforward, sans serif type is an appropriate choice.

In addition to specifying type fonts, you may want to define some usage preferences.

✔ Research has proven that people read copy that uses both uppercase and lowercase letters with greater ease than they read copy printed in all capital letters. For legibility, avoid using all capital letters unless the headline or copy block is extremely short and therefore easy for the eyes to track.

✔ Especially if your target market has aging vision, try to keep text or body copy at no smaller than 12 points in size.

- This is 8-point type.
- This is 10-point type.
- This is 12-point type.
- This is 14-point type.

✔ Avoid reversed type (having your copy appear as white type on black or dark backgrounds, as shown in Figure 7-2) if you expect people to read your words easily. If, for design purposes, you decide to reverse type, keep the type size large.

✔ Keep column widths narrow, especially when you're presenting long blocks of text. Readers' eyes get tired when they have to track across wide spans, and if the eyes tire, your message gets lost in the process.

✔ Limit the number of type fonts that you combine in any single marketing piece, unless you're trying through your design to intentionally look cluttered.

Figure 7-2:
Reversed
type.

This is an example of reversed type.

Copy guidelines

Copy is the term used for the words, text, or content of your marketing materials.

As you establish your style guidelines, define how you want your copy prepared. Doing so will save you time, stress, and money when you ask professionals or staff members to prepare ad or brochure copy on your behalf. Here are some tips to include in your style guide:

- If certain words in your marketing materials require copyright (©), trademark (™), or registration (®) symbols, then list these words in your style guidelines.

- Indicate in your guidelines if your materials require a copyright line to appear in very small (usually 6 point) type at the bottom of your material.

- If you plan to send your printed materials over national borders, you may have to include a line reading "Printed in USA." Check with your attorney and include the instructions in your guidelines.

- Decide which words you prefer to have capitalized in your marketing materials. For example, perhaps your style preference is to say your business is located in "Southern California" and not "southern California." Or maybe you want your business to be called "The Candy Factory" and not "the Candy Factory." The only way you'll get it right is to write it into your image rule book.

- Determine whether you want to ban certain words. For example, a real estate developer may prohibit the word *lots* in favor of the word *homesites*. A public relations firm may rule out the term *PR* and insist the word be spelled out to read *public relations*. If you have style preferences, put them all in writing.

Chapter 8

Getting Strategic Before You Get Creative

*C*reative. The very word turns confident people queasy and rational people giddy. It prompts even the most buttoned-down small business owners to say outrageous things, such as "Let's dress up like chickens" or "Let's show our products as animated characters dancing the cancan," and well-intended but pointless things, such as "Let's cut through the clutter" or "We have to think outside the box."

Far, far less often are you apt to hear the creative conversation turn strategic, with statements like "Let's talk in terms that matter to our target prospects," "Let's define what we're trying to accomplish," and "Let's be sure this ad concept is capable of achieving our objective."

By focusing on your ad objective *before* dreaming up ad concepts — by getting strategic and *then* getting creative — you'll steer past the mistakes that shoot too many ad budgets into the great abyss where wasted dollars languish. This chapter shows how.

Good Ads Start with Good Objectives

Copywriters and designers are talented and creative, but they're rarely telepathic. They can't create an ad that meets an objective if their instructions include no indication of the ad's purpose.

So who is supposed to state the objective, set the ad strategy, and aim the creative process, anyway? Well, get ready, because that task falls to the person responsible for marketing, which is probably, well, *you.*

In blunt terms, good ads begin in *your* office.

Aimed versus shot-in-the-dark ad instructions

You can hit your ad target almost every time if you take careful aim. Read the following two examples of ad instructions and note the differences:

> Example 1: "We need to build sales. Let's run some ads."

> Example 2: "We need to run ads to convince teenagers that by shopping after school on weekdays they will enjoy our best prices in a club atmosphere because we feature live music, two-for-one café specials, and weekday-only student body card discounts."

Example 1 forces the ad creation team to guess what you want. It will likely lead to an ad creation process that involves round after round of revisions as the advertising team tries to read your mind about the target market, the promotional offer, the creative concept, the ad copy, and the media schedule.

Example 2 tells the ad creators precisely which consumers you're targeting, what you want to say, the offer you want to make, and the action you're hoping to achieve so that they can develop an appropriate concept and media plan — probably on the first try.

As the chief marketer for your business, you must give those who produce your ads the information they need to do the job right the first time around.

Dodging the creative landmines

There's an old saying among marketers that half of all ad dollars are wasted, but no one knows which half. You can move the dividing line between ads that work and ads that don't by planning in advance to avoid these three wasteful errors:

- ✔ **Mistake #1:** Producing creative ads without first defining objectives, leading to the production of entertaining ads that address neither the target prospect nor the advertising objective

- ✔ **Mistake #2:** Creating hard-sell ads without first reeling in the attention and interest of the prospect, resulting in ads that readers tune out or pass over altogether

> ✔ **Mistake #3:** Creating advertiser-centered ads that focus more on the advertiser and what that business wants to sell than on the consumer and what that person wants to buy

Setting Your Ad Strategy

Your *ad strategy* is a brief statement defining what you want to accomplish with your ad. It is the basis on which you will evaluate ad concepts, and it is the beacon by which the ad creators will navigate.

Any ad concept that doesn't meet the specifications of the creative strategy, no matter how engaging, attention-getting, and clever, should be considered dead on arrival. Advertising is great only if it works, and it works only if it accomplishes your objective while advancing your brand image.

Sample ad strategy format

To write an ad strategy, you need to know who you're trying to influence, what you're trying to get the market to do, and what message you want to promote to accomplish your aim. Use the following format as your ad strategy template by inserting the appropriate text for your business in the parentheses:

> **This** (ad/brochure/sales call/speech/trade booth display, or so on) **will convince** (describe the target market for this communication) **that** (describe the action that you hope to achieve) **will** (describe the benefit they will realize) **because** (state the facts that prove your claim). **To advance our brand image, the mood of our communication will be** (describe your brand tone).

Diagram of an ad strategy

Table 8-1 presents the strategy for a high-tech product being advertised to a highly defined target market. It is proof that even a complex strategy can fit into two sentences — one defining the strategy and the other defining the tone necessary to advance the brand image. To understand what we mean, first read all the statements down the left column in continuous, whole sentence form. Then analyze the sentences by paying attention to the boldface type and the explanations in the right column.

Table 8-1	Ad Strategy
Sample Strategy Sentences	*What the Phrase Does*
This **magazine ad**	Defines the nature of your communication, in this case, a magazine ad.
will convince **managers of front line telecommunications repair staff**	Describes the target market. This ad will be written to managers of front-line, hands-on telecommunications repair staff.
that **returning the provided reply card to obtain more information about our fiber optic tester**	Explains what you want out of the ad and provides everything needed to obtain the action you desire. This advertiser wants brochure requests and includes a postage-paid reply card for easy response.
will **give them the facts they need to decide upon and arrange the purchase of the best testing device on the market for fast, accurate location of underground fiber problems and line breaks**	Defines the prospect's buying process and the related plan. This ad offers a detailed product brochure because the prospect will need facts and figures to accompany his request to a purchasing agent.
because **only our tester houses such advanced reflectometry technology in a portable, weather-rugged case that repair staff can carry into the field in the worst weather conditions to test installed underground fiber and to locate break sites within five feet of the problem area.**	States the features as user benefits, not as a lineup of specifications. The benefit presented in this ad is that the instrument goes where it needs to go and does what it needs to do — with portability, reliability, and accuracy. Lead with the benefit; follow with the facts and features.
To advance our brand image, the mood of our communication will be **consistent with that of the field environment rather than the boardroom, using straightforward language to emphasize repair solutions rather than repair equipment.**	Establishes a brand mood and tone (refer to Chapter 7 for more information). The creative strategy will serve as the umbrella under which the strategy for each ad and marketing communication effort exists.

Writing a Creative Brief

Your ad strategy defines *what* you're trying to accomplish. Your creative brief details *how* you'll get the job done. Figure 8-1 provides a format to follow as you condense your instructions into a page of information to hand to those who will create your ad. Simply answer Questions 1 through 7 (you can find more advice on each step later in this chapter), and your briefing instructions will be complete.

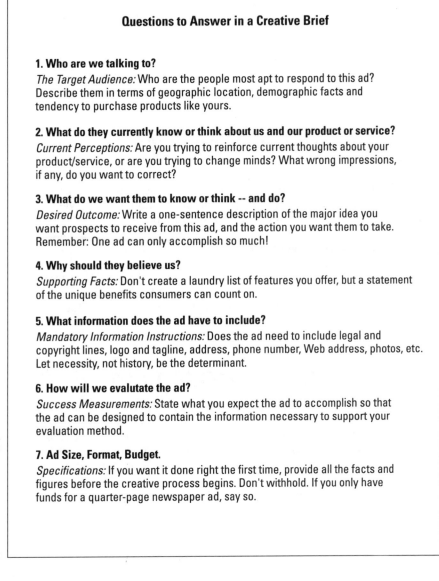

Questions to Answer in a Creative Brief

1. Who are we talking to?

The Target Audience: Who are the people most apt to respond to this ad? Describe them in terms of geographic location, demographic facts and tendency to purchase products like yours.

2. What do they currently know or think about us and our product or service?

Current Perceptions: Are you trying to reinforce current thoughts about your product/service, or are you trying to change minds? What wrong impressions, if any, do you want to correct?

3. What do we want them to know or think -- and do?

Desired Outcome: Write a one-sentence description of the major idea you want prospects to receive from this ad, and the action you want them to take. Remember: One ad can only accomplish so much!

4. Why should they believe us?

Supporting Facts: Don't create a laundry list of features you offer, but a statement of the unique benefits consumers can count on.

5. What information does the ad have to include?

Mandatory Information Instructions: Does the ad need to include legal and copyright lines, logo and tagline, address, phone number, Web address, photos, etc. Let necessity, not history, be the determinant.

6. How will we evalutate the ad?

Success Measurements: State what you expect the ad to accomplish so that the ad can be designed to contain the information necessary to support your evaluation method.

7. Ad Size, Format, Budget.

Specifications: If you want it done right the first time, provide all the facts and figures before the creative process begins. Don't withhold. If you only have funds for a quarter-page newspaper ad, say so.

Figure 8-1:
Question guide to writing a creative brief.

Walking through the Creative Planning Process

Every time you create an ad, write a speech, make a sales presentation, create a brochure, or compose an important business letter, start by running through the questions on the creative brief to focus your thinking. For all major projects, commit your answers to writing by completing the form.

If you think you don't have time, make time anyway. Consider this the "preventive medicine" of advertising. If you apply an ounce of preventive energy in the beginning, you won't have a pound of problems to cure later.

Targeting your market

Start with everything you know about your prospects (see Chapter 2 for more information) and then boil your knowledge into a one-sentence definition that capsulizes the geographic location, the lifestyle facts, and the purchasing motivators of your target prospects.

Here is the target market statement for a real estate developer:

> The prospect is a resident of Montana, aged 40+, married with children living at home, with a professional career, upper-middle to upper income, and an affinity for travel, outdoor recreation, status brands, and high levels of service.

Dealing with prospect perceptions

Advertising is supposed to alter market perceptions and inspire action. But in order to change market perceptions, you need to start with knowledge about what your prospect currently knows and thinks about your business. Use your own instincts and those of your staff and colleagues to answer the following questions about what prospects know and think:

- ✔ Have they heard of your business?
- ✔ Do they know what products or services you offer?
- ✔ Do they know where you're located or how to reach you?
- ✔ Do they see you as a major player? If they were asked to name three suppliers of your product or service, would your name be among the answers?

> ✔ How do they rate your service, quality, pricing, accessibility, range of products, and reputation?
>
> ✔ Do you have a clear brand and market position or a mistaken identity in their minds?

Be candid with your answers. Only by acknowledging your shortcomings can you begin to address them through advertising.

A new destination resort might write the following prospect opinion assessment:

> The majority of our prospects are not aware of our existence, but among those who know our name, we are known to provide an experience competitive with the best resort offerings in our state. We need to reinforce the opinions of our acquaintances while extending awareness to our prospects and especially to those opinion leaders whose recommendations are most valued by our affluent and socially connected target market.

Stating your desired outcome

Some advertisers use the tired phrase "more bang for the buck" as they work ineffectively to pack a dozen thoughts into a 30-second radio commercial or onto a print ad smaller than an index card.

Don't be greedy. Present one clear idea in your ad, and chances are good that you'll *communicate* one clear idea. But if you try to present two or three messages, you're likely to communicate nothing at all.

Four out of five consumers read only the headline in a print ad; they absorb no more than seven words off a billboard; and they take one idea away from a broadcast ad — providing that they don't tune out or skip over the ad altogether.

What single idea do you want readers or viewers to take away from your ad? As you answer, follow this process:

1. **Step out of your own shoes and stand in those of your prospect.**

2. **Think about what that person wants or needs to know.**

3. **Develop a single sentence describing what you want prospects to think and what motivating idea you want them to take from your ad.**

Here is the desired outcome for a computer retailer targeting senior citizens:

> We want senior citizens to know that they're invited to attend our Computer 101 open houses every Wednesday afternoon this month where they can watch computer and Internet demonstrations, receive hands-on training, and learn about our special first-time computer owner packages that include in-home installation and Internet hook-up.

Watch what you ask for! Be sure that you can handle the outcome you say you desire.

You've probably heard the saying that a good ad can kill a bad product faster than it could die on its own. If you aren't geared up to answer the phone, handle the foot traffic, or fulfill the buying demand that your ad generates, then you have failed strategically even though you succeeded — wildly — on the advertising front.

Consider this example: A one-man painting company decided to rev business by placing a series of very clever small-space ads in the local newspaper. The ads touted impeccable service, outstanding quality, affordable estimates, and prompt response. The ad series won attention, action, and advertising awards. The problem is, the painter couldn't keep up with the phone calls, the estimates, or the orders. Prospects — who had been inspired by the great ads to paint their homes — called the painter's competitors instead.

The moral of the story is to expect a miracle from good advertising and to be prepared to get what you ask for.

Making your case

To be believable, ads need to make and support a claim. *The easy way* is to list your features (the oldest moving company in the east, under new management, the only manufacturer featuring the X2000 widget, ten-year winner of our industry's top award, yada yada yada . . .). *The effective way* is to turn those features into benefits that you promise to your customers. The difference between features and benefits is that features are facts, while benefits are personal outcomes.

Table 8-2 shows you exactly what this crucial difference means.

Table 8-2	Features versus Benefits		
Product	*Feature*	*Benefit*	*Emotional Outcome*
Diet soda	One calorie	Lose weight	Look and feel great
Flower arrangements	Daily imports of exotic blooms	Send one-of-a-kind attention-getting floral presentations	Satisfaction that your gift stands out and draws attention
Automobile	Best crash rating	Reduce risk of harm in accidents	Security that your family is safe
Miniature microwave oven	1.5 cubic feet in size	Save dorm room space	Make room for the floor's only big-screen TV

Every time you describe a *feature* of your product or service, you're talking to yourself. Every time you describe the *benefit* that your product or service delivers, you're talking to your prospect, because consumers don't buy the feature — they buy what the feature does for them. Here are some examples:

- ✔ Consumers don't buy V-8 engines. They buy speed.
- ✔ They don't buy shock-absorbing shoes. They buy walking comfort.
- ✔ They don't buy the lightest laptop computer. They buy the freedom to work wherever they want.

Follow these steps to translate features into benefits:

1. **State your product or business feature.**
2. **Add the phrase "which means."**
3. **Complete the sentence and you are forced to state the benefit.**

   THE FEATURE + "WHICH MEANS" = THE BENEFIT

Here's an example using the diet soda mentioned in Table 8-2: Diet soda has one calorie (that's the feature) *which means* you can lose weight and look and feel great (that's the benefit).

Naming your "have-to-haves"

Ad designers call it "death by a thousand cuts" when marketers respond to every creative presentation with the words, "Yes, but we have to include . . . ."

If you know that your ad needs to feature a certain look or specific information or artwork, say so up front — not after you see the first creative presentation. And keep the list of have-tos as short as possible. Here are some guidelines.

- ✔ **Have-to #1:** Every ad has to advance your brand image with consistency. Refer to Chapter 7 for information on establishing the creative strategy and image style guide for your brand. Provide copies of the style guide when you present the ad team with the strategy for the particular ad assignment.

- ✔ **Have-to #2:** Be sparing with all other have-tos. Every time you start to say, "we have to include . . ." stop and check yourself with this self test:

  - Is this element necessary to protect our brand?
  - Is it necessary to protect our legal standing?
  - Is it necessary to prompt the action the ad must achieve?
  - Is it necessary to motivate the prospect?
  - Let necessity — not history — guide your answers.

Deciding how you'll measure success

Small businesses are critical of their ads — after the fact.

After an ad has run its course, the advertiser may criticize its effectiveness, saying something like "That ad didn't work, it didn't make the phone ring, and it sure didn't create foot traffic." Yet if you ask to see the ad under question, you'll find that it includes no reason to call, no special offer, a phone number that requires a magnifying glass, and no address whatsoever.

If you want consumers to take action when they see or hear your ad, set your expectation *before* the concept is created and define your measurement standard in your creative brief.

Specifying your specifications

Know the specifications of your job before you start producing it — and especially before you assign the production task to others.

- ✔ Set your budget and be frank about how much you can spend on production and media buys. Advertisers often worry that if they tell their creative partners the truth about their budgets, the designers or writers or agencies will spend it all — whether they need to or not. So they often try to conceal budget information in an effort to control costs. But the strategy usually backfires. If suppliers *don't* know the budget, they *will* spend it all — and then some — simply because no one gave them a not-to-exceed figure to work with. The solution is to hire suppliers you trust, share your budget with them (along with instructions that the budget cannot be exceeded without prior approval), and then count on them to be partners in providing a cost-effective solution. (See Chapter 9 for information on how to control costs when working with advertising agencies and freelance talent.)

- ✔ Obtain the media deadlines and material requirements if you have already committed to media buys. Attach a media rate card to your creative brief so that your designer can see the specifications directly from the publication and not through your translation.

- ✔ Define the parameters of non-media communication projects. For example, if you're asking for speechwriting assistance, know the length of time allocated for your presentation. If you're requesting materials for a sales presentation, know the number of people expected to attend and therefore the number of handouts you'll want to take with you.

The nitty-gritty details seem like a boring sideshow to the creative process until a great idea lurches to a halt because it fails to fit within the necessary specifications. What the creative team doesn't know can cost you dearly in enthusiasm and cost overruns if you have to retrofit creative solutions to fit production realities, so communicate in advance to keep everyone happy.

Creating Ads That Work

Good ads grab attention and lead consumers exactly where they want to go. Here's how:

- ✔ Good ads present *what* the prospect wants to buy.
- ✔ They present it *how* and *when* the prospect wants to buy it.
- ✔ They affirm *why* the prospect wants to buy it.

Good ads persuade, convince, and nudge prospects into action, and they do it without any apparent effort. Great ads manage to meld the verbiage with the visual and the message with the messenger so that the consumer receives it all as a single, compelling idea.

Creative teams will tell you that making an ad look so simple takes a lot of time and talent — and they're right.

If you're spending more than $10,000 to place an ad or more than $100,000 on annual media buys, consider bringing in the pros to help you out. Turn to Chapter 9 for advice about hiring freelancers or an advertising agency to amp up your creative horsepower.

Whom to involve

You may not be the best person to generate your own ad ideas. You may be too deeply set in routine terminology and too closely tied to the message you want your business to convey to step back and think in creative terms that will move your market to action. Consider saving your own time to set the strategy and evaluate concepts. Turn the actual creation of ads over to those experienced in the field, including some or all of the following professionals:

A *copywriter* is a person who writes the headline and motivating copy or, in the case of broadcast ads, the ad script. This person needs to be a good communicator who is capable of writing simply, clearly, and directly to your target prospects, using a single-minded approach to grab and hold the prospect's attention and to achieve the ad objective.

A *designer* is a person who arranges your ad so that it is visually appealing, using a layout that draws the viewer's eye to the correct starting point before guiding it on an effortless movement through the ad elements.

A *producer* is necessary if you're creating a radio or television ad, a video, or any kind of multimedia show. The difference in quality, impression, and impact between do-it-yourself and professionally produced broadcast ads and videos is big and undeniable. The local cable company can produce an ad for you (in which case it serves as the producer, so you'll want them in your early creative sessions). Realize, however, that especially when it comes to broadcast ad production, you get what you pay for, so think three times before agreeing to pay nothing. Free is a very good price, but in return you risk running an ad that looks and sounds like all the other media-produced creations.

Where to start

Ideas aren't exactly responsive to pressure, so ease yourself into the creative process, starting with a review of everything there is to know about your brand, your business, your product, and your market.

- ✔ Write down your positioning statement and tag line (see Chapter 7 for more on tag lines) to focus on the meaningful niche in the marketplace that the product you're advertising fills.

- ✔ Review your Unique Selling Proposition, or USP. This is the compelling proposition that consumers associate only with your business. It draws people to you and distinguishes you from your competition.

- ✔ List good things you've heard customers say about your product or service.

- ✔ Recall words that you use during sales presentations.

- ✔ Dig around for every product fact and figure you can get your hands on. It's impossible to know too much about what you're promoting. Buried in the details may be the very fact that will unleash a winning concept.

- ✔ Define the kinds of people who definitely *won't* want your product. (Defining nonbuyers is a good way to uncover things about those who *will* buy.)

- ✔ Think of all the reasons why a prospect will want to take action. Think of one likely prospect and consider that person's perceptions, desires, and needs.

- ✔ Make a list of everything that you're trying to achieve. What do you want people to think? How do you want them to change? What do you want people to *do*? Do you want them to feel differently, to tell a friend, to pick up the phone, to ask for more information, to purchase the product?

Landing on the Big Idea

The *big idea* is to advertising what the brake pedal, gas pedal, *and* steering wheel are to driving. (Now do you see why they call it *big*?) Here's what the big idea does:

- ✔ It stops the prospect.
- ✔ It fuels interest.
- ✔ It directs prospects toward the desired action.

"Think Small" is an historic example of a big idea. Volkswagen used it to stun a market into attention at a time when big-finned, lane-hogging gas guzzlers ruled the highways. "Think Small" — two words accompanied by a picture of a squat, round car miniaturized on a full page — stopped consumers, changed attitudes, and made a car dubbed "The Bug" chic.

Big ideas are

- ✔ Attention-getting
- ✔ Memorable
- ✔ Compelling
- ✔ Persuasive
- ✔ Capable of conveying the benefit you promise
- ✔ Appealing to your target market

A good idea qualifies as a big idea only if it meets *all* of the qualifications. Many advertisers quit when they hit on an idea that's attention-getting and memorable. Think of this: A slammed door is attention-getting and memorable, but it's far from compelling, persuasive, beneficial, or appealing.

Brainstorming

Brainstorming is an anything-goes group process for generating ideas through free association and imaginative thinking with no grandstanding, no idea ownership, no evaluation, and definitely no criticism.

The whole point of brainstorming is to put the mind on automatic pilot and see where it leads. You can improve your brainstorming sessions by trying the following tips:

- ✔ Flip through magazines for inspiration.
- ✔ Look at competitors' ads.
- ✔ Look at your own past ads.
- ✔ Think of how you can turn the most unusual attributes of your product or service into unique benefits.

✔ Doodle. Ultimately an ad is a combination of words and visuals. See where your pencil leads your mind.

✔ Widen your perspective by inviting a customer or a front-line staff person to participate in the brainstorming session.

If you decide to turn ad creation over to members of your staff or to freelance or agency writers and designers, you may or may not decide to participate in the brainstorm session. But if you do attend, remember that there is no boss in a brainstorm. Every idea serves as a springboard to another idea, so bite your tongue every time you want to say "yes, but," or "we tried that once and . . ." or "get real, that idea is just plain dumb." Remember, in a brainstorm session, every idea is a good idea.

At the end of the brainstorm, gather up and evaluate the ideas:

✔ Which ideas support the ad strategy?

✔ Which ones present the consumer benefit?

✔ Which can be implemented with strength and within the budget?

Any idea that wins on all counts is a candidate for implementation.

Golden rules

Chapters 11, 12, and 13 are all about creating and placing print ads, broadcast ads, and direct mail ads. Follow these rules for *all* your ads — regardless of the medium, the message, the mood, or the creative direction:

✔ Know your objective and stay on strategy.

✔ Be honest.

✔ Be specific.

✔ Be original.

✔ Be clear and concise.

✔ Don't overpromise or exaggerate.

✔ Don't be self-centered or, worse, arrogant.

✔ Don't hard-sell.

✔ Don't insult, discriminate, or offend.

✔ Don't turn the task of ad creation over to a committee.

Committees round the edge off any strong idea. They eliminate any nuance that any member finds questionable. An old cartoon that circulates in ad agencies has the punch line "a camel is a horse designed by committee."

Evaluating Your Advertising Efforts

Getting small businesses to want to assess their advertising is easy, which is why armchair quarterbacking is such a popular after-the-ad-runs activity. The problem is that if you want to be certain about which ad concept is pulling well, or which media buy is working best, you have to plan early — back when the plays are being called — not after the fumble has already occurred.

The easiest way for small businesses to monitor ad effectiveness is to produce ads that generate responses and then to trace those responses to various messages, offers, and media placements.

Generating ad responses

To track responses, include a response mechanism in your ad, choosing from the following suggestions:

- Give the prospect a reason to respond. Offer a brochure, a free estimate, or some other incentive to contact your business.

- Make response easy by featuring a toll-free number or including a pre-paid reply card or, in the case of direct mailings, an addressed envelope.

- If you plan to evaluate ad performance based on phone calls, create an ad that presents a reason to call and gives prominent placement to an easy-to-read phone number.

- If you plan to evaluate based on an increase in foot traffic or cash register activity, present a compelling and time-sensitive offer and be prepared to track the origination of customer activity during the promotion period.

Keying responses

A *key* is a code used to facilitate an advertiser's ability to track the ads that produce an inquiry or order. Here's how to key your ads:

- Add a unique extension to your phone number, keyed to indicate response to a certain medium or ad concept. Train all who answer the phone to quickly record the extension number before processing the inquiry.

- Add a key to coupons that you include in print ads and direct mailers. For direct mailers, the key might indicate the mailing list from which the inquiry was generated. For print ads, the code could match up with the publication name and issue date. For example, BG0214 might be the key for an ad that runs on Valentine's Day in *The Boston Globe*.

> ✔ Feature different post office box numbers on ads running in various publications or on various stations. Alert those who open your mail to attach all envelopes to inquiries so that you can monitor not only the number of responses per medium but also the effectiveness of each medium in delivering prospects that convert to customers.

Here are a couple ways that you can use ad keys to evaluate your advertising effectiveness:

> ✔ You can test a headline or ad concept by placing a number of different ads that all present the identical offer. Then track responses to measure which ads perform best.

> ✔ You can compare the cost effectiveness of various media buys by measuring the number of responses against the cost of the placement.

As you measure ad effectiveness, expect lag times between ad placements and consumer responses. Magazine ads, especially, take longer to show results because they're received and noted over a longer period of time than either newspapers or broadcast media.

The best test of whether your advertising is on target is whether your business is growing in both sales and profitability. If the answer is yes, you can be confident that you're getting the right messages to the right prospects and that you're taking the right actions to convert the interest generated by your ads into lasting customer relationships.

Chapter 9

Getting Help for Your Marketing Program

● ●

In This Chapter

▶ Figuring out when to seek professional marketing help

▶ Using in-house talent

▶ Deciding whom to hire

▶ Selecting an ad agency

● ●

*Y*ou're a small business marketer. Most likely you're not a trained marketing strategist, a media buyer, an award-winning designer, or a stop-'em-in-their-tracks copywriter.

You're also human. You have 24 hours in every day, and perhaps you've suddenly realized that even by giving up sleep you can't come up with enough time to run your company, develop your products and services, build your customer base, maintain your business relationships, *and* produce and place your own ads.

Or maybe you have the time, but you lack the professional touch or creative talent to create great ads, brochures, Web sites, or promotions on your own.

Or, best of all, maybe you've arrived at the point where your business has simply grown so large that you can no longer implement its marketing programs on your own.

Perhaps all you need is some help from a designer, a copywriter, or a media buyer. Or maybe it's time to graduate to "client" status by hiring an advertising agency to help polish and project your image. Either way, you need to know where to find marketing professionals, how to manage the screening and selection process, and how to participate in a relationship that works to your immediate and lasting advantage. That's what the following pages are about.

Knowing When It's Time to Get Help

When it comes to marketing, getting help is an indication of success. It means that you've decided to strengthen the image and message you project in the marketplace. It also means that you're willing to invest some of your hard-won profits into this business-building effort.

As with most business investments, you can't afford to dive in too soon, nor can you wait too long. Here's how you'll know when it's time to bring in the pros:

- ✔ **When you're creating a long-life marketing piece:** If you're creating a new logo, an important ad campaign, a major marketing brochure, or some other piece that will represent your business for months or years to come, invest in professional assistance if you're at all uncertain that your own talents aren't up to the task.

- ✔ **When doing it yourself takes you or your staff away from more profitable activities:** Focus on doing what you do best, and contract with marketing professionals to do what they do best. You'll profit doubly by building your business while investing in professionally produced marketing materials.

- ✔ **When your annual budget for marketing communications reaches $50,000:** Add up what you've budgeted for brochures, advertising, direct mail, and other outreach efforts. If the total exceeds $50,000, consider hiring creative professionals to build a strong message, look, and coordinated campaign for your company.

- ✔ **When the budget for any single marketing effort exceeds $10,000:** If you're going to put significant dollars behind a single direct-mail program, brochure, or ad placement, don't risk your investment trying to do it yourself unless you're certain of your internal capabilities.

Knowing Where to Turn for Help

With growing success, your needs will exceed the time or the talent that you have to devote to producing your marketing program. As you lift the weight off your own shoulders, here are some ways to get help:

- ✔ You can tap in-house talent.

- ✔ You can turn to local print shops or media ad departments for free or almost-free production services.

- ✔ You can hire freelancers, who are independent contractors available by the hour for short-term projects.

- ✔ You can hire an advertising or public relations agency to handle your work as a major project or as an ongoing assignment.

Tapping in-house talent

Many entrepreneurs take the first step away from doing it all themselves by assigning the coordination of marketing functions to an employee or associate. Others make the decision to add a staff person to handle the marketing task.

Before you take either of these steps, weigh the following cost considerations. Sometimes trying to save the expense of hiring outside professional talent by assigning the task to those already on or added to the payroll can result in a false economy if the in-house talent isn't up to the task at hand.

Assigning the marketing task to a staff member

Before you add the role of marketing management to the responsibilities of an existing staff member or associate, here's what you need to do:

- ✔ Write a job description for the ideal person to handle your marketing. Look at the experience and attributes you define as necessary. Before assigning the task in-house, be sure that the designated staff member meets the criteria.

- ✔ If the staff member doesn't possess the expertise to perform the assignment well, consider what kind of training will be necessary and the cost of the training.

- ✔ Consider which current responsibilities you will shift, and to whom? The staff person who will take on the marketing duties probably doesn't have idle time in which to perform the new marketing assignment.

- ✔ Define what kind of materials and resources this person will require in order to do the job. For instance, you may need to invest in design or production-tracking software, professional publications, occasional professional education opportunities, and support staff.

Hiring a marketing manager

When you hire a person to handle your marketing program, you may very well be able to delay the decision to hire an agency — because you'll have a person on staff who can handle the coordination and marketing management role. But as you budget for the position, realize that no one person can do it all — design, copywriting, Internet marketing, public relations, and media planning and buying. Plan accordingly by budgeting for freelance talent in addition to the line item that you budget for your new marketing manager.

Include the items in the following checklist in your budget:

- ✔ Recruiting and hiring costs
- ✔ Annual salary of the marketing manager or coordinator
- ✔ Annual benefits package

✔ Office equipment and supplies

✔ Professional enrichment costs

✔ Support staff

✔ Cost of outside talent for expertise not supplied by the marketing manager — including design, copywriting, production management, media planning and buying, Web site and broadcast ad production, strategic planning, and other marketing tasks

Forming an in-house agency

A general rule used in marketing recommends allocating 15 percent of the marketing budget for creative and production services. This guideline stems from the fact that most mass media organizations pay recognized ad agencies 15 percent of media buys as commissions. Historically, agencies have used the revenue from these commissions to cover the costs involved to produce their clients' ads.

Some companies calculate the commissions that their ad budgets will generate and decide to form an in-house agency so that they can keep the money under their own roofs.

An *in-house agency* (also called a *house agency*) is a company department set up to function as an ad agency that serves only one client — the company of which it is a part.

To form an in-house agency, take the following steps:

✔ Establish an internal marketing department that has the expertise to plan, produce, and place ads.

✔ Establish your agency with media organizations to confirm that you qualify for the discount offered to recognized agencies. Check with the publications and stations that serve your market. Find out about the criteria they use to recognize an agency, and see that you meet the requirements.

✔ Plan to pay media bills promptly in order to qualify for the commission.

Small businesses flirt with the idea of forming an in-house agency because they want to qualify for the 15 percent media commission. But when it comes to commissions, you have to spend money — a lot of money — to make money. Until you're spending $150,000 on media buys, the commissions are hardly enough to fund the bare-bone costs involved in staffing your own ad agency. Do the math: Fifteen percent of $150,000 is $22,500, hardly enough to pay the salary and benefits of an assistant, let alone someone with proven expertise to write, design, and produce ads that can enhance your image in the marketplace.

Using free or almost-free resources

This section is short. You get what you pay for, and if you don't need much, then free is a wonderful price. If you're only adding a tag line to a preproduced industry broadcast ad or dropping your logo and address into a manufacturer's newspaper ad, then you hardly need to invest in high-priced assistance. Hand your instructions over to a media production department, ask for a proof, and keep your billfold in your pocket as you probably won't have to pay a thing.

Likewise, if you're reprinting an existing brochure with only minor type changes, or if you're creating something as simple as a rack card using an already established design template, then a designer at your print shop is apt to be an ideal and economical resource.

But . . . if you want a big creative idea, a unique concept, a striking design, or memorable creative quality, then budget accordingly and hire professionals who can spend the time and effort necessary to create a piece capable of enhancing and advancing your unique brand image.

Hiring marketing professionals

Entrepreneurs hear the term "advertising agency" and instinctively grab hold of their billfolds — with good reason. The myth is a reality when it comes to the feeling that advertising agencies — and freelance professionals too for that matter — are expensive. They charge hourly fees that start in the mid $50s and climb up to $150 in a hurry.

An ad produced by professionals may cost anywhere from $500 to $10,000, depending on whether you're looking at a simple black-and-white ad for the local daily or a splashy full-page, full-color ad designed to compete in one of the big, slick, showy monthly magazines. Staggering as the numbers are, don't let them scare you off. Not yet. First, do the following:

- ✔ Add up what you spend on media buys. Then calculate 15 percent of that total to find out the amount that an ad agency would receive in media commissions if the agency placed your ads for you. Those commissions could apply to your ad creation and production costs, thereby reducing the amount you would need to spend to retain the agency's services.

- ✔ Then do an objective analysis of your current advertising compared to that of your competitors. Ask yourself whether your business would profit in terms of image, impact, and market responsiveness if you invested more in ad creation and production.

- ✔ Finally, estimate the potential profit you might realize if your ads were even 5 or 10 percent more effective in inspiring market action.

If you decide that the impact of professionally produced marketing materials justifies the extra expense involved (and it usually does), you can turn to a full range of professionals who can help you out on an hourly basis. They include advertising and public relations agencies, graphic design studios, freelance or independent graphic artists and copywriters, and media planners and buyers.

- ✔ **Ad agencies, public relations firms, and design studios** are set up to handle entire jobs, from strategic and concept development through design and copywriting, production management, and overseeing printing, ad placement, and direct mailings. They have systems in place to handle multifaceted tasks and they have a team of professionals to assign to your job. They also serve as brokers — screening, selecting, and managing photographers, printers, and a wide range of marketing specialists on your behalf. Best of all, they assign a liaison, usually called an account executive, to serve as your primary contact and advocate. As a result, you have a team of people helping you, but you have to deal with only one person, who will hold all the others accountable on your behalf.

- ✔ **Freelancers** are specialists in particular fields such as strategic planning, copywriting, design, illustration, and desktop publishing. Freelancers work on an hourly basis and gladly accept project work, whereas agencies often prefer longer-term client commitments. One other major difference is that freelancers are individuals who provide solutions on an assignment basis. They are rarely part of a team. If your job requires the talents of a variety of freelancers (a writer, a designer, and a photographer, for instance), you need to retain responsibility for managing your budget and timeline and for coordinating interface between the various professionals.

In deciding what kind of expertise to hire, follow these tips:

- ✔ Hire professionals whose talents and fees fit your situation. If you want a photo of a new employee to send with a news release to the local paper, you hardly need to hire a photographer who charges $1,000 a day to take the mug shot. And you don't need a public relations consultant whose fee is $100 an hour to write a two-paragraph release.

- ✔ If you have a person in house who can serve as the point person who coordinates the various steps of the production and ad placement process, you can hire freelancers rather than an agency. But if you need management as well as creative expertise, turn to an agency that is set up to offer full service and to assume the coordination role.

Some general guidelines can help you select the right person for the job. For example, a designer is your answer if you need a logo, stationery, start-up image materials, a low-budget or fairly simple product brochure, or a single ad. A copywriter also can help if you need brochures or a single ad. A media planner or buyer is the person who can come to the rescue if you want someone to help you with media placement of preproduced ads. Public relations agencies are skilled at special event planning, public relations, publicity generation, or crisis management. A full-service ad agency is the best approach if you're undertaking several of these activities as part of your overall marketing program, or if you already have an ad agency relationship.

Choosing and Working with an Agency

The best agency relationships start with a careful selection process. Before you can select a marketing partner, here's what you need to know:

- ✔ **Your needs:** What kind of service are you seeking? Are you looking for an agency or creative group to help you with a single important project — perhaps the creation of an advertising campaign, a major brochure, an annual report, or a big promotion? Or are you establishing an agency relationship to help you build your image on a long-term basis? Know what kind of partnership you're after before contacting agencies. Some agencies welcome project work, while others prefer to limit their involvement to work with clients only on a long-term partnership basis.

- ✔ **Your priorities:** Some businesses want an agency with a reputation for delivering award-winning creative concepts. Others want to work only with agencies with demonstrated experience in a particular industry or market segment. Some seek economy above all else. Others want an agency with a name-dropping client roster, proven government or industry relations, or even strong social connections. Before beginning your search, decide exactly which aspects of an agency's offerings are most important to you, and then evaluate capabilities accordingly.

- ✔ **Your budget:** Define how much you plan to spend over the coming year on ad production, media placements, marketing materials, and promotional efforts. Then share the financial facts with your top-choice agencies. Small businesses hesitate to reveal budgets that they think might sound meager, plus they're afraid to "let the wolf in the hen house" by telling an agency how much money is budgeted. Advice: Let both concerns go. Establish a trusting partnership by being open from the get-go. If your budget doesn't fit an agency's client profile, it's best to know before you spend time trying to establish a mismatched relationship.

Defining your selection criteria

Before beginning the agency selection process, spend some time confirming exactly what kind of service you're seeking and what kinds of attributes you most value in an agency. Answer these questions:

✔ **What are you trying to accomplish?**

Put your objectives in writing. Are you trying to establish and build a brand? Do you want to introduce a product? Do you need to reverse a sales decline or jump-start stagnant sales? Is your objective to launch a long-term effort to build market share?

✔ **What do you value in an agency?**

Are you looking for an agency that specializes in a certain kind of media — such as broadcast, print, online advertising, or direct mail? Do you want an agency that welcomes and specializes in brochure and collateral material production? Is it important to you that the agency can develop and implement cooperative advertising programs?

Are you seeking an agency that is known for its award-winning creative work? Realize that clients pay for breakthrough creative advertising in two ways. First, it takes time and therefore money to develop and produce highly creative and attention-getting advertising. Second, it takes brave clients to approve highly creative concepts. Clients of award-winning agencies talk about the sweaty palms they experienced in approving both the concepts and the budgets for ads that went on to win not just awards but market share. Be sure that you're willing to invest on both fronts if "creative" is your highest advertising value.

✔ **What do you bring to the table?**

To get and keep the attention of a good agency, you need at least one and preferably two or all three of the following three attributes:

- **A good budget:** You need a budget big enough to do the job and to allow the agency a decent profit.

- **A product or service around which an agency can create high-visibility ads:** Face it. Agencies want to produce work that will be noticed by other clients. Certain kinds of products allow for more attention-getting and visible advertising than others do. Agencies throw in non-billable time and even forgo some profits if they can produce ads upon which they can build not only your reputation but theirs too. Such ads are the type that air with frequency on major stations or that run in high-circulation consumer magazines versus low-readership trade or business magazines.

- **A client mind-set that allows for creative excellence:** Agencies lose enthusiasm quickly for clients who deal out "death by a thousand cuts." If you want your agency to stay enthused and effective, be prepared to provide clear advertising objectives, to maintain a streamlined and efficient concept approval process, and to allow the agency the creative freedom to do great work on your behalf.

Creating your agency short list

To save your own time and also the time of the agencies you'll interview, start by making a short list of the firms that you believe fit your needs and provide a good match for the attributes you seek in a marketing firm. In creating your short list, follow these steps:

1. **Name your agency review committee.**

   The agencies deserve to know who will be making the decision, and the process will go more smoothly if you confirm the selection participants in the beginning and then stick with your decision. Don't turn the process into a popularity poll. This is a review and analysis. Be sure to involve on your selection committee those who will be working most closely with the agency once it is selected.

2. **Assign primary agency contact responsibility to one of your selection committee members.**

   Don't confuse the agencies with calls from a number of different people. Choose one person to provide answers to all agency contenders. Doing so helps ensure that all agencies get the same information and also helps you compare agency styles as interpreted by one of your team members.

3. **Decide how many agencies you want to interview.**

   If your project is fairly simple or your budget is pretty tight, you might start with a short list of only one. You have a better chance of getting the agency's attention by telling the agency that it's your top choice and by not asking the agency to "compete" for a budget in which there is likely very little profit. For larger budgets, you have more clout, so start with a short list of up to four agencies.

4. **Choose the agencies for your short list.**

   Begin by talking with companies that resemble yours in size and that have particularly strong advertising, and contact the owners or marketing managers to ask who produces their work. Or call trusted business colleagues to ask for agency recommendations. Your local newspaper or television advertising manager is another good resource, as are the sales representatives of major print shops in your area. They know which agencies consistently submit professional work on time.

Include on your short list only agencies that you feel you might really want to work with. Do some advance work by talking within your network of professional colleagues to answer the following questions about prospective agencies:

- Do they handle and care about accounts our size?
- Do we have confidence in their expertise and experience?
- Will their creative style fit our brand and company culture?

✔ Do they have the talent we need? Sometimes small businesses hire very small agencies or studios with the belief that smaller firms have lower overhead and therefore lower costs. But if your agency has to subcontract to get your job done, you may end up paying marked-up costs for services that it buys on your behalf.

Requesting proposals

Once you've settled on a short list of agencies and determined the agency attributes you are seeking, send a letter to each agency CEO. Include the following in the letter:

✔ Explain that you're seeking an agency and that you would like to invite the CEO's agency to present its capabilities and to discuss its interest in working with your firm.

✔ Describe your marketing objectives, your target market, and whether you're seeking help on a finite project or an ongoing relationship.

✔ Outline the agency information you would like submitted in advance of interviews. Ask for any or all of the following information: samples of agency work, biographical sketches of key staff, client list, list of clients gained and lost in the past two years, relevant case studies of agency work, a description of expertise in your industry or market area, billing procedures including hourly rates and commission or markup policies.

✔ Detail your timeline. Ask the agency CEO to let you know within a certain number of days whether the agency will participate in your agency search. State the day on which the agency's capabilities summary should be submitted to your office (try to give the agency at least three weeks to prepare this written response). Give the dates on which you will be scheduling interviews, along with the day that you will make your decision and begin work with your new agency.

✔ Provide the name of the person to contact initially and throughout the agency search process.

Here's what *not* to do when requesting a proposal:

✔ Don't get overly prescriptive as you describe your needs. Tell *what* you want to accomplish through the agency relationship but not *how* you want to accomplish it. Leave room for the agency to bring its point of view and expertise to the task.

✔ Don't ask the agency to submit speculative work (in other words, free sample solutions) as part of its agency response. It isn't fair, and it isn't a good indication of an agency's abilities. Agencies work *with* clients, not *for* them. If you get ready to hire an agency but you want to "sample" the firm's style, propose a budget and be ready to play your role as the client — working with the agency on a solution to your marketing need.

✔ Don't withhold information. If an agency asks for the names of others being considered for your account, share your short list. If they ask what you've done in the past that has and hasn't worked, give a brief summary of previous efforts. Keep track of how you feel about the way that each agency asks questions and interacts with your company, even during the pre-interview period. Your impressions will be useful as you weigh the issues of chemistry and compatibility.

Agency presentations and interviews

The agency presentation and personal interview is the final step in the agency selection process. Follow these tips:

✔ Schedule up to two hours for each agency, with roughly half allocated to the agency's presentation and half allocated to an informal question-and-answer period.

✔ Consolidate all interviews in a two-day period so that no more than 48 hours elapses between the first interview and the final analysis and decision.

✔ Try to tour each agency before the presentation unless the presentations are held at the agencies. Doing so gives you a sense of how each agency works as a team and the atmosphere in which they create.

✔ Keep the interviews as relaxed and informal as possible. The goal isn't to put anyone on the spot or to watch rehearsed performances, but to learn how the agency interacts — among itself and with your team.

✔ Complete a worksheet following each presentation. This can be as simple as a grid that lists the agency attributes that are most important to your business and a means of ranking each agency on a 1–10 scale. For example, if "broadcast media planning" is important to your business, list that category on your worksheet. Then, following the agency presentation, you would rank the agency from 1–10 on how well it convinced you of its expertise in this area. Following the final interview, you can compare your impressions of each firm's capability to determine which one seems to best address your needs.

Putting the client-agency agreement in writing

Most agencies prepare a contract that defines the role the agency is to assume for the client, the compensation arrangement, ownership of work produced under the contract, and how the relationship may be terminated. If your new agency doesn't offer you such a contract or memo of agreement, ask for one and be certain that you both sign and keep a copy on file.

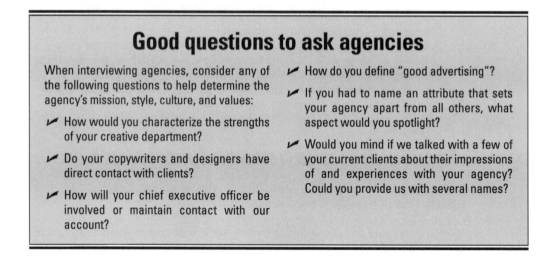

Good questions to ask agencies

When interviewing agencies, consider any of the following questions to help determine the agency's mission, style, culture, and values:

✔ How would you characterize the strengths of your creative department?

✔ Do your copywriters and designers have direct contact with clients?

✔ How will your chief executive officer be involved or maintain contact with our account?

✔ How do you define "good advertising"?

✔ If you had to name an attribute that sets your agency apart from all others, what aspect would you spotlight?

✔ Would you mind if we talked with a few of your current clients about their impressions of and experiences with your agency? Could you provide us with several names?

There is no single standard contract, but all contracts should define certain issues and agreements, including but not limited to the following points:

✔ **The products, services, or brands that the agency is to work on.**

✔ **The responsibilities that the agency is to assume for the client:** The contract might list the services that are to be provided, or it might cover the issue with a broad brush by stating that the agency is to provide "services customarily rendered by an advertising agency." This section of the contract often defines certain agreements that protect the interests of the client, including but not limited to the following: a stipulation that the agency may not act as an advertising agency for any products that compete directly with the products of the client; a clause stating that the agency must obtain written client approval before purchasing any services or media buys in excess of a certain dollar amount; a statement that the agency must be responsible for obtaining rights to photographs, artwork, copyrights, and other property rights that it uses on the client's behalf.

✔ **The client's obligations to the agency:** This part of the contract includes a definition of the client's role, including the client's agreement to provide information as needed to allow the agency to do its job, the client's agreement to pay for work in progress if a job is canceled by the client prior to completion, and an agreement that the client will determine ownership of materials that it provides to the agency for use in client advertising. If the contract covers a yearlong period (versus a project), the client often agrees not to hire another agency to work on the products or services covered by this contract without prior approval.

✔ **Agency compensation:** No one likes to talk about money, but if you dot all the i's in the contract, your client-agency relationship will be easier forever after. The contract should define whether you will pay a fee, a percentage commission of your budget, or a combination of the two. It should define how the agency will be reimbursed for purchases it makes on your behalf, including whether those charges will be billed with or without markups or commissions (see the following section for an explanation of how commissions and markups work). The contract describes the markup and commission structure, how the client can qualify for prompt payment discounts offered by media or suppliers, how the agency will be paid for work that exceeds the scope of the general agreement and budget, and the time frame within which client payments are to be made to the agency.

✔ **Ownership of materials:.** This just may be the single most important part of the contract. Just because you pay for advertising materials produced for your company by your agency doesn't mean that you necessarily own them. Be sure that your contract covers this issue. Ideally, it says that any material presented to your company by the agency becomes the property of your company upon payment for the services rendered. Be aware, though, that even if you own the agency's work on your behalf, you don't necessarily own unlimited rights to the artistic materials included in that work. Photos, illustrations, original artwork, and even voice and acting talent are usually purchased with limited usage rights. When the agency is buying outside art or talent on your behalf, you need to ask whether the purchase covers limited usage rights, unlimited usage rights, or outright ownership.

✔ **The term of the relationship:** The contract might remain in existence until it is "canceled by either party," or it might cover a finite period.

✔ **How the contract can be terminated:** This is the "prenuptial" part of the contract. It tells how the agency will be paid during the termination period, how contracts that can't be canceled will be handled, and how client materials will be returned from the agency.

Most likely, the agency will do the preparation work and get the contract to you so that all you need to do is review it carefully (preferably with your attorney), sign it, and keep it on file for future reference. As you sift through all the legalese, keep repeating the mantra "An ounce of prevention. . . ."

Understanding how agency fees are calculated

Agency math confuses most clients. The following explanations will help you understand agency charges.

Many agency charges include a 15 percent commission. For example, when an agency buys a $1,000 newspaper ad for a client, the newspaper allows the agency a 15 percent commission. Therefore, the agency bills the client $1,000 and pays the newspaper $850, keeping the $150 commission to offset costs involved in producing the ad.

Newspaper ad charge to client	$1,000
Less 15 percent commission to recognized agency	-$150
Payment to media	$850

But what if the agency works with someone who doesn't offer a commission? Say that an agency buys an $850 printing job for a client and the printer offers no commission. In this case, the client *marks up* the bill to allow the same margin that would have been realized on a media buy. To make the math work, though, the agency needs to mark the charge up not by 15 percent, as you'd guess, but by 17.65 percent.

Payment to printer	$850
Plus 17.65 percent markup per contract agreement	+$150
Printing charge to client	$1,000

Working with your agency

The best possible advice for building a great client-agency relationship is simply trust your agency — share your marketing plan, your budget, and your hopes. That's as close to the Golden Rule as you can get. In everyday terms, building a great relationship means that you do the following:

- Provide all the information your agency needs to do the job right the first time.
- Don't waste time. Boil your input. Don't make your agency read encyclopedia-length documents to figure out your marketing plan, advertising strategy, or positioning statement.
- Be frank about your budget. Don't act like a high roller (money is *always* an object). At the same time, don't withhold funds for fear the agency will spend it all unnecessarily.
- Spend your time questioning project estimates rather than arguing after-the-fact over the bills.
- Hold up your end of the bargain by providing information and approvals when you said you would.

✔ Be available.

✔ Pay on time.

✔ Pay for your changes. If you change your mind when you see the final proof, asking the agency to hold to their initial estimate is hardly fair. Someone has to pay for the last-minute rush, the new proof, and the extra hours involved.

✔ Be open to ideas.

✔ Be constructive with your criticism.

✔ Set up a decision-making process and then stick to it. Eliminate the words "let's just run it by so-and-so" from your vocabulary. Ads never get better as they go through a committee process.

✔ Stay involved. Agencies will tell you that a direct correlation exists between great agency work and great interest at the top levels of the client organization. That doesn't mean that you should be co-creating ads. It does mean that you should care about the objective, the strategy, and the creative rationale.

✔ Review the whole relationship once a year with both sides present.

✔ Be the agency's best client. How? Just follow the preceding advice and send over an occasional note or gift of thanks.

Part III
Getting the Word Out

The 5th Wave   By Rich Tennant

Listen up—I brought in a consultant to help figure this thing out. Old MacDonald, these are the boys. Boys, say hello to Old MacDonald.

QUACK. QUACK.

MOO. MOO.

OINK. OINK.

In this part . . .

When it comes to advertising, the money can really fly. Part III puts you in the pilot's seat by arming you (with facts about advertising terminology, ad creation, and media selection) and showing you how to aim (your message, that is) directly at your target market. The chapters in this part also reveal how you can telegraph your marketing message *without* media advertising — by using direct mail, promotions, sales calls, public relations, and publicity.

Consider this part your basic training in marketing communications — your personal, hands-on guide for steering your message into (and not just toward) precisely the right market for your business.

Chapter 10

Mastering the Basics of Advertising and Media Planning

Advertising is the stand-in mouthpiece for your business in the market-place. It goes where you can't — carrying your message into the homes, offices, televisions, computers, mailboxes, and car radios of your prospects and customers. When it is successful — when it is creative, entertaining, understandable, and compelling — advertising goes even farther. *Great* advertising goes right into the minds and hearts of customers, which is where brands live and thrive.

Contrary to popular opinion, though, great advertising rarely makes the sale for your business. Advertising paves the way but the sale happens later, after your prospect is motivated by your ad to call or visit your business, to request more information, or to actually buy your product.

This chapter offers the information you need to set reasonable expectations for your advertising and to make wise media selections and placements. The field of advertising is baffling and complex, but the following pages should make it feel a whole lot less foreign.

Moving the Market through Advertising

Ask any small-business person what advertising is and you'll probably hear the word "expensive" somewhere in the answer. That's because advertising is the means by which businesses, organizations, and individuals buy their way into prospects' minds.

By definition, advertising is how businesses inform and persuade potential and current customers through messages purchased in mass media such as newspapers, magazines, television and radio stations, and Internet Web sites.

Most ads promote the overall image of a company or a specific product or promotional message.

Image versus product advertising

Marketers talk about brand advertising, product advertising, promotional advertising, call-to-action advertising, and a list of other terms capable of setting your head spinning. Basically, ads fall into two categories: ads that promote a company's image and ads that aim to prompt a consumer action, as described in the following two definitions:

> If an ad's sole purpose is to build awareness and interest, it is considered an *image ad.* You'll often hear image ads called *brand ads or institutional ads.*

> If an ad's sole purpose is to present an offer and prompt a corresponding action, it is considered a *product ad.* Product ads are often called *promotional ads, response ads,* or *call-to-action ads.*

Image-plus-product advertising — the have-it-all approach

Brand advertising is an indulgence that many small businesses — which need each ad to deliver prospect action — cannot afford. Yet product advertising works best if the prospect already has a favorable impression of the advertiser's company, which is achieved through brand advertising.

It's a classic Catch 22, but one with a good solution.

Instead of choosing between brand ads and product ads, choose total-approach ads that build awareness and interest, present your offer, prompt prospect action, *and* advance your brand and position. To create ads that do double and triple duty, follow these steps:

1. **Establish a creative strategy to reign over the creation of all ads, brochures, and communications in your marketing program.**

   See Chapter 7 for step-by-step advice on how to define a purpose, approach, and personality, and look for your communications — and how to build a strong brand image as a result.

2. **Establish a creative brief to guide each new ad or other communication effort.**

   See Chapter 8 for a sample form you can follow before launching the preparation of any new ad.

3. **Hand your creative strategy *and* your creative brief to those who will produce your ad.**

   Insist on a final product that meets your image objectives *and* your product advertising objectives. As a result, you'll get an ad that builds your brand *while* promoting your product, which is like having your cake and eating it, too.

Talking to the right people

You wouldn't spend your business days calling on people who aren't able or likely to buy your products, and you shouldn't spend your money advertising to unlikely prospects either. Before you commit your budget to any form of advertising, know your prospect and do everything you can to talk to only that kind of person.

Your prospective customer is

- ✓ Someone who matches the profile of your best existing customers. (See Chapter 2 for information on profiling your customers.)
- ✓ Someone who wants or needs the kinds of products or services you offer.
- ✓ Someone who can easily access your business, whether by a personal visit or by a phone, mail, or Internet contact.
- ✓ Someone who is able to make the purchase from you, by reason of financial ability or ability to meet any qualifications required to buy or own your product.

Realize that the Internet makes it possible for your business to serve people literally all over the globe. But before you consider the world your market, turn to Chapter 17 to assess whether you offer the kind of product people will reach through cyberspace to buy from you.

The awareness-interest-desire-sale scenario

Much as you'd like to have each ad serve as a magic wand that brings you huge numbers of customers, the reality is a little more practical.

The process of converting a prospect to a customer usually requires multiple advertisements, promotions, and personal presentations. In rare instances, this conversion can occur through one communication — perhaps via a single infomercial or direct mailer that leads the prospect through all the steps in one fell swoop. But be aware that single-communication, on-the-spot selling usually occurs only with certain kinds of high-appeal, low-cost, low-involvement, or low-risk products.

Figure 10-1 shows the steps that prospects take as they move from awareness through to the sale.

Figure 10-1: How advertising moves your prospects from awareness to the decision to buy.

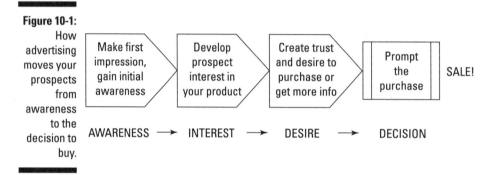

Prospect-to-customer conversion

To win the prospect-to-customer conversion, plan your advertising to move prospects through the steps in the awareness-interest-desire-sale scenario illustrated in Figure 10-1 and described in the following list:

- ✔ The goal of an introductory ad may be nothing more than to gain awareness and to prompt the prospect to request more information.

- ✔ When the customer responds to the introductory ad, the goal may be to prompt the prospect to request a brochure or to schedule an appointment.

- ✔ The goal of the brochure or appointment may be to prompt the prospect to schedule a face-to-face meeting.

- ✔ The goal of the meeting may be to prompt the prospect to request a proposal, a demonstration, or a site tour, depending on the nature of your offering.

- ✔ The goal of the proposal, demonstration, site tour, or other sales presentation is to achieve a positive buying decision — at which point you will have successfully converted the prospect to a customer.

Don't try to jump the gun in the race to turn prospects into customers. Plan each ad or communication to move prospects not necessarily to the sale, but to the next step they will be willing to take on the way to making the buying decision.

Say that a brand-new preschool named Kidville has just opened and wants to enroll 50 toddlers in its program. Because the school has no reputation and no existing awareness, the owners would be expecting the market to leapfrog over the buying process if they ran ads saying, "Announcing Kidville. Call to register children between 2 and 5 years old."

They would be more apt to succeed with an advertising strategy that works to build awareness, interest, and trust in the new preschool, all leading up to the effort to enroll children. They would be wise to opt for ads that communicate a message closer to: "The brand-new home and playground of Kidville Preschool is ready to serve 50 lucky 2- to 5-year-olds. Please join us Thursday afternoon for an open house and tour, or call any time for a personal appointment."

The first approach "calls for the order." The second approach advances a personality and builds rapport before asking for buying decisions. Which would you respond to more comfortably?

Customer conversion guidelines

It doesn't matter how many *people* you reach with your advertising. It matters only how many *qualified prospects* you reach and how you use your advertising to move them through the steps that turn them into customers.

Think about Kidville (mentioned in the preceding section) again for a moment. The owners may decide to run their ad in a local newspaper with a circulation of 100,000 people. But if only 2 percent of the readership has 2- to 5-year-olds in need of day care, the ad is only reaching 2,000 Kidville prospects. And if only half of those readers have the need or finances to afford preschool, then the number of qualified prospects for Kidville's offerings shrinks to 1,000.

But not all of those 1,000 prospects are going to turn into customers. Table 10-1 shows what happens along the way to shrink 1,000 prospects to a handful of customers.

The strength of your media selections, your advertising messages, and the reputation of your business and brand help you to hold on to more prospects at each step, but in general terms, you can count on a conversion process similar to the one shown in Table 10-1.

Table 10-1	Where Do All the Prospects Go?
Where Prospects Disappear	*Why Prospects Disappear*
The majority of prospects never get "caught" by your ad in the first place.	If your ad reaches 1,000 qualified prospects, chances are slim that you will gain the awareness of more than several hundred. The others, though they may fit your prospect profile, will simply tune your message out because it doesn't adequately grab them, because they're too busy to listen to or read your offer, or perhaps because your ad just plain got lost in the media clutter.
Many who become aware won't have interest.	Even after you grab the awareness of a few hundred prospects, only a portion will have interest in your message. The others may be committed to a competitor; they may not be in the market for your offering at the time; or your offering or message just may not motivate them.
Of those with interest, only a few have the desire to look further into your offer.	For every few hundred prospects that are interested in your message, only a few take action, either by getting more information or by starting the buying process. The others may decide, based on the specifics of your product, price, offer, or presentation, that they just aren't interested enough to part with their time or money.
Of those with desire, only a rare few decide to buy.	Out of those who get more information or begin the decision-making process, only a lucky handful become customers. The others may opt out based upon product availability, pricing, the nature of your offer, or some other factor.

Capturing Prospects with a Media Plan

Table 10-1 illustrates the harsh reality that many prospects disappear on the route between your advertising and your cash register. But with an orderly media plan, you can increase the top number — the number of prospects you bring into your sphere of influence — and almost automatically you'll increase your bottom-line number of customers as a result.

As you build a strong media plan, make decisions based on the answers to these five questions:

✔ **What do you want your ad to accomplish?**

Advertising can create awareness, interest, and a desire to purchase your offering, but, except in rare occasions, advertising doesn't create a sale.

As you make media decisions, be specific about your advertising objective. If you want to develop general awareness and interest, use media that reaches a broad and general market. On the far end of the spectrum, if you want to talk one-to-one with those who have already expressed interest in your product, you'll want to bypass mass media in favor of direct mail or other one-to-one communications, as presented in Chapter 13.

✔ **Who and where are the people you want to reach?**

Profile your market by using the information in Chapter 2 and select only media that are proven to reach those people.

If you know that your prospects are teenagers, ask the publications or stations for hard numbers on what percentage of their circulation or audience reaches that age group. If your prospects have a particular interest — for instance, they snowboard, own pets, or drive four-wheel SUVs — ask for a demonstration of how the medium in question reaches that group, and which sections or programs would capture the highest percentage of people with that affinity. The more precisely you can define your prospect, the more precisely you can choose your media vehicles. When it comes to advertising, trying to be all-inclusive is a bankrupting proposition.

✔ **What are you trying to say, and when do you need to say it?**

If you have a complex offering and are trying to show it in action, you'll want to use television or perhaps print ads that allow for clear reproduction of a series of photos. If you have a tremendous amount of explaining to do, you'll probably want to rule out radio or television, where you're timed by the second. If you have a very immediate message, such as a one-week special event, steer away from monthly magazines that are in circulation long after your offer is history.

✔ **How much money is in your media budget?**

Set your budget *before* planning your media. Doing so forces you to be realistic with your media choices. By following this advice, you also save an enormous amount of time because you don't have to listen to media sales pitches for approaches that are outside your budget range.

✔ **How much of this can you do yourself? Do you need professional help?**

See Chapter 9 for advice on when and how to bring in marketing professionals to help you with everything from making media decisions to creating ads that move markets to action.

Table 10-2 provides a quick overview of the cost realities and advertising advantages of each form of mass media, and the following section explains the pros and cons that accompany various media choices.

Table 10-2	Mass Media Comparisons		
Media Vehicle	*Cost Realities*	*Advertising Considerations*	*What This Medium Does Best*
Newspapers reach a broad market within a concentrated geographic area.	Inexpensive cost per thousand readers.	Inexpensive ad production.	Daily or weekly deadlines allow for quick-turn ad decisions. Announces sales, news, and offers to a majority of adults within a geographic area on a frequent and prompt basis.
Magazines reach a target market with specific characteristics and interests.	Advertisers pay for access to highly targeted audience.	Advertisers must invest in ad design and production.	Ad commitments are due months in advance of publication date. Magazines remain in circulation for long periods of time. Develops awareness, credibility, and interest in complex or high-investment products.
Directories reach prospects at the time of their purchasing decision.	Media costs are based on number of categories and ad sizing decisions; production costs are minimal.	Ad commitments are made well in advance, and ads remain in market for more than a year with no chance for revision.	Establishes credibility and provides reason to choose one business over others at the moment the prospect is ready to take action.
Outdoor advertising reaches a captured audience within a geographic area on a repeated basis.	Placement costs are based on traffic counts. Often involves investment in sign design/production.	Prime locations are reserved well in advance. Ad commitments usually span at least a month-long period.	Builds name awareness, product interest, and credibility through a single-sentence message.

Media Vehicle	Cost Realities	Advertising Considerations	What This Medium Does Best
Radio reaches a defined local audience — if they're tuned in — with a verbal message.	Ad time is inexpensive and negotiable, but costs most during peak listening times.	Repetition of ad is important. Last-minute decisions and short-term schedules are possible.	Reaches involved listeners to build quick interest and prompt responses to newsy or urgent messages.
Television reaches a defined audience — if they're tuned in — with visuals and sound.	High-audience buys are expensive. High-credibility ads often involve significant production budgets.	Repetition of ads is important. Local ads compete for attention with top-quality national ads.	Engages viewer emotions and empathy while explaining or demonstrating products and building credibility.

The media menu

Mass media is the term used for communication vehicles that reach many people simultaneously. Advertisers divide mass media into four traditional categories and one new category:

✔ **Print media:** Includes newspapers, magazines, and directories.

✔ **Broadcast media:** Includes television and radio.

✔ **Outdoor media:** Includes billboards, transit signs, building murals, and signage.

✔ **Specialty media:** Includes items imprinted with an advertiser's name and message.

✔ **New media:** This new category includes Internet banner ads, Web casts, Web pages, and interactive media.

The opposite of mass media is one-to-one communications, such as personal presentations, telemarketing contacts, direct mailings, and other means of contacting your prospect individually.

Mass media pros and cons

Each time you get ready to project an ad message, confirm your audience, your objective, and your budget to guide your media selection process. Use the following summary of advantages and drawbacks as a guide.

Newspapers

Newspapers — particularly metropolitan and suburban area newspapers — are the number-one choice for small businesses trying to reach local markets.

Here are the advantages of newspaper advertising:

- ✓ **Broad coverage:** Newspapers can reach a lot of readers within a geographically concentrated area.

- ✓ **Engaged readers:** Newspaper subscribers expect and look for ads and are willing to spend time absorbing substantial amounts of ad information on product features, pricing, promotions, locations, and phone numbers.

- ✓ **Targeted sections:** Advertisers can place ads in the sports, travel, food, home, or other section that best matches prospect profiles.

- ✓ **Geographic zones:** In most newspapers, businesses can place ads only in copies that reach specific geographic areas within the overall newspaper circulation area.

- ✓ **Predictable timing:** Newspapers are usually read promptly upon receipt, allowing for timely delivery of ad messages.

- ✓ **Minimal advance planning:** You don't need to give much notice to place ads.

- ✓ **Flexibility:** Most newspapers sell ad space by the column inch, so you can buy a space as small as one column wide by one inch deep, or any multiple of that size up to a full page or even a *double truck,* which is an ad that spreads over two facing pages.

- ✓ **Low production and placement costs:** Black-and-white ads in particular can be produced relatively quickly and inexpensively, and newspaper placement costs are among the lowest of all mass media, although multiple placements are considered necessary to achieve adequate levels of consumer impact.

Here are the drawbacks to newspaper advertising:

- ✓ **Limited ability to target prospects:** Advertisers pay to reach the full (or zone) circulation even if only a minor portion of the readers fit the prospect profile.

- ✓ **Minimal youth audience:** Newspaper readership is heaviest among the 35+ age group, and weakest among younger age groups.

- ✓ **Short life span:** Newspapers are usually read quickly and discarded.

- ✓ **Two-dimensional presentations:** Newspapers cannot provide the attention-grabbing sound and action of broadcast ads.

✔ **Print quality limitations:** Unless you produce and pay to place four-color ads, plan to limit art selections to high-contrast black-and-white photos and line illustrations.

✔ **A jam-packed environment:** Although many newspapers are stringent about maintaining a positive balance of news over ads, still the pages are filled with headlines, stories, photos, and ads. All these elements contribute to visual "clutter" and compete for the reader's attention. Generally only the largest and best-designed ads win.

Magazines

Most magazines fit into two categories:

✔ **General interest magazines:** These are also called consumer magazines or "glossies," because of their shiny, high-grade paper and premium-quality printing. They're the publications that dominate the average newsstand. They are read by target groups with various lifestyle interests, such as crafts, travel, cooking, sports, fitness, fashion, celebrity lifestyles, home decorating, and others that form almost an endless list.

✔ **Trade magazines:** These publications are also called "business to business" (B2B) and "vertical" magazines (because they reach vertical versus broad or horizontal markets). They're read primarily by people in targeted industries and services.

Here are some advantages of advertising in magazines:

✔ **Targeted readership:** You can reach people with defined interests.

✔ **Engaged readers:** Magazine readers generally dedicate time to read the contents carefully.

✔ **Credibility:** Readers tend to associate the credibility of the advertiser with the credibility of the publication.

✔ **Geographic zones:** An advertiser can buy only a portion of the magazine's full distribution.

Inquire about regional zones that reach only northwest, southwest, or central states, for example. Some magazines even allow the purchase of select metropolitan areas, while others bind editions for particular professional subscriber groups.

✔ **Classified or directory ad sections:** For advertisers who can't afford to buy or create magazine display ads, many magazines offer classified ad and directory ad sections at a dramatically lower placement rate.

✔ **Merchandising materials:** These are items such as ad reprints, poster-size versions of the ad, and easel-back display cards provided by magazines as added-value enhancements to advertisers. Consumer magazines in particular like to offer them to encourage advertising placements.

Many small businesses place an ad only once or twice in a major magazine, and then they leverage their investment by using the merchandising materials long after the magazine is out of date.

✔ **High-quality printing:** Magazines can deliver superb color and photo reproduction of your ad. Magazines also offer a wide range of creative enhancements, including fold-out pages, fragrance chips, and sound devices — most of which cost a small fortune in return for the hope of making a big impact. But even without the razzmatazz, well-designed and well-produced magazine ads can stop readers with near-perfect presentations of show-stopping photos, along with lengthy copy (if appropriate) and reply cards to prompt responses.

✔ **Long life span:** People read magazines in leisure hours and at a relaxed pace. When readers are done, they often keep issues or pass them along to others.

Magazine advertising does have its drawbacks:

✔ **High production and placement costs:** A full-page, full-color consumer magazine ad can run into tens of thousands of dollars. Although you can cut media costs by placing only in a regional edition, you still need to invest in quality design, photography, and production to create an ad capable of competing well in the upscale magazine environment. For advertisers with limited resources, large-circulation consumer magazines are rarely a cost-effective way to reach prospects, although they are a powerful way to establish awareness and build credibility.

✔ **Unpredictable response schedule:** Count on magazines for long-term awareness and interest rather than for immediate response. Magazines land in mailboxes and on newsstands over a several-week period, and they may not be opened or read for weeks after that.

✔ **Long lead times:** Magazine ad placement commitments are usually required months before the magazine actually reaches the consumer.

Directories

The most visible directory is the Yellow Pages, and there's an old saying that "Small businesses *are* the Yellow Pages," and here's why.

Directories offer these advantages:

✔ **Action-oriented readers:** Directories tend to reach people when they're ready to buy or at least ready to get information leading to a buying decision.

✔ **Credibility:** If a small business is listed in a directory, readers assume that the company is established in the marketplace.

✔ **Low production costs:** One ad — and usually a fairly small and simple ad — lasts a full year.

Here are the drawbacks of directory advertising:

- ✔ **An overwhelming number of categories:** Deciding where to list an ad can be a difficult and expensive proposition.

- ✔ **Competing directories:** These pop up daily, and even the stalwart directories are breaking into subdirectories that compound advertiser costs and decisions.

- ✔ **Long lead time:** Directories require ad commitments far in advance of publication, and ad materials remain in the marketplace for at least a year with no ability to pull out or make alterations.

- ✔ **Competing ads grouped together:** Similar businesses line up in directories, making it easy for prospects to comparison shop and forcing advertisers to compete via ad size, color, and claim in an effort to win the prospect's decision.

Outdoor and transit advertising

Outdoor advertising is a love-it-or-hate-it reality that includes roadside billboards, bench signage, transit vehicle ads, and other means of putting ad messages into the great outdoors.

Advantages of outdoor advertising include the following:

- ✔ **Unavoidable and repetitious:** Passersby can't change channels when they see your sign. You have a captive audience that tends to travel the same route daily, so you also drill your message in via repetition or frequency.

- ✔ **Geographically pinpointed:** You know in advance exactly where your sign will sit, so you can make your message directional (for instance, "Take Next Exit").

Here are the drawbacks of outdoor advertising:

- ✔ **A moving market:** Unless the sign is at a stoplight or railroad crossing, people are apt to read it while moving 35 miles per hour — or more. Keep messages to seven words that can be grasped in a couple seconds. With transit signs you have more time, but also a greater need to either entertain or inform.

- ✔ **A diverse market:** Many viewers may not be potential customers.

- ✔ **Presentation difficult to control:** Your ad is susceptible to vandalism, weather erosion, and dirt, and the environment may not suit your brand image.

- ✔ **Expense of high-traffic locations:** If your ad is posted where masses of people will see it, you're going to pay much more than for an ads placed on side roads and back alleys.

✔ **Long lead time:** Boards need to be reserved early, and most companies require multimonth commitments, making outdoor advertising a poor choice for short-term, time-sensitive announcements.

Radio

Radio advertising offers these advantages:

✔ **Rate flexibility:** You can bargain, barter, and ask for bonus spots. If a radio ad is left unsold, it is lost revenue that can't be recaptured — like an unoccupied hotel room — so radio sales reps are willing to wheel and deal.

✔ **Highly targeted audience:** National auditing services provide demographics for each station to help you determine whether the station reaches those who fit the age, gender, and lifestyle of your prospect profile. You can target your buys based on listener profile, geographic reach, time of day, and program format.

✔ **Last-minute decisions:** As long as ad time is available (which isn't always the case during Christmas and political election campaigns), you can schedule your ad up to hours in advance, and you can update your ad almost to the last minute before it airs.

✔ **Immediate:** Many listeners are in their cars when they hear radio ads, which is why live remote broadcasts work to build traffic for advertisers. Radio also delivers immediate messages in support of other media advertising. For instance, your ad can say "Check out our ad in Sunday's paper," or "Check today's mail for our half-off coupon."

✔ **Ad length choices** range from sponsorships ("This weather report is brought to you by . . .") to 15-second, 30-second, and 60-second commercials.

✔ **Intrusive and involving:** Especially if ads are creative and well produced, they can draw listeners in, create mental images, and advance direct offers. Most good ads include a clear call to action.

Radio advertising does have its drawbacks:

✔ **Now you hear it, now you don't:** The listener can't rewind it to hear your phone number a second time. Or, if you rely on the station announcer to read your message live on the air, you can't do any after-the-fact editing or repair work. And if the listener was tuned out when your ad played, you don't have a second chance to reach that person until you pay to air the ad again.

✔ **A distracted audience:** Listeners have access to many stations, plus they can opt to listen to CDs or books-on-tape or talk on their cell phones.

✔ **Necessary and costly repetition:** Most advertisers pay to air their ads many times weekly on a number of different stations in an effort to reach target prospects at least three times. They also invest in the production of a number of different ads to avoid boring the market with a single ad played over and over again.

✔ **Station switching:** The listener can change stations if your ad isn't adequately compelling during its first few seconds.

Television

Sometime in the late 1950s, the television replaced the fireplace as the center of the household, and homebodies have been transfixed by it ever since. It is the most intrusive, costly, and powerful advertising medium and one that requires careful thought and commitment.

Consider these advantages of television advertising:

✔ **Abundant airtime:** Between cable and broadcast TV, hundreds of ad slots are available hourly, even in the smallest media markets.

✔ **Targeted audiences:** You can place your ads to reach viewers in certain geographic areas, viewers during certain day parts, viewers of certain programs, or viewers of certain networks, like MTV or ESPN, that match your prospect profile.

✔ **Image-enhancing:** TV is considered the advertising major league. A well-produced ad transmits a prestige that goes beyond the message. Print advertisers use the term "as seen on TV" for a reason. Television ads build credibility, glamour, and excitement for advertisers.

✔ **Emotion-evoking:** Television brings together sight, sound, special effects, color, and well-cast actors to create a sensual impact on viewers.

Drawbacks of television advertising include the following:

✔ **Professional ad creation required:** This is show-and-tell at its best. You need to create an ad that illustrates your message while using the fewest possible words and only one or two selling points — while still managing to mention your name a few times and keeping the overall ad clear, entertaining, and memorable. Television advertising usually calls for an investment in professional assistance.

✔ **Fragmented audiences:** Viewers have endless choices in addition to all the TV stations; alternatives include videos, video games, computer games, the Internet, and movie rentals.

✔ **Commercials galore:** Heavy advertising makes TV a cluttered environment.

✔ **Low-cost ads:** If you do a low-budget ad, it can look amateurish and sometimes even sloppy next to the high-cost national advertiser commercials.

✔ **Complex buying time arrangements:** Buying airtime is complicated and usually merits investment in a media planner or expert buyer.

The Making of a Media Schedule

After you decide on the right media to use, it's time to create a schedule.

Your budget is a key determinant as you plan your schedule. But the same number of dollars can be spent many different ways, depending on how you decide to balance three scheduling considerations:

- ✔ Reach
- ✔ Frequency
- ✔ Timing

Balancing reach and frequency

Reach is the number of individuals or homes exposed to your ad. In print media, reach is measured by circulation counts; in broadcast media, reach is measured by gross rating points (see Chapter 12 for more information on broadcast ad terminology). *Frequency* is the number of times that an average person is exposed to your message.

Reach creates awareness, but frequency changes minds. Your schedule needs to achieve enough reach (that is, your message needs to get into the heads of enough readers or viewers) to generate a sufficient number of prospects to meet your sales goals. But it also needs to achieve enough frequency to adequately impress your message into those minds — and that rarely happens with a single ad exposure.

If you have to choose between reach and frequency — and nearly every small business works with a budget that forces that choice — opt to limit your reach by targeting your market areas carefully, and spend as much as you can on achieving frequency within that area.

The case for frequency

Ad recall studies have proven repeatedly that people remember ads in direct proportion to the number of times they are seen. Here are some facts about frequency:

- ✔ One-shot ads don't work — unless, perhaps, you invest a quarter of a million dollars to air an ad once on the Super Bowl. Even then, part of the audience will be away from the tube, replenishing the guacamole dish or grabbing more beer from the refrigerator.

✔ You need to run your ad as many as nine times to reach your prospect even once. Why? Because each time your ad runs or airs, a predictably large percentage of prospects won't be "present." Either they aren't reading the issue of the magazine or newspaper your ad is in, or they aren't tuned in to the TV or radio channel when your ad plays. Or, perhaps they miss your ad because they're distracted or because at the moment of contact your reactive approach or offer doesn't grab their attention.

✔ You need to run your ad as many as 27 times to reach your prospect 3 times, which is usually the number of exposures it takes before an ad message sinks in.

You will tire of your ad long before your market has even started to notice it. Frequency will wear on you (and your agency if you have one!) long, long before it will wear on your prospects, who see your ad only once for every couple of dozen times you look at it.

✔ Frequency increases an individual's responsiveness to an ad message.

✔ Frequency increases the number of people who take note of an ad message.

✔ Frequency increases advertiser recognition.

✔ Frequency increases overall responses to an ad.

The case for media concentration

Frequency and concentrated ad campaigns go hand-in-hand. A concentrated ad campaign is one that gains exposure through a limited number of media vehicles.

Instead of running an ad one time in each of six magazines that reach your target market, a concentrated campaign schedules your ad three times each in two of the publications. Or instead of running a light radio schedule and a light newspaper schedule, a concentrated campaign bets the full budget on a strong schedule that builds frequency through one medium or the other.

Reversing the forgetting curve

Here's some information to remember — if you can!

In the late 1880s, German researcher Hermann Ebbinghaus quantified the rate at which people forget. You may not need formal statistics to confirm that most people forget 90 percent of what they learned in class within 30 days.

Get this: Most of the forgetting takes place in the very first hour after contact with new information,

and by the time two days have passed, only 30 percent of the information is retained.

This "forgetting curve" is why ad repetition is so important to marketers. Through schedule frequency, prospects encounter your message, and just when they are about to forget it, they encounter the information again . . . and again.

A concentrated ad campaign offers several benefits:

- ✔ Concentrating your ads makes media buying more efficient because you can take advantage of volume discounts.

- ✔ Concentrating your ads can give you dominance in a single medium, which achieves a perception of strength and clout in the prospect's mind.

- ✔ Concentrating your ads limits ad production costs, which eat up a major portion of small budgets.

- ✔ Concentrating your ads ensures a higher level of frequency.

Timing your placements

No small business has enough money to sustain reach and frequency on a continuous basis, 52 weeks a year — 24/7 in 21st century lingo. Instead, advertisers eke out their dollars by using one of the following scheduling concepts, illustrated in Figure 10-2:

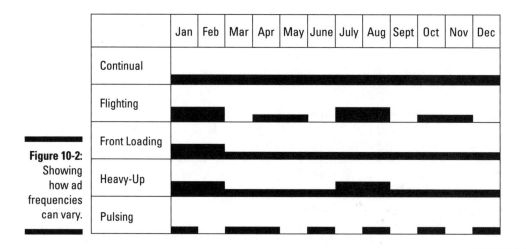

Figure 10-2: Showing how ad frequencies can vary.

- ✔ **Flighting:** You run or air your ads for a certain period of time and then go dormant before reappearing with another but lesser "flight" of ads. To succeed in flighting, start with a heavy enough schedule to make a strong market impression. That way, when your ads disappear for several weeks, your business will benefit from the residual awareness. Then you come back in with a light schedule to rekindle awareness, go dormant, and then reappear with a heavy schedule.

> ✔ **Front-loading:** You run a heavy schedule to saturate the market with your message and then pull back to a more economical schedule that aims to maintain the awareness you bought during the early days. Front-loading is often used to promote openings and new product announcements and to jump-start idle markets.
>
> ✔ **Heavy-up scheduling:** Heavy-up schedules are similar to front-loaded schedules, except that they rely on saturation advertising schedules (also called "blitzes") to be repeated several times a year.
>
> ✔ **Pulsing:** This is a simple on-and-off schedule. You're in the media, then you're dormant, then you're on, then you're dormant, with no blitzes and no variations.

In any of these schedules, you can take advantage of media "off times" by sending one-to-one communications (see Chapter 13), arranging publicity (see Chapter 15), or going dormant on one type of media while you heavy-up on another.

As long as you present a compelling message, a consistent image, and communications that reach your target market with frequency, you have the formula for achieving awareness, interest, and consumer action.

Chapter 11

Creating Ads for Newspapers, Magazines, and Directories

. . . .

In This Chapter
▶ Creating, negotiating, and producing newspaper and magazine ads
▶ Writing good headlines and head copy
▶ Making phone book and directory ad decisions

. . . .

*T*o many small businesses, *advertising* means one thing: placing printed ads in newspapers, magazines, and directories.

Direct mailers, brochures, and sales literature also present your message in print, and they are discussed in Chapters 13 and 14. But if you're paying to present your message in print in the mass media — in local newspapers, industry and trade magazines, targeted consumer publications, or telephone books and other directories — this chapter arms you with the tricks of the trade and the information you need to negotiate the buy, create the ad, and produce the materials that will carry your message to the market.

Creating Print Ads

In every print ad, the headline and copy work together to capture attention, appeal to the target market, promote the benefits of the product, and advance your brand.

The *headline* is the major introductory statement in a print ad. It is the large-type sentence or question that aims to stop readers in their tracks, to target the right prospects, and to pull them inside the ad to read, as commentator Paul Harvey would say, "the rest of the story."

Copy is the term for the words that fill the body of an ad. Good copy is written directly to the prospect. Its point is to connect with and persuade the reader. Instead of following the standard rules of grammar, copy usually is written to sound like people talk. It is conversational yet crisp, poetic yet to the point, and, above all, convincing.

Packing power into headlines

Four out of every five people who see your ad will read only the headline. Here's where the rest of the readers go:

- ✔ One reader will see your headline and move on because he doesn't have time to study the details this time round.

- ✔ A second one will see the headline and rule herself out as a prospective customer because she doesn't want or need what you're offering, can't buy what you're offering at this time, or just plain isn't interested.

- ✔ The third reader may find your headline all that's needed to reinforce an existing (hopefully positive) opinion.

- ✔ The fourth (should you be so lucky) will find the headline all-encompassing and sufficiently powerful to trigger the desired consumer action.

- ✔ The fifth one is stopped by your headline and inspired to dive into the ad copy in a genuine desire to learn more. Oh lucky day!

Attributes of a good headline

In any written marketing communication, your headline has to pack marketing power. It is your only chance to communicate with 80 percent of your prospects, and it's your hook for baiting the other 20 percent into your marketing message. If your headline doesn't grab and inspire, your body copy doesn't stand a chance. Here what your headline needs to do:

- ✔ Flag the attention of your prospect by saying, in essence, "Stop! This message concerns you."

- ✔ Appeal to your target prospect individually and immediately.

- ✔ Promote an answer or solution to a problem.

- ✔ Convey a meaningful benefit.

- ✔ Advance your brand image.

- ✔ Include your name if possible.

As if the preceding lineup isn't already a heavy load, the headline has to manage to accomplish all of the above steps in words that people can read and grasp in five seconds.

Luckily, headlines come with a lot of creative elbowroom:

- ✔ They can be short or long, as long as they're irresistibly compelling.

- ✔ They can sit anywhere on the page — at the top of the page, in the middle, or along the bottom.

- ✔ They can present a single word, a stand-alone phrase, a complete sentence, or a question.

Headline how-to's

Consider calling on the talents of a professional copywriter if you don't already have a relationship with an advertising agency. (See Chapter 9 if you want to look for a creative partner.) Then follow these headline tips:

- ✔ **Lead with your most powerful point.** Too many advertisers use a clever come-on for a headline and then divulge the benefit somewhere toward the end of the copy — where no one may see it. Flip the sequence. Pack punch into your headline and use your copy to back up your claim.

- ✔ **Turn features into benefits.** If you say that your product saves time, you've stated a feature. If you say that the consumer can save the equivalent of two days of vacation, you've stated a benefit. If you add that the extra vacation days are a free bonus with every purchase, you've fuel-injected the message.

- ✔ **Present headlines that use both upper- and lowercase letters.** Statements set in all capital letters are harder to read and, as a result, are easier to overlook.

- ✔ **Don't end your headline with a period.** The last thing you want is to encourage the reader to stop at the end of the headline!

- ✔ **Be believable.** There's an old line in advertising that states "if it sounds too good to be true, it probably is." Beyond that, media ad departments screen ads and reject ones that advance deceptive messages.

Amping up your headline language

As you develop headlines, consider the following advice:

- ✔ **Positive statements carry power.** Consider the difference between "save time" and "work less"; or between "feel great" and "reduce pain." In each case, one presents a desired outcome; the other brings up a nagging problem.

- ✔ **Use strong, compelling language.** Once you think that you've landed on a headline, go through and push each word further. If your headline says "stomach," ask yourself whether the word "guts" would be more forceful. Instead of saying "Are you concerned . . . ?" ask "Are you worried . . . ?" Avoid technical terms and always use words that most people will understand.

✔ **Use the word *you*.** It's the most magnetic word in advertising. McDonald's built a brand on it. (Remember "*You*, you're the one . . ."?) Every time you get ready to write "we," turn the spotlight to the consumer by using "you."

✔ **Tell *how*.** People are attracted to the feeling of interaction conveyed by the word *how*. Write a headline that includes "how to . . ." or "how you . . ." to up the chances that the prospect will continue on to the first line of the ad copy.

✔ **Use power words.** Whenever you can, grab your readers' attention with the long-proven power of words such as *free, new, save, better, now,* and other words that communicate that your offer is special and worth reading about.

Writing convincing copy

The first sentence of your ad copy only has to do one thing: It needs to make the reader want to continue on to the second sentence. The second sentence needs to lure the prospect into the third sentence. And so good ad copy goes, carrying consumers through your ad, building credibility and trust, and convincing readers of the merit of your message until, finally, it makes an irresistible offer and tells exactly how to respond.

As you lead prospects through your ad, work to accomplish the following points:

✔ **Tell your basic story.** Provide a description of your offering, your unique selling proposition, the benefits that a buyer can count on, and information that backs your claim.

✔ **Provide an action inducement.** Offer and describe a proposition or offer.

✔ **Sweeten your offer.** Add a guarantee, special financial terms, trade-in opportunities, a promotional price or package, special options, a free or limited-time trial, or other offers to increase consumer responsiveness.

✔ **Add a deadline.** For example, consider a limited-time offer, a promotion that involves only the first 100 respondents, or the statement "while supplies last."

✔ **Explain what to do next.** Don't assume that prospects know your address, which exit to take, what area code and number to dial, your Web address, or other details about how to reach you. Explain what, why, when, and how to respond.

As you review your copy, imagine that you're face-to-face with your prospect and that the person is saying, "Well, let me think about it; right now I'm just shopping." Then add statements of value, action inducements, or other ideas to overcome prospect hesitation.

Good ads treat the prospect as an intelligent consumer and feature the product — rather than the advertiser or the ad concept — as the ad's hero.

Presenting prices

The way that you present your prices can inspire your prospects — or it can confuse or underwhelm them. Use the information in Table 11-1 and the following list to show your prices in the most favorable light:

- ✔ Don't be apologetic, using terms like "Going Out of Business."
- ✔ Don't let your offer get too complex.
- ✔ Don't be misleading.
- ✔ Do present prices so that they look visually attractive and straightforward.
- ✔ Do make the price compelling. In today's world of outlet malls, online bargains, and warehouse stores, "10 percent off" isn't considered an offer at all.
- ✔ Do support your pricing announcements with positive reasons and added benefits. Price alone is never reason enough to buy.

Table 11-1	Pricing Presentation Do's and Don'ts	
Don't	*Do*	*Why*
We've just cut our nightly rates — $89 mid-week. Some restrictions apply.	Announcing a new St. Louis number to remember — $89 per night	The second approach makes the deal sound noteworthy, whereas the first approach provides no positive rationale and implies that "small print applies."
Sofa and Loveseat $1,995.00	Sofa and Loveseat $1,995	When prices are more than $100, drop the decimal point and zeroes to lighten the effect.
25% off two or more	½ off second pair	Complicated discounts are uninspiring, plus "½ off" sounds like double the discount of 25% off when you buy two.

(continued)

Table 11-1 *(continued)*

Don't	Do	Why
30% off	Regularly $995; now $695 while supplies last	⅓ off sounds more compelling than 30% off; but showing a $300 reduction is strongest of all. "While supplies last" ads incentive and urgency.
$6.99 each	$13.99 — Buy One, Get One Free	Sometimes a low price conveys low value. Consider doubling the price but making a powerful two-for-one limited-time offer.
$14.95 plus shipping/handling	$17.95. We pick up all shipping and handling	The word "plus" alerts the consumer that the price is only the beginning. Calculate and include shipping and handling to remove buyer concern and possible objection.
State and local taxes extra	State and local taxes apply	"Extra" goes into the same category as "plus" when it comes to pricing.

Making design decisions

Advertisers, advertising agencies, and the media have spent enormous time and money to determine what does and doesn't work in the design of print advertisements. There is no pat formula — life in the marketing world isn't quite that easy — but when readers are asked which ads they remember positively, certain design traits emerge, as discussed in the following sections.

A picture is worth a thousand words

Whenever you can, include an attention-getting visual element in your ads, following these tips:

✔ **Use art.** Ads with stopping power nearly always have a photograph, an illustration (a drawing, cartoon, or other custom art), or both. Sometimes the art presents the product; sometimes it shows the product in use; or sometimes it is merely relative to the product through "borrowed interest."

For example, an ad for a restaurant could feature art of the entry door (the product), a photo of diners at a nicely set table (the product in use), or an illustration of a sprig of rosemary or a bundle of herbs (borrowed interest).

✔ **Let your visual *show* what your headline and copy is *telling*.** But you don't have to be literal. An ad for housekeeping services could feature a mop, broom, and vacuum cleaner. The ad may be more effective, however, if it communicates the benefit of more free time by showing a person in a bubble bath, feet propped up on the rim, open magazine in hand, in an immaculately clean setting.

Keep it simple

Simplify your design. Doing so helps readers focus on the important points of your ad. Here are some ways to keep your ad design strong and uncluttered:

✔ **Frame your ad with wide-open space.** Isolate your ad from those around it while providing the visual relief toward which readers naturally gravitate. If you need a reason to sacrifice a chunk of your ad to plain old white space, ask yourself where your eyes went first on this page. Be generous with open space.

✔ **Make your ad easy to follow.** If a prospect's eyes sweep quickly from the upper left corner to the bottom right corner, will he be able to grasp your message and see your name and logo before exiting to the next page? If your ad lacks an obvious starting point or if two design elements compete for dominance, the reader is apt to pass the ad over altogether.

Designing every ad to advance your brand

Small businesses have small budgets to start with, and then they reduce the impact of their investment by changing the look of their ad from season to season or, worse, from week to week. Here are some ways to advance your brand:

✔ **Find an ad look and stick with it.** Settle on a recognizable format that readers can link to your name and brand.

✔ **Prominently present your name.** Huge advertisers can get away with postage-stamp-sized presentations of their logos because their products and ad looks are so familiar. Small business budgets don't allow for that level of awareness, so make your name apparent — through your logo and possibly through inclusion of your name in your headline as well.

✔ **"When in doubt, leave it out."** This adage offers good advice for do-it-yourself ad designers (and all other designers, too). As you consider tossing in an additional type font, a different type size, a border, or any other design element, remind yourself that good design is usually the result of subtraction — not addition.

Knowing your type

You can choose styles of type right from your computer screen, but choosing the *right* type is an art that makes a tremendous difference in how your ad looks and, even more important, how easy your message is to read. You may find it helpful to know some of the terminology used when dealing with type.

A *typeface* is a particular design for a set of letters and characters.

✔ Garamond is a typeface.

✔ Helvetica is a typeface.

✔ Times New Roman is a typeface.

A *type family* is the full range of weights and styles available in a typeface. For example, you can stay within the Helvetica type family and select bold, italics, and light versions in a great number of sizes. Helvetica, **Helvetica Bold,** and *Helvetica Italic* are all part of the Helvetica type family.

A *font* is the term used for a full set of characters (letters, numbers, and symbols) in a particular typeface and size.

✔ This is a 12-point Garamond font.

✔ This is a 10-point Garamond bold font.

✔ This is an 8-point Garamond italic font.

Limit the number of typefaces and sizes that you use in an ad. The general rule is to choose one typeface for your headlines and one for body copy.

✔ **For headlines,** which are meant to be attention grabbing, designers usually choose typefaces that are capable of standing out while also communicating clearly. Choose sans serif typefaces, which have no decorative lines at the ends of the straight strokes in the characters. Probably the most popular sans serif typeface is clean-cut Helvetica.

✔ **For body copy,** which needs to be easy to read, designers most often opt for serif typefaces like Garamond, Century, or Times Roman, because they're designed with flourishes (serifs) that serve as connectors

Translating the terminology

Even if you pay the pros to produce your ads (and if you can, you should!), it still helps to know the language of print ad design and production:

✔ **Ad proof:** The checking copy of your ad and the last thing you'll see before the presses run. Read the proof carefully; especially check for type set in all capital letters, which is where many typos slip through. Read your phone number twice; check your address; and see that all mandatory information (copyright lines, trademarks, photo credits, and so on) is in place. Then hand the ad to the best proofreader in your organization for a second review before you initial your approval to the publisher.

- ✔ **Display advertising:** Print ads that use a combination of space, art, headline, copy, visual elements, and the advertiser's logo in a unique design that aims to draw reader attention and to communicate quickly and clearly.

- ✔ **Four-color:** The production term for the process used to achieve full-color printing, because (flash back to second grade art class for a moment) all colors can be created from the primary colors of blue, red, and yellow (or in print terms, cyan, magenta, and yellow). Plus black is needed to print true black in type and other details. Even the most elaborate photo can be "separated" into these four colors and then reproduced by laying one ink over the next until the image is rebuilt to match the original.

- ✔ **Spot color:** The use of color highlights in an otherwise black and white ad.

Reading rate cards

Every publication has a rate card, which defines pricing, mechanical and copy requirements, and deadlines. Here are some definitions of key terms:

- ✔ **Bulk or volume rate:** The reduced rate offered to businesses that commit to place a certain amount of advertising over a contract period. Increased volume means decreased rates.

- ✔ **Cash discount:** A discount allowed by media to advertisers who pay promptly. Watch your bill and reduce the cost of your media charges by up to 2 percent by settling your bills quickly.

- ✔ **Closing date or deadline:** The deadline by which your advertising material must be to the publication if your ad is to appear in a certain issue.

- ✔ **Column inch:** Newspaper space is measured in column inches. A column inch is one column wide by one inch high. Column inches have pretty much replaced the ad measurement of the *agate lines,* which equals $\frac{1}{14}$ of an inch. If you see ad rates in agate lines, multiply by 14 to arrive at the price per column inch.

- ✔ **Cost per thousand (CPM):** This is the cost of using a particular medium to reach a thousand households or individuals. (You'd think that the abbreviation for "cost per thousand" would be CPT, but the accepted term instead uses the Roman numeral for "thousand" — M. Just FYI!) By calculating CPM, you can compare the relative cost of various media options.

   The CPM formula: Media rate ÷ circulation or audience × 1,000 = CPM

   Example: If a full-page newspaper ad costs $2,200 and the circulation is 18,000, the CPM is $122.22. ($2,200 ÷ 18,000 × $1,000 = $122.22)

✔ **Combination rate:** The discounted rate offered to advertisers buying space in two or more publications owned by the same publisher or by affiliates in a syndication or publishing group.

✔ **Earned rate:** The rate that you actually pay after all discounts are applied.

✔ **Flat rate:** The cost of advertising with no discounts.

✔ **Frequency discount:** A reduced advertising rate offered by media to advertisers who run an ad a number of times within a given time period.

✔ **Local or retail rate:** A rate offered to local or retail newspaper advertisers that is lower than that paid by other advertisers. If you are placing ads in an out-of-town paper but selling your product through or in connection with a local business, see whether the local business can place your ad or if you can receive the local rate by mentioning the local business in your ad.

✔ **Make-good:** This is a no-charge repeat of your ad, which you can request if your ad ran with a publisher error or omission.

✔ **Open rate:** The highest price you'll pay for placing a particular ad one time with no discounts. Also called the *one-time rate* and the *basic rate*.

✔ **Pick-up rate:** Many newspapers offer a greatly discounted price when advertisers rerun the identical ad (no changes) within a five- or seven-day period.

✔ **Short rate:** This is the amount you'll owe to the publisher if you don't earn the rate for which you contracted. For instance, if you sign a contract to run a certain amount of advertising, but over the contract period you run less advertising than anticipated, you will owe the publisher the difference between the rate for which you contracted and the rate you actually earned.

Placing Newspaper Ads

Small businesses spend more on newspaper ads than on any other medium.

There are more opinions about what works in newspaper advertising than there are newspapers, and with thousands of newspapers in circulation, that adds up to a lot of differing ideas. Some advisers will tell you to avoid the Sunday edition and the day that the grocery store ads appear because they're crammed with ads and yours will get lost in the chaos. Others will counter with the fact that those big and busy issues are crammed with ads because they're the best-read papers of the week. Some people will tell you to place clever, small-space ads with high frequency; others will advocate dominating the paper with big-format ads even if you can afford to run them only on a few carefully chosen dates.

Most of the advice you hear is absolutely right — but only some of the time. So how do you proceed?

- ✔ Know your target prospect so that you can make an educated guess about what days and sections of the paper that person is likely to read.

- ✔ Know your ad strategy (refer to Chapter 8 if you have any doubts) so that you can time your placement to accomplish your advertising objective.

- ✔ Know how newspaper advertising works so that you can prepare a schedule that allows you to take advantage of the various media discounts.

Scheduling your placements

Myths are rampant about which day gets the most readership, but the fact is this: From Monday through Friday, the number of people who open their papers varies only 3 percent, with Tuesday's paper outpulling the others because in most markets it is the issue that carries the food ads. If you want your ad to generate results, heed these tips:

- ✔ Place your ad on the day that makes sense for your market and message, and not on rumors about which day is the "best" day to advertise. Here are some examples:

  - • If your target prospect is an avid price shopper, don't miss the issues of your paper that are full of grocery ads.

  - • If your target is a sports fanatic, advertise in Monday's sports section, where your prospect will read the weekend sports recaps.

  - • If you're promoting weekend dining or entertainment, advertise in the Thursday and Friday papers and in entertainment sections — unless you're trying to pull business from out-of-town markets, in which case you'd better run your ad closer to Tuesday and Wednesday to give your prospect time to make weekend travel plans.

  - • If your ad features an immediate call to action ("Call now for a free estimate"), don't choose the Sunday paper if you're not open to handle the responses.

- ✔ Advertising in the Sunday paper usually costs more — and delivers more. The number of single-copy sales is 10 to 40 percent higher on Sundays than on weekdays. What's more, readers spend nearly an hour with the Sunday paper compared with 20 minutes spent with weekday papers, and Sunday's paper tends to have a longer shelf life. Even if your newspaper charges a premium for Sunday ad placements, if you calculate the cost per thousand you'll find that the cost of reaching readers is cheaper on Sunday than on any other day.

Sizing newspaper ads

I could lead you through lots of technical stuff about ad sizes, but everybody gets the main idea: More readers note full-page ads than half-page ads; and more note half-page ads than quarter-page ads; and so forth down the line. Pretty simple, isn't it?!

The good news for small-budget advertisers is that while partial-page ads pull fewer readers, the reader numbers don't drop as fast as the cost of the space. For example, while a full-page ad pulls about 40 percent more readers than a quarter-page ad, the quarter page ad costs roughly a quarter of the price. By knowing your budget and needs, you can work out the right size-cost solution with the advertising salesperson. But here's some general advice:

- ✔ **If you have to choose, opt for frequency over size.** Plan the largest ad that you can afford to run multiple times and don't worry if the most you can afford is only a partial page.

- ✔ **Match your ad size to the size of your message.** If you're opening a major new location, go for the biggest ad you can afford. But if you're promoting a simple $5.99 product, a big splashy ad is likely to be overkill.

- ✔ **Aim to dominate the page.** Even partial-page ads can have a page-dominating affect. Consider spanning the entire width of the page with a ⅓-page horizontal ad. Or run a half-page vertical ad (4 columns wide by 12 inches high).

- ✔ **If you're not the biggest, be the most consistent.** Ask your newspaper representative about a Top-of-Mind Awareness (TOMA) program that offers sometimes outrageous discounts in return for the commitment to run even the tiniest ads several times a week, 52 weeks a year.

Requesting your ad placement

"Right-hand page, as far forward as possible" is repeated like a mantra by print advertisers. But there's no solid proof that an ad on the right page of an open publication does any better than an ad on the left page, and the same can be said for other hallowed rules about ad placement. In fact, research shows that newspaper ads placed above the fold pull no more readers than those placed below the fold, and ads next to editorial content pull the same as those next to ads. It all depends on the ad — not on the placement.

Before worrying over where your ad is going to be placed in the publication, think first about the content and look of your ad. Ask yourself this question: Have you created a strong message and an ad designed to draw attention regardless of where it appears in the paper?

Once you know you have a strong ad, decide whether you will reach your prospects if your ad runs anywhere in the paper (called a "run of paper" or "ROP" placement) or whether you need to request — and pay extra for — a "preferred position." The following advice will help you make your placement decisions:

✔ Make an "if possible" request when you place an ROP ad. Most newspapers do their best to honor reasonable placement requests with ROP orders — at no extra charge but on a space-available basis. Ask for placement in the front section, sports section, business section, as far forward as possible, or any other preference. Be willing, though, to settle for what you paid for — which is placement anywhere in the paper. Realize that most readers flip through nearly all of the paper on a daily basis, which is why most advertisers are confident rolling the dice with ROP ads.

✔ Look into special section rates for display ads placed in the real estate section and the classified section, as well as in special interest supplements that target your specific market.

✔ If your ad has a coupon, alert your ad representative in advance so it can be placed on the outer edge of the page to make clipping easy and so it won't be positioned back-to-back with another coupon on the flip side of the page.

✔ Leverage your budget. Work with your newspaper to arrive at a preferentially priced contract rate based on the nature of your business and your advertising volume. Ask about a contract addendum assuring that a certain percentage of your ROP placements will be in a preferred placement.

Taking advantage of the classified section

The classified section is the bargain basement of the newspaper. It's where you'll find great ad prices and readers who are intent on taking action.

Classified ads come in two types:

✔ **Small-print classified ads:** These ads are typeset by the newspaper and arranged into interest categories.

✔ **Classified display ads:** These ads feature unique layouts including headlines, illustrations, special type styles, and advertiser logos. They're available in sizes much smaller than those accepted in the rest of the paper, and they stand out on the otherwise all-type section pages.

Classified ads follow the same guidelines as all other print ads:

- ✔ Use a headline. Give even the shortest small-print ad an interest-grabbing statement or question, set in capital letters, to draw readers in.

- ✔ Write your ad to talk directly and personally to a single target prospect.

- ✔ Avoid abbreviations unless you're certain that most people will understand them.

- ✔ Place your ad in a number of classified categories if it appeals to more than one interest area.

- ✔ Tell how to contact you, and give the reader a reason to call — to request an estimate, to learn the price, to view the product, to schedule an appointment, or to take some other action.

Placing Magazine Ads

With a full-page color ad in *Time* magazine costing close to $200,000, you may wonder why small businesses should even bother considering magazine advertising. The reason is that thousands of small circulation (and vastly more affordable) magazines exist — plus many of the best-known magazines print regional or even city editions in which you can place an ad for a fraction of the full-edition price.

Most small businesses limit their magazine ads to targeted publications that serve particular business or interest groups, or — especially in the case of those in the resort industry — to city or regional travel magazines.

Selecting magazines

Review which magazines serve your industry or your target market. A good reference is the *Standard Rate and Data Service (SRDS)* collection of advertising directories, available on the reference shelves of most public libraries. The catalogs feature data provided by business and consumer magazines, as well as by broadcasters, direct mail houses, and other media resources. You can research a specific magazine, or you can look up an interest area to find the various magazines serving readers in that category.

Say that your business sells software to small banks, and you want to run ads in magazines read by small institution bankers. You can go to the *SRDS Business Publications Advertising Source Directory,* turn to the "Banking" section, and find 20 pages of magazines ranging from the *ABA Journal* to *U.S. Banker.* For each publication, you can find the editorial profile, editorial personnel, ad representatives, page dimensions, deadlines, and rates including commissions, discounts, and color charges.

Scheduling placements

In scheduling magazine ads, consider the following:

✔ **Frequency matters.** Be sure that your budget is big enough to place your ad in the same magazine at least three times over a three- to six-month period. Or if you want to advertise during a single month, choose three magazines with similar readership profiles and run your ad in each one, building frequency for your message not through multiple placements in a single magazine, but through what is called "crossover readership" between publications.

✔ **Magazines have long lead and response times.** If you're placing ads for spring vacations, your magazine ads will have to run well in advance of the March and April vacation months to allow your prospects time to read your ad, request information, and make travel plans. Unlike newspaper and broadcast advertising, response to magazine ads is not immediate. It builds over a multiweek period and continues for months and years into the future.

✔ **Full-page ads reign, but partial-page ads can compete well.** Consider using square one-third page ads or vertical one-half page.

Be aware that partial page ads almost always share the page with other advertisers and often end up toward the back of the magazine. On the flip side, they also share the page with editorial content, which means that readers are likely to spend more time on the page.

✔ **Concept and design will make or break your ad.** Definitely, *definitely,* invest in professional copywriting, design, and production to create an ad that looks good in the competitive magazine ad environment.

✔ **Success stories are built on frequent placements of small well-designed black-and-white ads.** If you can't afford the production and placement of a full-color ad but you want to reach a magazine's readership, run a small black-and-white or classified ad in the magazine. Use the space to invite readers to "request our color catalog," or "visit our Web site" or other offers that use the small ad space to lead readers to a larger, full-color marketing message from your business.

✔ **Work with magazine ad reps.** Build a relationship even before you place an ad. Explain your business, your desire to reach the magazine's circulation, and your budget realities. If you have an ad that is produced and ready-to-go, ask to be contacted if high-discount *remnant space* (last-minute unsold ad space) is available. Also inquire about regional editions or any other means of placing your ad at a reduced rate.

✔ **Take advantage of merchandising aids that accompany your ad buy.**

The magazine may have a "bingo card" that invites readers to circle numbers for additional information from advertisers. All you have to do is offer a free brochure or other item. You'll receive labels for all respondents — a great way to gather inquiries and build a database of prospects to whom you can send direct mailings (see Chapter 13).

Ask for mounted tear sheets of your ad for display in your business. They'll be mounted on boards reading "As Seen In XYZ Magazine."

✔ **Reprint color ads for use as direct mailers.** Color ad production is expensive. Amortize the cost and leverage the credibility of being a major magazine advertiser by turning the ad into a direct mailer (see Chapter 13).

Yellow Pages and Directory Ads

If consumers are apt to start a search for a business like yours with a phone call, you need to be in the Yellow Pages.

If you rely predominantly on personal referrals rather than walk-in business, obviously you won't want a big display ad. But even so you'll want at least a listing, to help customers who forget your business name or who want to look up your address or phone number.

Research conducted for the Yellow Pages Publishers Association finds that

✔ Nearly half of those looking up a business in the Yellow Pages are looking for how to contact a specific establishment.

✔ Six out of ten consumers turned to the Yellow Pages to solve a need with no particular business preference.

Yellow Pages and directory ads are important because they get your name in front of prospects who are clearly in the market for the kinds of products or services you offer. To get your money's worth out of your directory ads, though, you have to do some careful advance planning. Use the following as a checklist:

✔ **Choose the right classifications.** Ask yourself, "If I were looking for a business like mine, what categories would I check?" Sales reps suggest that you list under a number of headings, but use your own customer knowledge to restrict your choices. Each category you add costs more money, so limit your entries only to the sections your prospects are most apt to check.

✔ **Choose the right size.** In Yellow Pages, biggest isn't always best. First, check what your competition is doing. In many categories (and particularly in service business categories), the most established and respected firms run the smallest and most subdued ads. Consider how many businesses compete in your category in your market area, realizing that if your crowd isn't very big, you hardly need a large ad to stand out in it.

✔ **Choose whether to add color.** Study the section where your ad will run. See whether color is necessary to compete on the pages. Consider whether adding color will contribute or detract from the image you want to project. If you opt for color, read the rate card carefully, because color charges vary from one directory to another but always mount up quickly.

✔ **Choose the right directories.** Small businesses hate to be left out of any listing, but before spending dollars on independent and upstart directories, ask for proof regarding how well they will be distributed and used.

✔ **Create the right ad.** Regardless of size or color, what your ad says determines its success.

✔ **What should your ad say?** According to consumer research, people want *solutions* to their problems and to *trust* the businesses they choose as a result of Yellow Pages searches. Write your headline and copy accordingly, following the advice in the preceding section on "Creating Print Ads." As you prepare your ad, remember that it will appear adjacent to ads for your competitors — so present the beneficial attributes that set you apart and make you the best choice.

Consumers consider the following kinds of information valuable:

- Offers of brochures, catalogs, demonstrations, estimates, and so on
- Listings of products or brands (including logos)
- Special qualities and services
- Professional endorsements or affiliations
- Length of time in business
- Hours of business
- Map or directions to the business
- Parking instructions
- Phone, fax, and toll-free numbers and Web site address
- Street address
- Credit card options
- Bonding, licenses, and related information

✔ **How should your ad look?** Remember that directory readers are also seeing your other ads and marketing materials. Use your own designer, and not one provided by the directory, to create an ad that matches your brand image. By all means include a headline, following all the advice on headline creation in the earlier section on "Creating Print Ads." Include a differentiating border and a layout that gives prominence to the one thing that consumers most want when they use the Yellow Pages — your phone number and address.

If you place a display ad, remember to include a line in your regular listing that says "See our display ad on page XX." And if you don't place a display ad, consider an "in-column ad" that expands your alphabetical listing into a bordered presentation for your business.

Chapter 12

Broadcasting Your Message on Radio and TV

In This Chapter

▶ Figuring out how much airtime to buy

▶ Understanding broadcast media terminology

▶ Adhering to broadcast ad guidelines

▶ Producing radio and television ads

▶ Advertising with infomercials

*W*ith television sets in more than 98 percent of U.S. homes, and radios in the dashboards of 95 percent of all cars on the road, it's unquestionable that your customers are tuned in to the broadcast world. If you want your advertising to meet them there, this chapter helps you prepare your strategy and master the terms and guidelines that apply to broadcast advertising, whether on radio or television.

Venturing into the broadcast advertising arena is a lot like taking a first-time trip to a foreign territory. The language is new (*avails, dayparts, GRPs, TRPs, flights, reach* — yikes!) and the rules are different from other, more familiar kinds of advertising.

Count on the following pages to help you translate broadcast lingo and plan your foray into the world of radio and television ad production, scheduling, and placement.

Buying Airtime

If you're placing ads on just a few stations in your own hometown market, you can probably handle the task on your own. But if your marketing needs involve multiple market areas, or if you're spending more than $10,000 on a media buy, use a media buyer to wheel, deal, apply clout, and bring the kind of muscle that comes from experience in the field. (See Chapter 9 for help choosing and hiring media buying professionals.) You'll pay an hourly fee or a percentage of your overall buy, but you'll save time and confusion and almost certainly obtain a better schedule and price. Media planning and buying usually come as part of the service when you use an advertising agency for ad creation.

If you're going to do it yourself, begin by requesting a rate kit for each station you believe will reach your target market. The rate kit contains the following:

✔ Audited research including statistical profiles of the age, gender, and consumer buying patterns of the station's audience

✔ Descriptions of network affiliations

✔ Summaries of advertising success stories

✔ Sample advertising packages

✔ Rate cards

Use the rate card as a cost guideline. In broadcast, nearly all prices are negotiable. They vary depending on availability, time of day, time of year, and the advertising commitment you're willing to make to the station.

Station advertising sales representatives will assemble media schedules and package offers for you. Take time to evaluate not just the bottom lines but how well each station's audience matches up with your prospect profile and how well the proposal compares with those from other stations.

Station and ad buying terminology

So that you don't get dizzy tuning into an entirely new language, get acquainted with the following terms before talking with media representatives:

✔ **Area of dominant influence:** Also known as *A.D.I.* The area that a station's broadcast signal covers.

✔ **Availability:** Also called *avail.* A broadcast advertising time slot that is open for reservation. With the exception of the holiday and political seasons, most stations have plenty of avails even at the last minute.

✔ **Call letters:** A station's identification, for example (borrowing from the old TV sit-com), WKRP in Cincinnati.

✔ **Dayparts:** Segments of the broadcast day.

Radio time is generally segmented into the *morning drive time* (6 to 10 a.m.), *midday* (10 a.m. to 3 p.m.), *afternoon drive time* (3 to 7 p.m.), *evening* (7 p.m. to midnight), and *late night* (midnight to 6 a.m.). The drive times draw the most listeners and the highest ad rates.

TV time is priced highest during *prime time,* which runs from 8 p.m. to 11 p.m. The next most expensive ad buys are in the hours adjacent to prime time, which include *early fringe* (5 to 8 p.m.) and *late fringe* (after 11 p.m.).

✔ **Flight:** A schedule of broadcast ads concentrated within a short time period, followed by a *hiatus,* or period of inactivity. Ad flights create awareness that is followed by a *carryover affect* that causes prospects to think that they "just heard" your ad even when it has been off-air for several weeks.

✔ **Increments:** Stations sell ad time in lengths — called *increments* — of 10 seconds (written as :10s and called "tens"), 15 seconds (:15s), 30 seconds (:30s), and 60 seconds (:60s).

Most radio ads are :30s, although :60s are usually only slightly more expensive and sometimes no different in price. If you opt for the longer ad, be sure that you really need the time to convey your message. An ad that makes a good impression in 30 seconds can bore the socks of a listener when dragged out for a full minute. Shorter ads (:10s and :15s) are often used as reinforcements, rotating into a schedule of :30s or :60s to build frequency through short reminder messages.

Well over half of all television ads are :30s.

✔ **Network affiliate:** A station that is affiliated with a national broadcast network (like ABC, NBC, CBS, and FOX), usually resulting in higher news credibility and larger audiences. A station not affiliated with a network is called an *independent station.*

✔ **Sponsorship:** Underwriting a program in return for on-air announcements (called *billboards*) that tell the sponsor's name and tagline or brief message.

On commercial stations, advertisers can sponsor specific news reports such as the helicopter traffic update or the daily weathercast. Or they can sponsor a public service message, for example, "This safe driving reminder is brought to you by the doctors and nurses of St. Vincent's Hospital."

On public broadcast stations, sponsorships provide the *only* way to "advertise." Many financial planners, medical and legal professionals, and other service providers use program sponsorships to gain awareness without looking promotional. When you hear, "This program is brought to you by a generous grant from . . ." you're listening to a sponsorship announcement.

✔ **Spot:** The term "spot" has several meanings in broadcast advertising:

- It refers to the time slot in which an ad runs. For example, "We're going to run 30 spots a week."

- It refers to the ad itself. For example, "We're going to produce three spots to rotate over a month-long schedule."

- It refers to television time purchased on specific stations rather than on an entire network. For example, "We can't afford a million dollar Super Bowl network buy, so we're going to spend $500 to make a spot buy on our local channel."

✔ **TAP or Total Audience Plan:** A TAP is a radio package that includes a number of ads aired in each day part, allowing the station to decide on the schedule as long as it plays the agreed-upon number of your ads in each time period. Ads that run as part of TAPs are called *rotaters*. TAP programs are usually the most affordable packages offered by stations. Still, negotiate the deal. Ask about weighting the schedule toward the day parts when your prospects are most apt to be listening, or see whether the station will throw in additional spots to enhance the schedule. It's okay to beg — just don't get greedy!

Achieving broadcast reach, frequency, and rating points

Reach is the number of people who hear your ad or, in the case of television, the number of households that are tuned in when your ad airs. *Frequency* is the number of times that an average prospect is exposed to your ad. The rule of thumb is that a broadcast needs to reach a prospect 3 to 5 times before it triggers action, which usually requires a schedule of 27 to 30 ad broadcasts. Chapter 10 has more information about how reach and frequency work together in advertising schedules to put your message in front of enough prospects enough times to make a marketing difference.

Increase advertising impact by opting for frequency over reach. Instead of airing ads on ten stations (wide reach), choose two of the stations and talk to the same people repeatedly (high frequency).

It takes *reach* to achieve awareness, but it takes *frequency* to change minds.

How much is enough?

The age-old question among broadcast advertisers is how much and how often ads need to air. This is where rating points come to the rescue. A *rating point* measures the percentage of the potential audience that is reached by a broadcast ad. If an ad airs during a time that is calculated to reach 10 percent of the potential audience, then it earns ten rating points.

The ratings are based on actual market performance, measured through surveys conducted by firms such as Arbitron and A. C. Neilsen. The findings have an admitted margin of error, but they remain the best way to compare broadcast audiences within a market area. Stations subscribe to the findings and share the numbers with advertisers as part of their sales efforts.

Decoding the rating points

In scheduling ads, you'll hear reference to two kinds of rating points. *Gross rating points,* or *GRPs,* are the total number of rating points delivered by an ad schedule, usually over a one-week period. If you air 30 ads in a week, each reaching an average of 5 percent of the total potential audience, your schedule will achieve 150 GRPs. *Target rating points,* or *TRPs,* are measured exactly like GRPs, *except* they count only the audience that matches your target audience. If your target market consists only of men age 35+, then your TRPs are measured as a percent of the men 35+ who hear or see your ad. GRPs measure your *total* reach; TRPs measure your *effective* reach.

Most media planners agree on the following scheduling advice:

- ✔ **150 GRPs/month is the rock-bottom minimum.** If your budget can't cover a schedule with 150 GRPs over a month-long period, the effort likely won't be worth the investment.

- ✔ **To build awareness, schedule at least 150 GRPs for three months in a row.** You can divide your schedule into 50 GRPs every week or 75 GRPs every other week, but commit to a multimonth schedule if you expect broadcast advertising to result in good awareness for your business.

- ✔ **Buy up to 500 GRPs/month if you're trying to blitz the market.** For grand openings and major promotions, you need the kind of major market impact that comes only from high frequency and concentrated broadcast buys. A "heavy-up" schedule involves as many as 500 GRPs.

You can make a broadcast buy without ever mentioning rating points, but don't. Stations will gladly present you with people-language proposals — for example, "30 spots at an average price of $25 each." But what are you really getting for your money? Follow up with a request: "Would you calculate how many gross rating points that schedule delivers? Also, what percentage of the audience fits our target profile of men age 35+?"

Bartering for airtime

Barter is the exchange of merchandise or services rather than monetary payment for broadcast advertising time. For example, a restaurant might trade for ad time by catering a station's holiday party, or a hotel might swap ad time for weekend lodging packages for use in on-air drawings. Here are a couple ways to barter for airtime:

- ✔ You can trade a product or service that the station wants or needs — either for its own use or for use in on-air promotions.

- ✔ You can trade your product to a third-party business that then trades a like value of time or product to the station. (For example, you trade $1,000 of plumbing services to a contractor who then trades $1,000 of contracting services to a station's remodeling project, and the station gives the contractor $1,000 of airtime which you get as your end of the deal.)

Unless you're making a direct trade with the station, bartering takes time and expertise. For assistance, look online or in the Yellow Pages for "Barter Services," or inquire with your media planner about making barter contacts.

If you decide to barter for your ad buys, here are the advantages:

- You can buy airtime without spending actual money.

- You can leverage your budget. You may be able to trade for airtime at one and a half to two times your product value (for example, $1,500 of airtime for $1,000 of product). Even a straight trade ($1,000 of airtime for $1,000 of product) saves money over a cash buy because your product price includes profit.

- Your ad buy will likely cost even less than the amount you provide in trade, because the product you provide in trade may not be fully redeemed — which puts money back on your bottom line. For example, when a theater trades airtime for movie ticket certificates, the manager knows that a percentage of the certificates will never be used. (Include an expiration date in your trade agreement. You don't want to end up paying for this year's advertising out of ad budgets in years to come.)

As you make barter purchases, proceed with exactly the same care you would exercise if you were make cash purchases of media time, following these steps:

- See that the schedule delivers adequate reach and frequency.

- Verify that the station reaches your target audience.

- Be sure that the timing matches your marketing plan.

- Be careful that any on-air promotions involving your products are consistent with your business image and contribute to the strength of your brand.

Following Broadcast Ad Guidelines

Whether you're producing a television ad or a radio ad, some general broadcast advertising guidelines apply.

Establishing your own broadcast identity

Over time you want listeners or viewers to recognize your business before they even hear your name. Consider the following identity-building techniques:

- **Sound:** Have the same distinct announcer serve as the voice in all your ads.

- **Style:** Establish a broadcast ad style, for example an ongoing dialog between the same two people or ads that always advance a certain kind message.

- **Music:** Use notable music as background in all your ads.

- **Jingles:** Jingles are musical slogans that play in broadcast ads. Be prepared: Some people love jingles, some hate them, and sooner or later almost everyone tires of them. Before investing in a jingle, be sure of two things. First, air enough broadcast ads to achieve and benefit from an association between the jingle and your name. Second, develop a jingle appropriate to your brand image. Any station or studio can direct you to jingle producers.

Writing your ad

Don't write your own ad and don't let the station write it either. Instead, write your own strategy and ad objective and bring in professional help to develop your concept and write your ad. Follow these tips:

- **Be strategic.** Start by setting your ad strategy (see Chapter 8).

- **Know your objective.** Write a creative brief (again, see Chapter 8) summarizing who you want the ad to talk to, what you want it to accomplish, and what market action you want it to inspire.

- **Develop your ad concept.** Your concept should be capable of grabbing and holding audience attention without stealing the spotlight from your ad message (see Chapter 8). This is where a professional writer really earns her fee. It's your name and offer that you want to convey. Your creative concept is your approach, not your message!

- **Grab audience attention.** You have three seconds before your audience is gone — out to the refrigerator or over to another station.

- **Tell a story in seconds.** In a 30-second ad, you have about 20 seconds to inform, educate, entice, and entertain — and even less if you cede time to a jingle or other sound effects. The other seconds get divided between an attention-getting opening and your ad identification and call to action. Be sure to do the following in your ad:

- Feature your name (or product name) at least three times.

- Feature your call to action at least once, preferably twice.

- If you include an address, provide an easy locator (for example, "across from the train station").

Turning your script over to the producers

When it's time to begin production, radio or TV stations usually offer to help you out again, and this time you may want to take them up on it. When you use the talents of radio or TV stations, follow these steps:

✔ **Review work samples.** As you watch or listen to each ad, ask yourself: Would my impression of this company be enhanced by this ad, or would this ad create a negative image about the company's commitment to quality? If you like what you see and hear, inquire about pricing, which at station-based studios is likely to be free or close to it.

✔ **Make your selection.** Plan to produce your ad at one studio and then provide all stations on your schedule with duplicate copies, called *dubs*. Don't allow each station to air its own version of your ad. Frequency works only when people hear the same ad repeatedly.

✔ **Obtain a budget.** Know what costs lie ahead. Request detailed allocations for studio time, tape and materials, music fees, talent, editing time, other costs, and ad duplication. Particularly, review the costs and usage restrictions for music, sound effects, and talent, following these tips:

- **Music and sound effects:** Most studios have access to libraries of rights-free or nominally priced music and sound effects. Study the costs and, as you make selections, confirm the usage rights. Some rights are outright (you can air the ad wherever and whenever you want at no additional fee), while others cover only the designated exposure and are renewable (meaning you pay again) for further use. Prerecorded music that is available through music libraries is referred to as *needle-drop* and usually comes with a moderate fee based on the amount of exposure the piece will receive through your advertising.

- **Talent:** Your ad will involve at least an announcer and likely actors as well. For locally aired ads, you'll probably hire directly or use talent provided by the studio. If you use members of a union such as the Screen Actors Guild, be prepared for higher rates, piles of paperwork, *and* more experienced talent. When using non-station talent or recording outside the studio, be careful to obtain talent releases. Figure 12-1 presents a simple format, although you should check with your production company and even your attorney to be sure that you're using an appropriate form.

TALENT & MODEL RELEASE FORM

Project: _____

Business: _____

For valuable consideration I do hereby authorize (name of company) _____ or those acting on its authority to:

■ Record my participation and appearance on video tape, audio tape, film, photograph, or any other medium

■ Use my name, likeness, voice, and biographical material in connection with those recordings

■ Exhibit or distribute such recording in whole or in part without restrictions or limitations for any educational or promotional purpose deemed appropriate by (name of company) _____

I have read this agreement before signing below, and understand its contents.

Name (Print) _____

Address _____

City, State, Zip _____

SSN (for paid talent only) _____

Phone number _____

Signature _____ Date _____

Signature of parent or guardian if talent is under 18 years of age

_____ Date _____

Witness signature _____ Date _____

Figure 12-1:
Sample
talent
release
form.

Roar of the greasepaint gotcha?

Think long and hard about serving as your own ad talent. Even if you're your firm's best advocate, you aren't necessarily its best spokesperson. Do you have the best voice and appearance to serve as your own on-air talent? Can you commit the time? Can your advertising build a story around you, thereby making your appearance part of your message and not just a substitute for paid talent? Do you *want* to be the spokesperson? If you're considering selling your business in the future, will your presence in your advertising help or hinder that effort?

✔ **Meet with the talent.** Before rolling the tape or cameras, ask the talent to perform a dry run of the ad. Listen as the talent reads or enacts your script. Take time to correct the pronunciations of your name and products if necessary, and alter sentences that contain tongue twisters. Trim time-gobbling extra words and do a final read to be sure the ad sounds right and fits within the allocated seconds.

If you don't like what you see or hear, speak up. Announcers can adjust their voices to sound younger, older, happier, sadder, or like they're talking to children versus adults, or to a single person rather than a whole group. A good ad agency or production facility director can handle much of the talent direction for you, representing not only your thoughts and ideas but bringing an additional layer of expertise and professionalism to the task.

✔ **Attend the editing session.** Editing is where dollars burn quickly. Be on hand to make and approve decisions on the spot to avoid the need for a repeat session.

Review your ad in your car or living room. Get out of the studio with its perfect sound system and lack of interruptions. Sit in your car, preferably in traffic, or in your living room while kids race through after school. Turn your ad on while others are around to see whether they stop to watch or listen. Turn it on half way through to see if it still presents a coherent message for your business. Then review it not once but a dozen or more times to see whether it can hold your interest without driving you to distraction.

Producing Radio Ads

In 30 or 60 seconds, a good radio ad grabs attention, involves a listener, sounds believable, creates a mental picture, spins a story, calls for action, and manages to keep the product on center stage and the customer in the spotlight — all without sounding pushy, screamy, obnoxious, or boring.

Done perfectly, a radio ad is a one-on-one conversation with a single target prospect, written and produced so well that a target prospect hears the introduction and says, in essence, "Ssshhh, be quiet, you guys, I need to hear this. It's talking to me."

About the only thing radio ads can't do is to present a three-dimensional product to see, touch, taste, or feel. They can do the next best thing, though, which is to use words and sounds to conjure up mental images and leave the consumer ready to take action to obtain the real thing.

Writing to be heard

In radio advertising, your "headline" is your opening statement, and the rest of the script tells your story. See Chapter 11 for general headline and copy advice. The difference is that radio ads need to be even more intimate and closely focused than other ads because the *only* way you'll get and hold attention is with your words and sounds. Here's how to write successful radio ads:

- ✔ **Stick to a single theme.** When your time is up, you can expect your listener to remember only one message, along with your name and — if you're lucky — how to reach you.

- ✔ **Use straightforward language** that is written exactly how people talk.

- ✔ **Write to the pace people talk.** Don't write to the pace at which they read.

- ✔ **Include pauses.** People need time to think, and the announcer needs time to breathe.

- ✔ **Cut extra verbiage.** You wouldn't say "indeed," "thus," "moreover," or "therefore" if you were explaining something exciting to a friend, so don't do it in your radio script, either.

- ✔ **Rewrite elaborately constructed sentences.** Don't expect listeners to track through phrases linked together with "who," "which," "where," and "what." Instead of saying, "The new fashions, which just came off the Paris runways where they made international news, are due to arrive in Chicago tomorrow at noon," try saying, "The newest Paris runway fashions arrive in Chicago tomorrow. At noon you're invited to the national premier of the world's leading looks."

- ✔ **Call for action.** Tell readers what to do next. Prepare them to take down your phone number ("Have a pencil handy?"), or at least take the time to repeat the number. Most important, though, be sure they remember your name. That way, at least they can find you in the phone book or online. (Warning: Don't use radio time telling people to "look us up in the Yellow Pages," especially if your competitors overshadow your presence.)

Radio do's and don'ts

As you prepare your radio ads, use the following checklist of good ideas to employ and landmines to avoid:

✔ Do use music.

✔ Do stick with a single theme in each ad.

✔ Do make a simple offer that calls for immediate action.

✔ Do use radio to generate leads by making no-risk offers for free estimates, free brochures, or free information.

✔ Do limit yourself to 30 seconds unless you're sure that you can hold the prospect's attention for a full minute.

✔ Do limit your 30-second ad to 60 to 70 words *unless* it includes an intentionally rapid-fire conversation.

✔ Do use radio as a complement to other advertising, including statements such as "Look for our coupon in Friday's paper."

✔ Do say your name three times.

✔ Do match your ad to the format of the stations you air it on. If you choose to advertise on a country western station, you'll hardly want an ad with new-age music in the background.

✔ Don't ask the ad to make the sale; use it to make the contact.

✔ Don't advertise products with a bunch of disclaimers.

✔ Don't fast-talk the prospect.

✔ Don't use incomprehensible jingles.

✔ Don't use weak attempts at humor.

✔ Don't talk to yourself. "We've been in business 25 years," "We're excited over our new inventory." "We're open until 10 p.m." Instead turn every statement into a consumer benefit ("Shop 'til 10 nightly") if you want to hold listener attention — and you do!

Producing TV Ads

People spend more time with the television set than with any other advertising medium. "I saw it on TV" has become a mark of having made it into the advertising major leagues. To get there, though, be prepared to make a financial commitment. Successful television advertisers have two things in common. First, they earmark adequate funds to produce good ads. Second, they fund media schedules that span at least a multimonth period. If you can do both those things — produce a quality ad and fund an extensive TV schedule — television advertising will deliver both awareness and credibility for your business.

If your market is limited to a concise geographic area, you can use the ever-increasing number of cable channels to air your ads at a fraction of the price of major network ad rates. But remember that even if the time charge is low, the production value of the ad you air needs to be high enough to represent your business well in the single most competitive advertising arena.

Overseeing creation of your TV ad

Notice that this section isn't titled "*Creating* Your TV Ad." *Don't* create your own television ad, your own marketing video, or any other moving-picture medium. Ever.

Why the insistence? Consider this: Your ad will play to an audience that has been trained to expect feature film quality and Nike-style concepts. To compete on a small business budget, you need a strong, simple ad concept and clean, well-edited visuals. The first step toward making a good impression is to get help from those who deal in television ads daily.

Hiring professionals

As you select a creative partner, rely on the following kinds of resources:

- ✔ **Advertising agencies:** Big agencies serve major advertising accounts on annual contracts. They often accept large project work as well, but if you want to receive major attention for a fairly small project, interview small agencies to evaluate their talents, expertise, costs, and availability.

- ✔ **Video production services:** Look under "Video Production" in the Yellow Pages, and you'll find businesses specializing in everything from wedding memories to digital production, editing, graphics, and animation. Look for a studio that offers creative services, script writing, production, and editing services.

- ✔ **TV station production facilities:** Local stations can create your ad for "almost nothing," but get a bid anyway. What is "nothing" to those who deal with TV advertising daily could be enough to break your bank.

Airing preproduced manufacturer ads

High-quality, ready-to-air ads may be available to you through your manufacturers or dealers. The ads feature the manufacturer's products, but they include time to add a tag line directing viewers to your business. If you go this route, consider the following:

✔ Look for ads featuring products with major sales potential for your business and for which your business is the exclusive regional representative.

✔ The ads are likely to be of higher quality than you could afford to produce on your own. By adding your own tag line, you'll gain advertising visibility while benefiting your business through association with a major national advertiser.

✔ When airing manufacturer ads, contact the manufacturer to discuss the possibility of obtaining cooperative advertising support in the form of shared costs for the media placements.

✔ Work with your local station to add or change your tag line. They perform the service for free or very close to it.

Television ad guidelines

You heard the advice loud and clear in the previous section: Don't even try to conceive, write, or produce your own TV ads. Bring in the pros and then know what to look for as you evaluate their ad concepts and schedules.

The advice in Table 12-1 shows you what to aim for and what to avoid.

Table 12-1	TV Advertising Do's and Don'ts
Do's	**Don'ts**
Do work to stir the emotions and imagination of your audience.	Don't create ads that feature only a lineup of facts about your product or business.
Do focus on the viewer and how your message will change the prospect's life.	Don't keep the entire focus on your product, company, or staff.
Do start strong. You have three seconds to grab the audience.	Don't save your punch line until the end — your audience may be gone by then.
Do get to the point quickly and then use the rest of the ad to back up your point and tell what's in it for the viewer.	Don't go for a slow build-up unless you're confident that your ad will be intriguing and entertaining enough to hold the viewer.
Do present your name visually *and* verbally.	Don't simply flash your logo. Much of the audience will be listening but not watching.
Do invest in a quality ad with staying power that you can air for months or even a year, updated with inexpensive tag lines.	Don't go for quantity over quality, creating a lineup of inexpensive ads that fail to create a positive image for your business.
Do place an adequate schedule of at least 150 gross rating points a month.	Don't invest in TV advertising if you can't air a quality ad with adequate frequency.

Do's	Don'ts
Do rely on visuals to tell your story, and use your script to support the message.	Don't resort to a "talking head," the TV equivalent of a classroom lecture.
Do start with a great idea that can be told visually and then use words, music, and sound effects as enhancements.	Don't start with a script and then find visuals to fill the screen while an announcer "reads" the ad.

Infomercials

Infomercials are the half-hour program-style ads that you come across when you're channel cruising during daytime and late-night hours. They promote housewares, financial and business opportunities, exercise and beauty items, self-help offerings, and such aptitude development products as memory enhancement and reading programs. Oh, and don't forget psychic services. Infomercials involve a direct exchange between the viewer and the advertiser. No retailers, travel agents, or other intermediaries are involved.

Infomercials solicit viewer action in two ways:

- ✔ Sales-generating infomercials invite viewers to call toll-free to place COD or credit card orders.
- ✔ Lead-generating infomercials ask viewers to call for free catalogs, brochures, or other offers.

Products featured in infomercials have markups that are high enough to absorb the cost of creating and airing the infomercial. For example, a product that sells for $19.95 should cost the manufacturer between $4 and $6, leaving room for a three- to five-time markup, which is the typical margin for an infomercial product.

Infomercials are high risk. There is no other way to put it. Experts in the field warn that the infomercial success rate is as low as one out of four.

The topic of infomercials comes up among small business advertisers in part because they generate direct and measurable results and in part because the ads look fairly straightforward and easy to produce. Looks can deceive, though. As with all other broadcast ads, viewers have been trained to expect a certain caliber of production value.

The average national infomercial production budget is more than $150,000, though you can find video production houses that will create your infomercial for a tenth of that amount or less, and you can air the program for dollars per showing on local-market cable channels. Be aware, though, that as you limit your costs, you also limit your reach and frequency, resulting in fewer contacts, fewer sales, and probably a proportionately lower return on investment than the big-budget infomercial advertiser gets.

Big budget or small budget, all infomercials have the following traits in common:

- They promote unique products that are not available through retail channels.
- They present products that are of interest and use to most viewers.
- They feature strong testimonials.
- They show easy-to-demonstrate solutions.
- They offer low prices that most viewers feel that they can opt for without great deliberation.

In creating infomercials, follow these ten rules:

1. Feature the product as king.

2. Solve a viewer problem.

3. Focus on selling, not on entertaining.

4. Use short sentences, short words, and short segments, broken at least three times during the program by your call to action.

5. Don't try to be funny.

6. Know your product position, your unique selling proposition, and the customer benefits you deliver (see Chapter 8). Then use your infomercial to give people a reason to believe what you're saying.

7. Use unscripted testimonials. Let customers ad lib their remarks but ask them to be specific with their praise. "It's amazing" has an iota of the sales punch of "I stood there watching the fine lines around my eyes fill in and disappear. I just stared at my mirror, and then I started laughing with pure joy."

8. Never fake product demonstrations. It's illegal. Enough said.

9. Evaluate the effectiveness of your infomercial the morning after it airs. Unlike other forms of advertising, infomercials don't work better after repeated viewing. Most viewers will respond after watching the program one time if they are to respond at all. If your infomercial lights up your phone lines, re-air it to reach yet more prospects. But if no one calls, don't wait to see what happens. Go back into the edit booth and start fine-tuning it, starting with the first three-minute segment, which is the portion that either grabs or loses most viewers.

10. Before you invest your budget, study other infomercials, meet with infomercial producers, and read direct marketing publications and Web sites. For a great starting point, go to the Smart Business Supersite, www.smartbiz.com, and enter the word "infomercials" to see the latest articles and books available.

Chapter 13

Mailing Direct to Your Market

. . . .

In This Chapter

▶ Building relationships using one-to-one marketing

▶ Creating and maintaining a mailing list

▶ Creating effective direct mailers

▶ Making compelling direct mail offers

▶ Venturing into the field of e-mail marketing

. . . .

*O*ne-to-one communications are the exact opposite of mass media advertising. *Mass media advertising* uses the shotgun approach (that is, you create a great ad and use newspapers, magazines, and broadcast media to spread the message far and wide), while *one-to-one communications* are far more precise: You aim your message only at specific and well-defined target prospects. When you employ one-to-one marketing, you bypass mass media vehicles and take your ad straight to the mailboxes or telephones of those individuals who are prime prospects for your product or service.

Most marketers believe that the two approaches work best as a tag team effort: You use mass media advertising to build the awareness, desire, and perceived value for a brand, and then use one-to-one marketing to call for the order and to form the basis of a lasting customer relationship.

If you can only afford to do one or the other, however, consider placing your bets on one-to-one marketing so that each dollar you spend is directed straight to a target prospect, and not scattered through mass media to reach prospects and non-prospects alike.

One-to-One versus Mass Media Marketing

Although the terms direct marketing, database marketing, direct-response advertising, and direct mail are often used interchangeably, they each represent different roles in the direct marketing field. For the record, here are the definitions:

- ✔ **Direct marketing:** Involves a direct exchange between a seller and a buyer — without the involvement of retailers, travel agents, or other intermediaries.

- ✔ **Direct mail:** A primary means of direct marketing communication that involves sending print ads (in the form of letters, postcards, or packages) directly to targeted prospects.

- ✔ **Direct-response advertising:** Includes all ads that invite consumers to take an immediate action, such as making a purchase or requesting additional information.

- ✔ **Direct sales:** A sales transaction that occurs over a distance and directly between the buyer and the seller. Mail order and e-commerce are the primary vehicles for direct sales. (See Chapter 17 for information on e-commerce.)

- ✔ **Database marketing:** Entails compiling detailed information about customers and prospective customers. This information is then used to create and send marketing messages that are focused on the specific needs of unique consumer groups.

- ✔ **Telemarketing:** Involves communicating with prospects and customers over the telephone — via *inbound calls* made by consumers to toll-free numbers that they see in ads or sales materials or via *outbound calls* made by a business to the homes or offices of target prospects.

Direct Sales: The Do-It-Yourself Distribution Channel

Just as you'd guess, direct marketers sell directly to consumers without involving any middlemen, retailers, or other representatives. Instead they use direct response ads, direct mailers, catalogs, and e-commerce (there's much more on this topic in Part IV) to deal one-on-one with prospective buyers. Following are three examples of how direct marketing tools can work to generate direct sales:

- ✔ **Direct response advertising:** A handcrafted-jewelry maker may advertise his wares by placing small black-and-white magazine advertisements. But instead of aiming to build general awareness, the ads would directly invite customer orders by instructing readers to call toll-free to make a purchase of the featured item or, alternatively, to visit the jeweler's Web site to view and order from his complete line. Either way, the instructions in the ad would lead straight back to the jewelry maker and not to any retailer or other intermediary.

✔ **Direct mail:** The self-publisher of a book featuring lists and ratings for summer youth camps may promote the book — along with a special promotional offer — to a subscriber list rented from a major parenting magazine.

✔ **Catalog distribution:** A kitchen accessories company may mail its catalog to the households of all past customers and ad respondents, as well as to subscribers of major gourmet and cooking magazines.

Managing an Ethical Direct Sales Program

The Direct Marketing Association warns against the two biggest direct sales landmines: nondelivery of merchandise and misrepresentation of offers. Every year a few direct marketers hurt the reputation of all by implementing programs that fail to communicate honestly or to deliver the products as promised. If you are going to sell directly, protect your own reputation and the reputation of all who participate in direct marketing by following this advice:

Be clear, honest, and complete in your communications. Your ad *is* the shopping experience for direct buyers, so make it thorough and consistent with what the customer will see upon receipt of his or her order. Be careful that the way you represent your product is accurate in terms of product description, price, terms of payment, and any extra charges. Don't make outlandish claims, and don't make promises that defy belief or that you can't live up to.

Describe the commitment involved in placing an order. Decide how you will handle returns, and communicate your policy in your marketing materials. Also be aware that there are laws enforcing honesty in direct mail marketing. If you promise that "satisfaction's guaranteed" (or if you make a money-back guarantee), Federal Trade Commission regulations mandate that you give a full refund without question and for any reason. If you offer a risk-free trial, then you can't charge the customer until the product is received and met with satisfaction. And if you do not plan to refund a customer's money under any circumstances, then your marketing materials must read "all sales are final."

State the estimated lag time between order receipt and product delivery. If the average order takes three to four weeks for delivery, you can avoid complaints and concerns by telling the customer in your marketing materials and at the time she places her order.

Get good customer data. Your ability to deliver relies on good customer input. In your marketing materials, ask respondents to print clearly (especially the name and address to which the order will be shipped) and use ink on the order form.

Describe payment options. Require that payments be made by check, credit card, or money order. Do not allow cash transactions. Credit card privileges increase response rates, so plan your policies accordingly.

Log consumer questions and complaints. If — in spite of your best efforts — your ads still cause misunderstandings, pull and revise them.

Marketing with Direct Mailers

All direct mailers, regardless of purpose, are alike in one way: They go straight to customers' mailboxes rather than reaching customers through the mass media. The unique aspects and benefits of using direct mail (as opposed to the mass media) are detailed in Table 13-1.

Table 13-1	Direct Mail/Mass Media Comparisons
Direct Mail	*Mass Media*
You target your prospects and send your ad only to those consumers.	You reach all consumers who read a publication, tune into a broadcast, or see an outdoor ad.
You can personalize each marketing message.	You can target your message, but it is very difficult (and expensive) to personalize it.
You determine your format and length, and can include samples, reply cards, or any other item you feel will inspire a response.	You fit your message into available ad units.
Your cost per contact is higher than with mass media, but your cost per response is lower than with any other medium.	Your cost per contact is very economical, but many unqualified or uninterested consumers are included in your audience.
Has a predictable response period, with most responses occurring within 10 days of a mailing.	Has a slower and less predictable response period, especially when using magazine or outdoor advertising.
Response rates are easily measured.	Response rates are difficult to measure.

Direct mail success factors

When it comes to measuring success, direct mailers are among the easiest of all marketing communications to monitor. With each mailing you know exactly how many pieces you're sending and therefore how many qualified prospects you're reaching. And because direct mailers almost always request an easy-to-track direct response (in the form of a sale, an inquiry, a visit to your business, or some other prospect action), within weeks you can count the responses to learn the effectiveness of your direct mail effort.

To increase your chances for success, realize that the most successful direct mailers all rely on these three make-it-or-break-it factors:

- ✔ **A targeted list.** A great list can outperform a mediocre one many times over. To be great, a list must reach genuine prospects for your product or service. (See Chapter 2 for help creating a prospect profile.)

- ✔ **A compelling offer.** The *offer* is the deal — the catalyst to which the consumer reacts. You can test the strength of your offer by sending some prospects a mailer with one offer and other prospects one with an alternative offer, and then measuring the difference in results.

- ✔ **An attention-getting format.** When it comes to formatting your direct mailer, no rules apply. Some great mailers involve nothing more than a regular or oversized *(jumbo)* postcard. Others involve only a good old-fashioned sales letter in a simple, white envelope. Some are elaborate packages that contain letters, samples, and a host of other enclosures (including brochures, CDs, or videotapes). Great mailers can be highly personalized or look like official correspondence. Just be sure that whatever approach you take is consistent with the brand image of your business (see Chapter 7) and that it is capable of meeting your advertising objectives (see Chapter 8).

Building your direct mail list

In direct mail — more so than with any other form of marketing communication — customer knowledge makes all the difference.

Direct mail programs are successful only when they involve mailing lists full of names of people who match your prospect profile to a tee (see Chapter 2). With all other forms of advertising, you can match media selections to your market profile in *general*. But because each direct mail contact involves — at least — the cost of ad production and postage, you need to be sure you're mailing only to people who match your market profile *exactly*.

The best mailing lists are extremely targeted: They include only people who possess characteristics that make them likely to buy from your business. In building your list, consider the following approaches:

- ✔ **Demographic lists** include only addresses of people of the age, profession, job title, and so on most apt to purchase your products.

- ✔ **Geographic** lists include only addresses in the cities or zip code areas that match your market area.

✔ **Demographic *and* geographic** lists include only the addresses of individuals in your targeted geographic market area who have certain demographic attributes that make them prime customer prospects.

You can either build your list by assembling names into a database in your own business, or you can purchase or rent lists from outside organizations.

✔ **House lists:** You create these lists on your own by using your own customer contacts, as well as the names and addresses of prospects that you receive from other sources.

✔ **Outside lists:** You purchase or rent these prepared lists from mailing service businesses and organizations, professional associations, magazines, or other list owners.

Creating house lists

If you market in a local or very clearly defined market area, you'll probably want to create your own list rather than buy one from outside your company. As you go about assembling the names for your list, follow these steps.

1. **Start with your proven customer and prospect base.**

   Begin with the names of current customers. Then add the names of those who, although they aren't yet customers, have expressed interest in your product by responding to your ads, entering contests, or in other ways sharing their name with your business.

2. **Turn to local business and community directories.**

   For example, a golf club that's seeking to build its membership roster might create a mailing list that includes names from other golf club membership directories, as well as the CEOs of all the businesses listed in the local chamber of commerce directory.

3. **Segment the names according to past purchasing patterns or interests.**

   This allows you to send tailored messages to people in portions of your overall list.

4. **Enter the names into a database.**

   There are a number of ways to proceed with this step. Buy (and learn to use) a sophisticated database program, turn to the mail merge program on your word processor, or employ the resources of professional database managers to keep your mailing list organized. (See the sidebar "Using mail specialists" in this chapter.)

Using outside lists

A number of mailing services and mailing list brokerage businesses stand by to help when you're ready to implement direct mail programs that reach outside your current contact base or when you want to add the knowledge of specialists in preparing and managing your mailing list development.

Before you contact outside resources to discuss renting a list, though, be ready to state your needs in specific terms. Clarify exactly whom you want to target. If you can define your prospect profile by stating where your most likely customers reside geographically and who they are in terms of age, income, family size, education, and other lifestyle facts (see Chapter 2), chances are almost certain that a list can be compiled to match it.

For help honing your prospect profile, you can turn to magazine ad reps in your industry or market area, the SRDS Direct Mail List Source, and the SRDS Lifestyle Market Analyst — all described in the following sections.

Magazine subscriber lists

Most magazines rent their subscriber lists. Contact an ad representative at the leading publication that serves your industry or market area to learn about list availability, costs, and prices. Ask whether the magazine breaks its subscriber list into various interest subscriber segments. You may learn that you can rent a portion of the list to reach only those subscribers that are most likely to be in the market for your product.

For example, say that you're marketing a great new travel bag, and you'd like to acquire a list of people who would be apt to buy it from you. You start by contacting a major travel magazine and inquiring about buying access to its subscriber list. Because you know that your bag won't appeal to *all* subscribers, you ask about the ways the list can be *segmented*. In this case, you want to target your mailer geographically, so you ask only for subscribers in the Midwest. You also want to send your mailer only to subscribers who list home addresses. (This eliminates the names of travel agents and others who receive the magazine in their offices.) The magazine ad representative tells you that the publisher can indeed segment its list geographically and by home versus office addresses. Furthermore, it can segment by subscriber income level — even by the type of travel the person prefers. You're on your way to a list tailored to your prospect profile!

The SRDS Direct Mail List Source

This guide, published by the Standard Rate and Data Service, is available on the reference shelves of most public libraries. It features data on thousands of mailing lists in hundreds of categories, including:

- Club membership lists
- Demographically targeted lists
- Magazine subscriber lists
- Professional association membership lists
- Lists of people with a history of purchasing certain kinds of products

An hour or so browsing the catalog will help you focus on the kinds of lists available — useful information to know before you enter discussions about list rentals with magazine publishers or mailing service professionals.

The SRDS Lifestyle Market Analyst

Also available at public libraries, this publication provides consumer profiles for residents of various towns and cities, for demographic groups, or for people with certain lifestyle interests. It can help you decide *where* to send mailers, *who* to send them to, and *what* your mailers will offer. Using the *Lifestyle Market Analyst,* you can look up

- ✔ **Cities:** Figure out where you want to market, and then use the available data to confirm (or redirect) your plans.

  For instance, if you looked up the profile for our hometown of Bend, Oregon, in the *Lifestyle Market Analyst,* you'd find that the average resident skis nearly three times as much as the average American. (You'd know this because you'd see an "index number" of 301 alongside the word "Skiing," which means that people in Bend ski 301 percent the rate of average Americans.) Bend residents also outperform national averages when it comes to camping, using recreational vehicles, hunting, fishing, bicycling, investing in real estate, sewing, and owning cats and dogs.

  But according to the statistics, the average resident of Bend, Oregon, ranks *below* average when it comes to buying fashion clothing (with an index rank of 76 on a scale of 100). Translation: If your product serves a customer with outdoor recreation interests, Bend could be a great market for your business. But if you market Chanel handbags or Versace gowns, you'd do well to concentrate on a market other than this one!

- ✔ **Lifestyle interests:** This section will tell you everything you need to know about the lifestyles of those who participate in the interest area your product serves.

  For example, if you're marketing a new sewing product, you'd want to know about those who participate in the field of sewing. So you could turn to the "Sewing" section in the *Lifestyle Market Analyst.* There, you'd find out that the average participant is 52.4 years old. (***Hint:*** Use large type — and drop any idea of an MTV marketing theme.) Most are married and also participate (at above-average rates) in crafts, needlework and knitting, devotional reading, and self-improvement. You also learn from the statistics that the top five market areas for per capita participation in the field of sewing are Glendive, Montana; Idaho Falls–Pocatello and Twin Falls, Idaho; Springfield, Missouri; and Bangor, Maine. To a manufacturer of a new sewing product who wants to know where to hold a special product demonstration, this information would be close to pure gold — don't you think?

- ✔ **Consumer profiles:** Here, the *Lifestyle Market Analyst* reveals details about the people who fit your target demographic description.

Say that your market serves prospects who are (predominantly) married people between 35 and 44, with no children at home. You flip to the section "Married, 35–44 Years Old, No Child At Home." There, you find out that the people who fit your prospect profile outperform other Americans when it comes to traveling for business, riding motorcycles, reading science fiction, joining frequent flyer clubs, drinking wine, owning a cat or dog, skiing, boating, and working on their cars. They are *not,* however, into entering sweepstakes, participating in civic activities, or playing video games. Armed with this information, you decide on an offer that features a frequent customer program rather than a sweepstakes or a contest.

Buying a list

Once you know the profile of the person who is most likely to buy your product, you'll want to obtain a list of names of people who fit your target market description.

To buy a list, you can either work directly with list owners — including magazine publishers, mailing service organizations, and others who compile lists for rental by marketers — or you can use a *mailing list broker,* which is a business that provides usage of preassembled or customized lists for use in your direct mail program. For the names of direct mail specialists in the field, you can look in the Yellow Pages — they'll be listed under "Mailing Lists and Mailing Services." You can also visit the Mail Advertising Services Association (MASA) Web site at www.masa.org. The site's "Mailer/Services Locator" allows you to enter your hometown to find the names of mailing service businesses in your area.

Before you use a list, be aware that the list owner will have set prices and minimum requirements. Expect to take all or some of the following steps:

- Pay anywhere from $50 to several hundred dollars for one-time use of 1,000 names — with higher prices for targeted industry and business lists.

- Buy a minimum number of names (usually the minimum number is well into the thousands).

- Allow list owners to conduct the mailing themselves — from their own facility. Some list owners insist on handling the mailing within their own operation largely to protect the value and usage of their list.

- Arrange for the list to be released to a bonded mailing house. Some list owners, rather than handling the mailing themselves, insist that the mailing be handled by a recognized mailing service to ensure against multiple use or resale of names.

- Ensure list owners the opportunity to review and approve your mailer before it is sent to the names on their list. This allows them to protect their contacts.

Using mail specialists

Mailing services go by many names, including direct response specialists, bulk mailers, database managers, mail processors, and list managers. They provide professional assistance in the following areas:

- Merging, updating, and maintaining databases

- Deleting duplicate addresses

- Standardizing addresses

- Inserting ZIP+4, carrier route, and delivery point bar code information

- Presorting your list by computer to qualify for the lowest possible postal rate

- Addressing envelopes with ink jet technology

- Bar-coding

- Folding, inserting, and sealing direct mail packages

- Label printing and affixing

- Packaging and sacking

- Generating postal reports and certification reports

- Delivering mailings to the post office

Look for mailing services in the Yellow Pages (under "Mail Services"), or contact the Mail Advertising Services Association (MASA) at 1421 Prince Street, Alexandria, VA 22314-2806; Web site www.masa.org.

If possible, rent two lists that meet your prospect profile and put the lists together to eliminate duplications (called a *merge/purge* operation). The names that appear on both lists are your best prospects. For example, a destination resort could buy the names of golfers aged 35 and over living in a targeted metropolitan area *and* the names of homeowners in the same area whose household income is $100,000 or more. After merging and purging the list, the resort would have a better chance of reaching people with the interests *and* the financial abilities to match the destination resort's customer profile.

Remember that when you purchase labels from a list owner, you are *renting*, not buying the names. You are not allowed to use the list beyond the scope of your agreement or to duplicate the labels for additional mailings. Once you conduct your mailing, however, individuals from the rented list will respond to your company for more information. From that point on, you may market to these respondents: By responding to your mailer, the individuals have basically given you permission to do so.

Deciding on your offer

Once you have the right list, the next important consideration is your offer. Your direct mailer offer must relate to — and build credibility in — your product or service. It should also be unique, valuable, and interesting to your prospect.

Don't use your existing promotional materials or items emblazoned with your company name or logo as your offer. People get promotional material (for free) daily: They certainly don't want to take the time to write and ask for it unless it is extremely unique or exclusive.

So what is a good offer?

Table 13-2 shows how a public relations agency that's seeking to build relationships with regional CEOs might weigh direct mail offers as bad, good, and better.

Table 13-2	Examples of Direct Mail Offers	
Bad Example	*Better Example*	*Improved Example*
Invite the CEO to request a free brochure that features case histories of some of the agency's recent public relations success stories.	Invite the CEO to request a free guide that features advice on "How to Write News Releases and Manage Media Interviews."	Invite the CEO to specify how many free copies of "How to Write News Releases and Manage Media Interviews" she would like for distribution to key staff members.
Why?	*Why?*	*Why?*
The CEO has every right to read the offer and say, "So what?" The brochure is a promotional piece. The "offer" asks the CEO to take the time to request the kind of sales material that other companies send out on an unsolicited basis.	The guide is a free resource that can benefit the recipient. It contains advice that public relations professionals usually sell by the hour. It also focuses on the needs of the CEO.	The CEO has a good reason to respond to this offer. Because only the CEO knows how many copies the agency can use, the response request has meaning. And the offer promises an item that is unique and of value to the CEO and the public relations company.

A good offer contains the following elements:

✔ **A great deal:** This can include a free sample or gift, a trial offer, a special price, or special payment terms — depending on the objective of your mailer and the nature of your product. In crafting your offer, be aware that the word "free" pulls more responses than discounts or other price offers. If possible, try to offer something free of charge (for example, a "free sample," a "free catalog," or an offer to "buy one, get one free").

✔ **A guarantee:** Offer an assurance that working with your business is risk-free and reliable, to improve your mailing results. For example, extend a money-back guarantee, a delivery guarantee, or a service guarantee. And then keep your promise — both for good business purposes and for legal reasons.

✔ **A time limit:** This will increase both interest and response — even if the deadline is only implied (such as, "Please reply by December 15").

Although every direct mailer wants a strong response rate, remember that your highest goal is to receive *quality* responses. If your offer is *too* great, it will generate responses from people who simply want your gift — and nothing more. So don't go overboard.

Creating your mailer

Your mailer should attract attention, be clear and likeable, and make an offer that is easy to understand and accept. Mailers come in all shapes and sizes, but the best ones are, first of all, *personal.* (The polar opposite of a personalized mailing is one that is addressed to "Occupant.")

You can personalize your mailer in a number of ways. For example, you can use personally addressed labels. Better yet, you can make the address look handwritten. (Mail houses have ink jet technology that makes this seemingly arduous task pain-free.)

If you're enclosing a letter (see the following section on "Writing direct mail letters), you can increase your mailer response rates by personalizing the salutation line. If your mailing is too big to allow for personalized greetings, replace the salutation with a headline. Just don't try to get away with a catchall greeting, such as the dreaded "Dear Friend" or, worse, "Dear Valued Customer." Also consider adding a personalized paragraph that mentions that particular consumer's past purchasing patterns to boost response rates even higher.

The best mailers also:

✔ **Make a clear offer.** Repeat your offer on every piece that you include in your mailing package: the envelope, the letter, the letter's postscript, and any additional enclosures. Reiterating your offer on the reply card will provide respondents with a last-minute reassurance regarding the request or commitment that they're making.

✔ **Make the reply mechanism free to the consumer.** Include a toll-free number or a postage-paid card or envelope so that the customer can respond at your expense.

✔ **Include a reply card in addition to a toll-free number to call.** Many people prefer to mail in their responses — even if you provide a toll-free number or Web address. As you produce your reply card, give people a chance to say "yes" or "no." Believe it or not, giving them the chance to decline your offer increases the chances of them accepting it. To save money on the cost of postage, contact your post office or a mailing service for help obtaining a Business Reply Postage Number to print on your reply cards. That way you'll pay only for the responses you receive — and you won't have to place a stamp on every card you mail out.

Writing direct mail letters

First things first: If your mailing is any larger than a postcard or self-mailer, *enclose a letter.*

People may try to tell you that "no one reads the letter" or that the letter "just gets in the way" of other, more exciting enclosures — but they're wrong. The letter is an essential ingredient of direct mail: Enclose one in every package.

In your letter, follow every single piece of advice for writing advertising copy (for a refresher, see Chapter 11), taking the following steps:

1. **Start with a strong first sentence.**

   Your opening line is your chance to establish rapport, focus your message, and entice the recipients to continue on to the next sentence. This should lead readers to the following sentence and right through to the all-important P.S.

2. **Tell your prospects what's in it for them.**

   Don't talk about yourself or your company, or about how great your product is. (No matter what, never ever begin your first sentence with *I, we,* or your company's name.) Reread your letter imagining that you are the consumer — not the advertiser. Ask yourself, "So what's in it for me?" If the letter delivers a compelling answer, you've hit the bull's-eye.

3. **Get to the point quickly.**

   Introduce your offer and explain — in the simplest terms possible — how easy it is to take advantage of your invitation.

4. **Explain your product and company.**

   Emphasize only the benefits that consumers will enjoy. They don't need a line-up of facts or features that matter more to you than to the market.

5. **Use as much space as you need to communicate your offer.**

Multipage letters can work beautifully — *if* they are superbly written. If you're trying to write your own letter (and you should think twice before deciding to do so), keep it down to one page. If you decide to go with a longer letter, include bulleted or highlighted items to catch the attention of readers with short attention spans.

6. **Finish with a P.S.**

An astonishing number of letter readers glance only at the opening line and the postscript. Use the P.S. to advance a final pitch of your offer.

For an amazing array of information on how to write and implement direct mailers, visit the Direct Mail Library in the Knowledge Center of the American List Counsel Web site, www.amlist.com.

Sending your mailers

"Know before you go" is the rule for direct mail design. To do this, download a copy of the U.S. Post Office mailing guidelines through www.uspsdirectmail.com or visit any of the nation's 85 Postal Business Centers. Professional mailing service consultants also have this information. Even if you do everything else yourself, you should partner with the pros when it's time to actually design, prepare, and send your mailers.

Meeting regulations

Mailers must match precise dimensions in order to be processed by post office equipment. Otherwise, they require special handling — which costs you both time and money. Confirm that your mailer complies with size regulations while it is still in the design stage — not once it's already printed and ready to be sent.

Take particular care when it comes to the address panel of your mailer. The post office reads addresses using high-tech postal character recognition equipment. If your recipient address doesn't appear in the correct place on the envelope, or if other design elements get in the way, your mailing piece will either take longer or cost more to process. In general, you should limit any creative license to the lower left-hand corner of the envelope. Leave the center of the envelope blank for the recipient address, the upper left-hand area free for the sender's return address, and the upper right-hand corner open for postage. For more specific advice, of course, refer to postal regulations.

Taking advantage of discounts

If you prepare your mailers to meet processing and delivery regulations, the post office rewards you with reduced rates, called *Standard A* or *bulk* rates. To take advantage of these discounts, you must

- ✔ Obtain a mail permit and pay an annual bulk mail fee.
- ✔ Send at least 200 addressed pieces in each bulk mailing. In each bulk mailing, all pieces must be in the same mail category, such as letters *or* packages, and *none* can contain checks or bills. (These must be sent using first-class postage.)
- ✔ Include the correct zip code on each piece.
- ✔ Presort the mail. *Presorting* means sorting your mail and bringing it into the post office (in trays or bags) with bar codes on the address panel.
- ✔ To simplify presorting, use a list that has been CASS (Coding Accuracy Support System) certified. When you purchase outside lists, ask to see the CASS certification certificate that the U.S. Postal Service provides.

You can receive further discounts by using ZIP+4 codes and adding bar codes that support the postal service's automated systems. Various kinds of bar codes earn different discounts. Inquire at the post office or ask a qualified mail consultant for explanations and to learn the requirements that you must meet in order to receive reduced rates on your bulk mailing.

Specifying instructions

When you send bulk mail, you can include instructions, or *endorsements,* that tell the post office what to do with mail that is undeliverable as addressed. Without a mailer endorsement, these items will be thrown away — so protect yourself by specifying your postal instructions.

For example, "Address Correction Requested" instructs the post office to advise you of the corrected address or the reason the mail was undeliverable. Although the item won't be forwarded to the new address, you will have the information you need in order to update your list. Adding another endorsement, however, can ensure that the post office forwards the mail or returns it to your business.

Each additional step that you ask the post office to take will result in an additional charge. The instructions you give depend on how much you want to pay for the service — and on your confidence in the accuracy of your list.

Following up

Half of all responses arrive within two weeks of the date that people receive a direct mailing.

How many replies should you expect? Brace yourself: 1 to 3 percent is considered a home run with a purchased or outside list. If you use internal lists that are full of highly qualified names, you can hope for 5 to 10 percent or sometimes higher.

Responding quickly

Don't wait even one week to get back to your direct mail respondents.

If you don't think you can handle the volume of responses in a timely manner, send your mailers out in *flights,* groups of several hundred every three or four days. This ensures that the responses are staggered, as well. No matter what, be prepared for responses — and handle them immediately.

In your response:

- ✔ Enclose a letter thanking respondent for the inquiry. Believe it or not, people can forget that they even sent in a card — so take a moment to refresh their memories.

- ✔ Enclose the item that you promised in your initial mailing, along with a description.

- ✔ Introduce your business, presenting a description in terms of benefits that matter to the consumer. (See Chapter 8 for advice on how features and customer benefits are different.)

- ✔ Offer the next step in the buying process. Enclose a rate card, an introductory offer, an invitation to call for an appointment, a coupon for service, or any other reasonable means of heightening interest to convert the prospect into a customer.

Creating a database of respondents

After responding to the prospect's request, file the name of each respondent into a database for follow-up. Before two months go by, make sure that you follow up a second time, via a mailing, phone call, or — if they've invited you to do so — an e-mail newsletter or update. (See Chapter 19 for information on the detrimental effects of sending unauthorized e-mail messages to your prospects.)

As you enter each name into your database, be sure to include

- ✔ The source of the lead
- ✔ The date of the response
- ✔ The respondent's name, address, and e-mail address

> ✔ Any information that can help you customize future contacts (such as the answers to any questions that you asked on your reply card)
>
> ✔ Additional space in which you can log follow-up activity

If you're a service business that has a select clientele and, therefore, a limited number of client prospects, you can keep this database manually. But if you are managing a larger number of leads, use a computer program or a database management company.

Sending a second mailing to non-respondents

Within 30 days of your first mailing, contact all recipients who have not yet responded. (If you are using an outside list, make sure that you purchase a two-time usage — and a duplicate set of labels — for this purpose.)

Research shows that this kind of follow-up with non-respondents increases your overall response rate dramatically. It also gives you much more value for the cost of the list rental, because the second-time usage is usually at a fraction of the cost of the initial usage.

Scouring your list

You need to keep your list up to date with current addresses of real prospects by editing it on an ongoing basis. Every time that you receive word of an address change, update your list immediately. And from time to time poll the individuals on your list to be sure that they are still in the market for your offering. The following sections tell you how.

Keeping addresses current

Address lists go bad at a rate of almost 2 percent a month. To beat the statistics, follow these steps:

> ✔ Request (and be willing to pay for) address correction information from the post office. Make the request by including your instructions in an endorsement on your mailer (see "Specifying instructions" earlier in this chapter).
>
> ✔ Take advantage of the *National Change of Address (NCOA)* file, a compilation of change-of-address records. Ask the owner of the list you're using or your mailing service to arrange to update your list by checking it against this file, which is licensed by the U.S. Postal Service.

Confirming prospect interest

On either a 12- or 18-month basis, send a mailer that includes the opportunity for prospects in your database to opt out of their relationship with you. It may sound crass, but the fact is that uninterested prospects aren't prospects at all — they're simply a marketing expense.

To determine the validity of the names on your list, you can occasionally add an opt-out option as one of the choices on your reply cards. For example:

- ✔ Yes, send me whatever great offer you are making in this mailing.

- ✔ I'm not interested at the moment, but please keep my name on your list for future invitations.

- ✔ No, I'm not in the market right now. Please remove my name from your list with the promise that you'll welcome me back in the future if my needs change.

Direct Mail — or Junk Mail?

People love to hate "junk" mail. Yet, every day, people open direct mailers. Why? Because not all promotional mail is junk mail — and consumers know how to tell the difference.

Direct mail earns the dubious distinction of junk mail when consumers feel that the offer isn't personal. For example, if a college student lives in an apartment and gets a mailing for landscaping services, she automatically determines that the mailing is junk mail — especially if she has received the same offer three times already. Timely and targeted messages that communicate information and an offer of value, however, are not junk mail. As a direct mail marketer, it's your job to toe the line.

E-mail Marketing

Somehow, it seems appropriate to follow the section on junk mail with a section on e-mail marketing. The sequence isn't meant to imply that e-mail mass mailings *are* junk mailers, but a good many of them spiral into the junk mail category and you'll want to be sure yours don't. So before you take a single step into the field of electronic direct mail, see Chapter 19 for a lineup of e-mail marketing advice, including a definition of "spam," the Internet world's disparaging definition of electronic junk mail. The advice from the online marketers regarding unsolicited e-mail is "When in doubt, don't." However, it's okay to send marketing messages via e-mail when the recipient

- ✔ Has *opted in* by providing an e-mail address and asking you to provide more information.

- ✔ Is a friend, colleague, supplier, customer, or prospect that has requested similar information in the past.

- ✔ Was referred to you by a colleague or by some association related to your business with the assurance that the contact will appreciate receiving your information.

If you are confident that your e-mail will land in welcome mailboxes, make it quick, to the point, and casual, following these tips:

✔ Use a short subject line (maximum of 5–7 words). This increases the chances that your message will be opened. Remember:

- If your mailing is based on a referral, use the subject line to say so. Doing so will move you out of the Spam category — and get your message opened.

- Create a subject line that alerts recipients that the message is aimed specifically at them. (See Chapter 11 for advice on writing good headlines.) Try subject lines that include geographic and lifestyle interest references — for example, "Calling All Sausalito Macintosh Users" is far more targeted than "Closeout Computer Prices."

✔ Limit your message to ten lines, if possible. Rather than trying to make a comprehensive sales presentation in an all-text e-mail message, link the consumer to your Web page. A short e-mail can also prompt the consumer to request an electronic newsletter. This allows you to offer far more information — to an already engaged prospect.

Because few marketing arenas are less tolerant of intrusion than the e-mail inbox, you must tread cautiously and build relationships in order to succeed. (For detailed advice on targeted e-mail marketing, see Chapter 19.)

Chapter 14

Brochures, Promotions, Trade Shows, and Other Communication Tools

. . . .

In This Chapter

▶ Producing brochures and marketing literature

▶ Choosing and using advertising specialties

▶ Planning and placing outdoor ads

▶ Preparing for trade shows

▶ Launching promotions that work

. . . .

Mass media advertising and direct mailings are the most obvious ways to promote your business, but within the communications toolbag are a lineup of other effective (and often far less expensive) communication vehicles to consider.

Brochures and fliers, free giveaway items known as advertising specialties, billboards and other out-of-home ads, and promotions are all-important alternatives to traditional advertising. Most come with low price tags, and for that reason many small businesses use them with a "nothing ventured, nothing gained or lost" attitude. But although large sums of money are rarely at risk when you print a stack of fliers or order pens imprinted with your name, your reputation may well be on the line instead. This chapter offers advice so that every marketing investment — however large or small — contributes to a favorable image of your business.

Producing and Using Literature and Printed Marketing Materials

People who aren't professional marketers consider "collateral" something you pledge when you're trying to get a bank loan. To marketers, though, the term *collateral* refers to brochures, fliers, sales folders, posters, and all the other printed items that carry your logo, message, and reputation into the marketplace.

When, why, and how to produce a brochure

Designers make a handsome living off all the small business marketers who say that they need a brochure but can't say *why* they need one. To many small businesses, getting a brochure is like getting a Web site. They think they need one because everyone else has one. But here is a far more sensible way to decide.

You need a brochure if prospects aren't easy to contact in person or by phone but would likely respond to literature about your business. Or, you need a brochure if your prospects would benefit from a printed piece that could be sent ahead of sales presentations or left afterwards to reiterate key points, or if they aren't easily or affordably reached by mass media but are likely to pick up brochures at information kiosks or other literature distribution points. You need a brochure if your service or product is complicated and includes many details that your prospects need to read and study in order to make an informed decision. On the same note, a brochure is the right idea if the price of your product, or the emotional involvement or purchase-approval process that your product undergoes prior to purchase, is so special that prospective buyers will be grateful to have your information in hand and in writing when they consult with advisers, associates, or spouses.

Before you decide to produce a brochure, be sure that you can answer yes to these questions:

- **Do you have an adequate budget?** Can you allocate enough money to create a brochure that will make a favorable impression for your business?

- **Will the brochure advance your image?** Can you commit to designing and writing a brochure that complements and enhances your company's image?

- **Do you know your distribution plan?** Do you know how you will use the brochure? The literature will do no good sitting in a back closet.

Types of brochures

Brochures run the gamut from elaborate folders filled with sets of matching literature to laser-printed cards that sit on countertops or in "take-one" racks. The following sections help you sort through the opportunities:

Capabilities brochure

A *capabilities brochure* is an "about our business" brochure that tells your story, conveys your business personality, and differentiates your business from your competitors. Especially if you're marketing a service business (such as a law or accounting firm, a financial services firm, or some other form of consulting business) or a business that offers high-emotion consumer products (for instance, a home builder), this type of brochure is a marketing necessity. Capability brochures are among the most expensive kinds of brochures to produce. For that reason, you'll want yours to have a "keeper" quality. For instance, a financial planner might include a net worth asset worksheet, or a home builder might include a checklist for how to get the most value out of a homebuilding budget. The goal is to include some reason for prospects to hold onto and refer back to the piece.

Product brochure

A *product brochure* is a printed piece that describes a specific offering of your business. Product brochures are useful if your offering requires more than spur-of-the-moment consideration. These brochures are designed for high-ticket products, products that are purchased with input from more than one person, and products that involve careful cost and technical comparisons before the buying decision takes place.

Rack cards

If you need inexpensive handouts that present current promotional offers and pricing lists, consider using *rack cards*. They have to fit into standard 4-x-9-inch brochure racks. Many small business marketers print three rack cards on an 8½-x-11-inch sheet of paper (*3-up* is the printing term), which they then cut into three cards each sized 3⅔ x 8½ inches. The most important thing to remember about rack cards is that only the top couple of inches are visible to the consumer — the rest is hidden under the brochure that sits under yours in the rack. So be sure that your name and a message announcing your customer benefit appear in that small top space.

Modular literature

Modular literature is a brochure format that involves a number of sheets or brochures — all using the same design and format — that can be assembled into a folder or used individually depending on the interest level of your prospect. A modular brochure format is a great way to go if your business offers a wide range of products that are each represented by separate spec sheets, if you have complicated price lists, if your business information changes frequently, or if your prospects have greatly differing interests or needs.

Targeting and writing brochures

Brochures serve as a means for introducing your business, for describing your offerings, and for conveying endorsements that help prospects feel confident in choosing to work with or buy from your business. The best brochures talk right to the prospect, anticipating their questions and providing answers before the person even thinks to ask.

Before writing your brochure, start by defining your target market and marketing objective. (Chapter 8 provides the steps for this process.) Then, for everything but the most basic rack card, seriously consider relying on the talents of a professional copywriter. As you develop copy, refer to these copywriting tips:

- ✔ **Include a headline.** Simply putting your name on the cover is too "I-oriented." Customers care about what's in it for them. Use your brochure cover to present a benefit-oriented headline (see Chapter 11 for headline-writing tips) that attracts your prospect's attention.

- ✔ **Use subheads.** By placing secondary headlines throughout the brochure, you communicate your message at-a-glance to those who don't have time to read it all.

- ✔ **Write directly to your prospect.** Know your prospect profile (see Chapter 2) and write brochure copy that delivers the benefits and reasons to buy that you would describe to your prospect in person if you could be there yourself.

- ✔ **Keep copy brief, friendly, and personable.** Avoid technical jargon or long feature-oriented descriptions. Turn every selling point into an easy-to-understand customer benefit.

- ✔ **Don't boast.** You wouldn't (or shouldn't) brag if you were presenting in person, so don't do it in your brochure, either. Avoid hyped-up superlatives (the best, the biggest, and all those other "est" words). Trying too hard to impress almost always backfires. Aim to write a brochure that informs, inspires, and establishes a friendship with prospects.

- ✔ **Let satisfied customers do some talking.** A convincing way to tout your excellence is to feature customer testimonials in your brochure. When deciding to feature customer endorsements, ensure that the customers are credible and clearly identified, their comments are compelling, they're honest (nothing is worse than testimonials that look scripted), *and* they give you permission (in writing) to use their quotes with attribution.

- ✔ **Tell what to do next.** People get so carried away trying to create a gorgeous brochure that they often forget the publication's purpose. Remember that a brochure is a marketing tool. It needs to compel prospects to take the next step. Do you want them to call to make a reservation or to schedule an appointment or demonstration? Should they return a reply card to request more information? Should they come to your business to take advantage of a special offer? Know what action you're trying to achieve and use your brochure copy to lead the consumer to the desired decision.

✔ **Make the next step in the buying process an easy one.** If you're asking for phone calls, include your toll-free number on every single page of the brochure. If you're encouraging the consumer to request more information (perhaps a video or an appointment), provide not only a phone number but a postage-paid reply card as well. Make your address, phone numbers, e-mail address, and Web site easy to see and read, and if you're inviting visits to your business, give office hours and a locator map, too.

✔ **Revise and proofread.** Share the copy with someone else, revise it again, read it out loud, make final revisions, and, finally, proofread it multiple times before turning it over to the printer. Your brochure serves as a salesperson for your business when no actual person can be present to tell your story, so tailor it accordingly.

Your brochure will be read most carefully by those who are ready to buy or who have just purchased and who now want to validate and confirm their decisions. Write your brochure as if you're talking to those committed consumers. By doing so, you minimize the tendency to oversell, instead focusing on the benefits and promises that customers can count on when they work with your business.

Designing brochures

Before you begin designing your brochure, spend a few minutes reading Chapter 7 for guidance in making type style, color, and logo usage decisions so that your printed materials all present a single uniform image for your company.

If you're creating the first brochure for your company, invest in the talents of a graphic artist if you don't have the ability yourself or within your company. (See Chapter 9 for more information.) Work with the designer to create not only a brochure but a design format or template that you can easily follow as you produce additional literature in the future.

In designing your brochure, know your budget before you begin designing. If you're operating on a shoestring budget, limit the use of photos and color and choose a moderately sized brochure in a shape that can be printed on lower-cost presses. Keep the following tips in mind:

✔ **If photos are essential to your story, budget accordingly.** Paper, production, and printing prices all increase when color photographs become part of your design. If you want to keep your budget low, opt for clear, high-contrast black-and-white photos and simple line art to tell your story.

✔ **Keep your brochure quality in line with the nature of your offering.** A laser-printed brochure on neon-colored paper may be ideal for a rental shop featuring the least expensive Halloween costumes, but it will never do for a restaurant striving to be *the* place to spend anniversary evenings. Save the heavy paper, rich embossing, and foil-stamped headlines for businesses that want their literature to "say" upscale and exclusive. Similarly, save the do-it-yourself quick-print literature for businesses that want to communicate bargain-basement economy.

✔ **Know your type and color guidelines.** Designers love to be creative. That's their job. So give them parameters in advance regarding what type styles and color choices fit within your brand image. In the end, you want to create a brochure that represents *your* business — not a designer's whim.

✔ **Make your company name visible.** If your brochure goes in a rack, be sure that your name is on the top part that sticks out above the brochure under yours. For multiple-page brochures, consider featuring your name and contact information (phone, address, and Web site) on every single panel.

Getting your brochure into the marketplace

Printers will rightfully tell you that printing the first brochure is the most expensive. After that, you're paying only for ink and paper, so print enough brochures to ensure that you won't feel a need to hoard them. Then get them into circulation by using these ideas:

✔ **"Announce" your brochure to your internal mailing list.** A new brochure is a great reason to be in touch with the friends of your business. Send copies to your customers, your qualified prospects, your suppliers, and associates. Include a cover letter thanking them for their partnership in helping you achieve the business success that you're proud to portray in your new brochure. Tell them that you want them — your most valued business friends — to be the first to preview the brochure. Enclose a few extra copies with the hope that they will share them with others who may be interested in your offerings.

✔ **Send copies to the editors at local and industry publications.** A new brochure isn't a news item, but it does present an opportunity to make a personal contact and to share useful information. When sending it to editors (and with luck you've already established editorial relationships — see Chapter 15), always attach a cover letter — not a news release. Use the letter to personalize the usefulness of the brochure to the editor. A home builder might include a sentence such as, "As you continue your coverage of growth in our area, please feel free to contact me. Our firm has records of the changing tastes of homeowners over the past decade, along with information on regional and industry statistics and trends."

✔ **Carry brochures with you at all times.** Encourage your staff to do the same. Don't hoard them. On the other hand, don't hand them out like Halloween candy. Target your distribution so that you get your literature into the hands of qualified prospects who will value your message and who can make referrals or buying decisions in your favor.

✔ **Send a brochure ahead of your arrival at meetings.** That way, your prospect has a chance to "know" you before meeting you.

✔ **Use your brochure as a step in the buying process.** When qualified prospects leave without buying, follow up by sending your brochure along with a cover letter that provides additional information that relates to the consumer's concerns or interests. Also, keep a list of pending prospects and use your brochure — along with copies of recent publicity, news announcements, or other timely information about your business — as a reason to be in touch on a regular basis.

Launching and maintaining free newsletters

Newsletters are informal, friend-to-friend communications that deliver newsworthy information, useful updates, reminders of what your business does, and ideas of interest and use to newsletter recipients. Newsletters can accomplish the following for your business:

✔ Build credibility and reputation

✔ Establish a means of frequent communication

✔ Deliver news from your company and your industry

✔ Answer customer questions, usually through a question-and-answer column

✔ Provide tips that enhance the credibility of your business while also building customer confidence and loyalty

✔ Share profiles of employees, success stories, and customers

✔ Provide reprints of industry information (with permission, of course)

Know-before-you-go newsletter planning advice

Newsletters work only when they're produced and distributed on a consistent basis, which means you have to commit to the long haul before you undertake the first issue. As you make your decision, consider the following:

✔ **Begin by defining the purpose of your newsletter.** Is it to keep an open line of communication with customers? Is it to share promotional offerings with current customers? Is it to enhance your reputation by sharing company news and success stories? You may have one or several objectives. Know what you expect from your newsletter before you design or write the first issue.

✔ **Establish how often you will produce and send your newsletter.** Your answer depends on two considerations: How often are you and your staff able to get a newsletter assembled and distributed? How often is your customer interested in hearing from you?

✔ **Determine how you will produce your newsletter.** Will you handle the task in-house or hire freelance talent? If you can't devote the time or don't have the writing talent yourself, get a bid for outside assistance (see Chapter 9 for help hiring professional talent) and be sure that you can afford to commit to and fund the project for at least a year.

✔ **Know the target market for your newsletter.** Decide in advance how you will assemble, maintain, and build your newsletter mailing list. You might start with a list that includes your customers, current prospects, and friends. Then work to expand the list by featuring the offer of a free newsletter subscription in future direct mail programs and other response-oriented marketing efforts.

See Chapter 19 for more newsletter planning tips, including how to write and distribute newsletters through e-mail while skirting the fine line that lands your mailing in the dreaded "spam" e-mail category.

Writing and designing newsletters

Here is the best news you'll get about newsletters: the most effective newsletters look newsy and current rather than expensive and labored, which translates to the fact that great newsletters don't have to be budget-breakers. In creating your newsletter, consider the following points:

✔ **Opt for many short items rather than a few long ones.**

✔ **Establish an easy-to-use format.** The more your newsletter looks like a brochure, the less it looks newsy. Decide on a template, keep it simple, and stick with the same look issue after issue after issue.

✔ **Include news items that invite reader responses to help you gauge the effectiveness of your newsletter.** If your company was featured in a news story, include the announcement in your newsletter and invite readers to call to request a reprint. Or if you've launched a frequent shopper program or unveiled a new product offering, summarize the news in an article and offer to send information on request. Find ways to inspire responses to verify that your newsletter is being well read.

✔ **Avoid presenting time-sensitive offers in your newsletter.** Newsletters have a long life and may be read well into the future, long after your offer has expired.

✔ **Use your newsletter to promote your Web site if you're trying to build site traffic.** Include your Web address along with your phone number, address, and other identifying information. Then give readers an incentive to visit your site. Here is an example from a fictitious resort:

"Our new online reservation service, inaugurated only six months ago, is already doing a brisk business. More than half of our site visitors click to view room photos and floor plans, and 38 percent of those who view our property online go on to make a reservation request. If you haven't seen our site lately, go to `www.yourhotel.com`. While you're on our home page, click to enter our Web-only sweepstakes for a free weekend stay. And if you'd rather receive our newsletter electronically than by mail, click on the newsletter request icon and enter your e-mail address, and we'll move your name off our regular mailing and into the electronic file. Either way, we'll see that you get our quarterly update on vacation packages and regional resort happenings."

✔ **Combine your sales messages with news updates so that readers will view your newsletter as an informative piece and not a promotional mailing.** For example:

"Rocky Mountain vacations are more popular than they've been in years, based on the number of calls and visitors to our toll-free reservation line and Web site. Phone calls in April 2001 were up a full 22 percent over April 2000, with Thanksgiving and Christmas reservations coming in at a brisk pace. Call us at 1-800-000-0000 just as soon as you know your vacation dates so we can book your stay."

✔ **Include your company identification** — your logo, phone number, mailing address, e-mail address, and Web site address — on every page of every issue to encourage communications.

Using your packages as advertising vehicles

For all the money that businesses spend on advertising, they often race right past the free opportunity that exists every single time they package up a product for a customer. Give yourself a free ride. Use on-pack and in-pack advertising as a no-cost means of advertising to existing customers.

Manufacturers can use this approach by affixing or printing ads right onto product cartons or enclosing materials in the box that invite the purchase of accessories, warranties, service programs, or other offers.

Retailers might drop into each shopping bag a tasteful invitation to join a frequent customer club, to request automatic delivery of future orders, or to receive a special offer on a future purchase (called a *bounce-back offer* because it aims to bounce a customer back into your business). For example, a pool or hot tub chemical supply company could enclose a brochure offering a monthly service program, automatic twice-a-year chemical delivery, or an annual maintenance visit. A shop selling infant and toddler clothes could enclose a form inviting participation in a baby shower registry program.

Building business with gift certificates

It is astonishing how many small businesses make a gift certificate request seem like a true inconvenience, when actually it is the sincerest form of customer compliment. If someone wants to give your business as a gift, roll out the red carpet. Here's how:

- ✔ **Create a gift certificate form.** This form can convey the details of the gift while also enhancing the gift's perceived value simply by its creative presentation. Use quality paper, a professional design that matches your company image, and a look that is appropriate to the nature of your business offering.

- ✔ **Deliver it to the gift buyer in an envelope or a gift box.** A gift certificate is a sale and also a current customer's effort to bring a new person into your business.

- ✔ **Keep track of the names of both the gift buyer and the gift recipient.**

- ✔ **When the gift is redeemed, write to both parties.** Reinforce your relationship with the gift buyer by sharing that the certificate was redeemed and that you and your staff were flattered by the gift choice. Send a separate letter to the gift recipient, welcoming that person to your business and enclosing an offer. Such an offer can be a free subscription to your newsletter, a special new customer invitation, a frequent-shopper club membership, or some other reason for the person to become a loyal customer of your business.

- ✔ **If the deadline is nearing on an unredeemed certificate, write or call the gift recipient.** Offer a short extension or invite a phone call order or some other gesture to build goodwill.

Papering the market with business cards

Even the highest-quality business cards cost only a few cents each. You'll be hard-pressed to find a more economical way to get your name into your marketplace.

To create a business card that makes a quality statement for your business, use a professional design, careful type selection, quality paper, good printing, a good straight cut (nothing looks cheaper than a card with a crooked cut), and good ink colors. Unless you're certain of their design talents, don't ask staff members or quick-print shop designers to create your card. Invest a few hours with a graphic designer to achieve a distinctive, professional design that enhances your company image. Be sure that the card features your business name and logo, a bulleted lineup of services or a slogan or tag line, and your phone number and other business contact information in a type size that is large enough to be read easily. Once you design a good business card, use it liberally, following these tips:

✔ **Print a supply of business card "masters."** These cards can be quickly imprinted with the names of new or promoted staff members. Doing this isn't necessary if you have an inexpensive single-color card, but if you invest in specialized ink colors, embossing, or foil stamping, plan for the future by printing a large supply all at once, dramatically reducing your unit cost as a result. Leave the unneeded supply uncut and in storage at the print shop. As you need more cards, simply imprint the names and titles in a single ink color.

✔ **Give a stack of cards to every employee.** First of all, it's great for staff morale. Second, employees can use their cards to introduce your business to their friends as well as to their business contacts, and you'll reap the cost of the cards many times over.

✔ **Consider printing a map to your business on the back of your card.** Maps are especially important if you're an out-of-the-way retailer or consumer service business.

✔ **Add value to your card by imprinting the flip side with useful information related to your business.** For example, a mailing service company might include a schedule of postal rates. A retail outlet or visitor attraction might print open hours. A fine dining restaurant might imprint the dates of the current year's holidays, so patrons won't forget Mother's Day, Father's Day, and even local events such as the high school proms or festivals.

If you decide to print on both sides of your card, remember that all the most pertinent information — your logo, name, title, and contact information — should appear on the front face of your card. Many people keep business cards in files in which only the front of the card is visible.

Weighing the Benefits of Advertising Specialties

Advertising specialties are ubiquitous little mind-joggers for your business. They include a wide range of giveaways including pens, pencils, refrigerator magnets, mouse pads, matchbooks, notepads, paperweights, pocket knives, calendars, calculators, T-shirts, golf towels, and a long list of other items that can be printed, engraved, embossed, or emblazoned with a business logo.

Specialty advertising items are usually cheap — and often they look it. Before investing in an advertising specialty, consider the following advice:

- ✔ Select only items that relate to your business and that are capable of advancing a reminder of the benefits you offer.

- ✔ Choose things that your prospective customers will want or need and things that they will notice, pick up, and keep for at least a short time.

- ✔ Opt only for items that will add to — and not detract from — your business image.

- ✔ Decide how you will feature your name on the item. The more exclusive your clientele and offering, the more discreet you'll want to make your presentation. The corner gas station and the one-of-a-kind designer boutique require two different designs. You have a better chance of making your ad specialty a keeper item if you settle on a name presentation that is attractive and scaled to the item rather than a gaudy design that monopolizes the item and assures its quick trip to the trash can.

- ✔ Know how you'll distribute the items before you place an order for advertising specialties.

For information on ordering from the unbelievably wide range of specialties available, start in your Yellow Pages, looking under "Ad Specialties" or "Promotional Products."

Communicating through Out-of-Home Advertising

Out-of-home ads include billboards, transit displays, waiting bench signs, wall murals, sports and recreational facility signs, vehicle signage, movie theatre ads, and even flyover signs. Look around your market area. See where your prospect is apt to be waiting, standing, or sitting, and you'll probably find an advertising opportunity, usually accompanied by the name of the company to contact for advertising information.

As you consider out-of-home ads, be aware that they are almost always used as support media and not as the sole or prime vehicle in your ad strategy.

The most frequently used form of out-of-home advertising involves billboards. Nearly every town (except those in billboard-free Alaska, Hawaii, Maine, and Vermont) has one or two companies that own most of the boards, so start there to find out about available locations, costs, and contracts. Whenever you see a billboard in a desirable location, look along the bottom of the sign to find the billboard owner's name so you can call for availability and cost information.

In scheduling billboard ads, a few key terms apply:

✔ **Circulation** is measured by the number of people who have a reasonable opportunity to see your billboard or sign message.

✔ **A full showing,** or *#100 showing,* describes the number of boards necessary to reach 100 percent of the mobile population in a market at least once during a 30-day period. A half showing (or #50 showing) reaches 50 percent of the mobile population. Anything less than a #25 showing is not considered adequate frequency for an advertising campaign, although the placement of one or two boards may be useful as directional signage.

In placing and creating billboards, two truths prevail.

✔ **Location is everything.** When you make an outdoor ad buy, you will receive a map or list of locations. Drive by the sites to be sure that they are in areas that reach your prospects and enhance your image.

✔ **Ads must pass the at-a-glance test.** Viewers often look at a billboard for five seconds and take away only two ideas — your name and the reason to buy your product. Design your ad using legible type (plenty large enough and with adequate spacing between the letters, words, and lines), strong color contrasts, and graphics that can be seen and understood in a flash.

Choosing and Using Trade Shows

Trade shows are industry gatherings that bring together businesses, suppliers, customers, and media representatives in a given field for a multiday extravaganza of selling, socializing, entertaining, product previewing, and competitive sleuthing.

Attendance at trade shows is a great way to maintain customer contacts, introduce products to your industry, develop and maintain media relations, and stay on top of industry and competitive developments. The only drawback — and it's a big one — is that even in the most targeted industry you have a lineup of trade shows from which to choose. Because attendance at even one show costs a significant amount of time, money, and energy, invest carefully, using this checklist:

✔ Choose the show carefully. Check on the number of presenters and attendees over recent years (see whether the number is going up, which indicates a well-regarded show). Also find out about the media sponsorships, another indication of the show's reputation.

✔ Know whom you want to attract to your booth, what you want to communicate, and what action you want to inspire.

✔ Know how you will capture visitor information for future use and how you will follow up with your trade show contacts.

Table 14-1 offers suggestions to guide your trade show planning.

Table 14-1	Trade Show Do's and Don'ts
Do	**Don't**
Do prospect before the show, using personal letters, direct mailers, and phone calls to invite and encourage prospects to visit your booth.	Don't count on prospects to seek you out or even to find you on their own. Big shows, especially, simply have too many distractions.
Do arrive at the show with pre-set appointments for meetings with your top-choice media reps, journalists, customer prospects, and vendors.	Don't expect to simply catch time with key contacts at the show. Take the time in advance to introduce yourself and establish scheduled appointments.
Do use your staff well. Be sure they wear business identification or, better yet, logo shirts or uniforms. Have a staffing schedule that lets you present with your best presenters, turning other team members loose to meet with suppliers and do competitive research.	Don't let your whole team hang out in your show booth — it gives the impression of a dull spot. Aim instead to have ongoing client or media meetings underway, a greeter visiting with passersby in the entry area, and other staff members out working the show.
Do have moderately priced handouts and logo items available for distribution, along with a means for collecting prospect names for follow-up. After the show, send a thoughtful letter and gift to prospects who were serious enough to complete a short form to qualify their interest.	Don't set up for "trick-or-treaters." You don't have to give something to every visitor, and you shouldn't waste money (or weight down your prospects) by giving out expensive or heavy literature or catalogs at the show. They'll appreciate the information more if it arrives by mail.
Do invest in a professionally designed booth that reflects your business image, your advertising, and your current message.	Don't try to do it cheap by using a self-designed booth plan and do-it-yourself graphics.
Do use lights, banners, moving displays, bright colors, floor carpeting, and counters to break your booth into parts, and other devices to draw attention and make your booth look like a hub of activity.	Don't be bland and don't expect a banner with your logo to double as a booth design. You need huge colorful photos, ad enlargements, and graphics that shout "new" to passersby.

Building Sales through Promotions

A promotion is marketing activity that aims to increase sales over a short period of time by offering an incentive that prompts consumers to take immediate action. Businesses stage promotions to encourage new customers to try your product or to entice current customers to try your new products. Promotions also are used to urge a different buying pattern, such as greater dollar volume per transaction, more frequent purchases, or purchases via a certain payment method. In addition, businesses use promotions to increase sales by offering limited-time special pricing or added-value offers and to stimulate business during slow times of the day or year.

Choosing your promotion incentive

The whole purpose of a promotion is to create consumer action over a short period of time. The objective is accomplished by offering one of the following types of action incentives:

- **Price savings:** Offer a percentage discount, a two-for-one offer, a buy-one-get-one-free deal, or some other appealing reduction. The bigger the incentive, the better, of course, but not if you're going to lose money. Come up with an offer that is enough to inspire customers but that doesn't give the store away.

- **Samples:** Businesses that are trying to introduce new products or win over a competitor's customers often use samples or free trials to prove their advantage and to get their products into circulation. In using samples, first be sure that your product will show well in comparative tests. Second, accompany the sample with a "bounce-back offer" using a coupon or offer that prompts the customer to make an after-sample purchase or to take an action (for example, signing up for a free subscription to your newsletter) to cement the new relationship.

- **Events and experiences:** Businesses use events to create crowd-drawing experiences that spur additional purchases from existing customers while drawing new customers and sometimes even media coverage.

- **Coupons and rebates:** A *coupon* provides an offer that a customer can redeem at the time of purchase. A *rebate* provides an offer that a customer can redeem following the purchase, usually by filling out and sending in a rebate form. Since the early 1990s, the redemption of coupons has been declining, with recent studies showing that of all the coupons in circulation, only about 2 percent are redeemed by consumers. Still, coupons are a popular promotion staple and a measurable way to offer price reductions and to reward frequent customers. If you use coupons, protect your profitability with small-print advisories such as "not valid with other special offers" and clearly stated expiration dates.

Promotions are especially important to restaurants, hotels, retailers, and consumer product businesses. They are less appropriate for service professionals or for business-to-business marketers who may lose a degree of esteem and dignity by sending out pricing or other buying incentives.

Staging cross-promotions and cooperative promotions

Promotions benefit from critical mass — which is why businesses team up to participate in cooperative or cross-promotions that bring together the media budgets, consumer incentives, customer corps, and staff energy of not one but two or several businesses or organizations.

In spite of the benefits involved when you form a promotional partnership, enter the alliance with care. Stop first to be sure you can answer "yes" to the following questions:

- ✔ Do the proposed businesses operate without directly competing with each other?

- ✔ Do the businesses serve customers with the same or very similar profiles?

- ✔ Do you trust the management of the partnering company?

- ✔ Have you committed the strategy, budget, timeline, and fiscal responsibilities to writing, and have all parties agreed to the responsibilities?

- ✔ Can you explain the promotion in a single sentence that will make sense to and motivate consumers — and do all parties agree to the identical description?

Promotion planning checklist

In staging a promotion, you need to know your objective in advance, including exactly the end you're working to achieve and how you will measure success. Use the following checklist as you make your plans:

- ✔ Know the target market that you intend to influence with the promotion.

- ✔ Know what incentive you'll offer, and be sure that it is capable of motivating your target prospect.

- ✔ Inform your staff. Nothing is worse for a consumer than to arrive at what was billed as a promotion only to learn that no one at the host business seems to know anything about it.

Keep the promotion description simple. If you can't explain the promotion and the incentive in a single sentence, the idea almost certainly won't fly.

Chapter 15

Getting Ink and Air: Public Relations and Publicity

*W*e want to smash two notions right up front. First, public relations is not simply whitewashing. Second, publicity is not free advertising.

With those two major misconceptions out of the way, you can count on this chapter to confirm what public relations *is,* what publicity *is,* and how you can use each of them to increase your company's visibility, to supplement and reinforce your advertising, and to enhance your reputation in your market and industry.

An old adage says that if you wait to launch a public relations program until you face an image problem, then you will have waited far too long. Use public relations and publicity to enhance a strong image, not to right a wrong or fix an image disaster.

Right now, when you don't *need* publicity, start planning your public relations program. Then keep it going strong every single day of your business life. The following pages tell you how.

The Relationship between Publicity and Public Relations

The same people who think that marketing is a dressed-up word for sales will tell you that public relations is a way to get publicity — and that publicity is a way to get free advertising. That's like saying that fashion is about hem lengths. There's a shard of truth in there, but it's hardly the full story.

The wide-angle view of public relations

The Public Relations Society of America defines *public relations* as activities that "help an organization and its public adapt mutually to each other."

Other professionals say that public relations involves activities that aim to establish, maintain, and improve a favorable relationship with the public upon whom an organization's success depends.

In *Small Business Marketing For Dummies* terms, we say that public relations involves doing the right thing and then talking about it — using publicity and other nonpaid communication opportunities to inform those whose positive opinions favorably impact your business.

Public relations consist of the following:

- **Media relations:** Establish and maintain editorial contacts, generate and distribute news releases and story ideas, and become a reliable and trustworthy news source. Publicity is part of media relations, and media relations are part of — but not all of — public relations, as this list aims to prove.

- **Employee or member relations:** Develop communications and rapport with internal audiences through newsletters, meetings, events, and programs that prove that your company's interest in doing the right thing starts at home.

- **Community relations:** Build ties to your market area by joining groups, serving on boards, spearheading charitable endeavors, or donating time, products, services, or funds to help out with projects that benefit your community. When you undertake efforts for community causes, first and foremost do so because it's the right thing to do. Second, do it because you and your business benefit by association and by the credit you receive for being a valuable citizen in your area.

✔ **Industry relations:** Establish contacts within your industry, join industry associations, attend industry events, and even serve as an officeholder in the group that represents your business arena. A strong industry role is beneficial in keeping your business on top of the latest news and also building credibility among consumers and editorial contacts.

✔ **Government relations:** Build relationships with elected representatives and acquaint them with the mission and vision of your company. Doing so helps create a favorable impression should they be asked to comment on your business or should you need their help in the future. (Just as with bankers, it's good to make friends with politicians long before you need to enlist their help.)

✔ **Issues and crisis management:** Sometimes your news will be confusing, and once in a while, it will even be damaging to your image. One function of public relations is to explain and build support for complex issues and to manage crises when they arise.

Focusing on publicity

When you get mentioned in the media, that's *publicity.* It sounds so simple, and yet a surprising amount of planning and effort goes on behind the scenes before a company gets a "free" mention in a newspaper or magazine, a television or radio station, online, or even in another company's newsletter.

Those of us who spend much time generating publicity know that "valuable" is a much more appropriate descriptor than the word "free." Costs are involved to generate news releases and supporting materials, make and maintain media contacts, stage news events, and implement programs worthy of editorial coverage. But if you can get your name in print through publicity, the benefit will outweigh the investment many times over.

Each time you succeed in generating publicity, you score a triple victory. First, you win valuable editorial mentions in mass media vehicles. Second, you win consumer confidence, as consumers find information they receive through the editorial content of mass media more believable than they find paid advertising messages. And third, you can use reprints of the coverage you obtain through your publicity efforts to add credibility to your other marketing communications, by enclosing copies in direct mailings, sales presentation, and press kits.

The power of the press is undeniable, and the power of an editorial comment on your behalf is worth much, much more than the cost involved to get it.

Orchestrating Media Coverage

To generate publicity, you need to start with a news item of interest. If an editor thinks his audience won't care about your story, it will never make it into print or onto the air. But if your story conveys timely and useful information — if it tells something new, or a different or easier way to do something — then you should package it up and get it to the media, applying the process described in this chapter. Be prepared to proceed with both tenacity and patience, however, because the art of getting your name into the news requires both!

Getting real with your expectations

The fable about the oil driller who tossed in the towel just feet before reaching liquid gold is a good analogy for what most small businesses term their "failed publicity programs." They send out five, maybe even ten, news releases, nothing happens, and they quit — disappointed and without a clue of how close they came to achieving the result they so badly desired.

To generate publicity for your business, commit to a long-haul program and keep the following in mind:

- ✔ **Don't expect instant or even consistent results.** Most news releases never make it into the media. Don't expect to bat 1.000, or .500, or even .250.

- ✔ **Tailor your story to individual editorial contacts.** Universal news releases — the same exact release sent to all media — are less apt to be used by the media than releases that are customized to specific audiences and news vehicles.

- ✔ **Don't try to get news coverage as a perk for your advertising investments.** To obtain news coverage, send well-written releases and avoid anything that smacks of editorial arm-twisting. Count on your advertising investment to positively impact your publicity effort only in that your releases will reach news contacts who already know your name and brand — thanks to the strong and consistent message delivered in your paid ads.

- ✔ **Don't peddle hype as news.** If the focus of your story is why you think your product is improved or better than that of a competitor, that's hype. But if your story announces a new occurrence of interest to the public, that's news. Newsworthy releases announce new products, technology or industry updates, financial results, special events, awards given or received, staffing or management changes, activities that benefit your community, reactions to legal or financial difficulties (see "Dealing with bad news," later in this chapter), and new activities that will benefit your community.

✔ **Don't hound the media.** Never demand an explanation for why a release didn't run. If you are truly concerned that your releases are being ignored, buy an hour or two of a publicist's time to request a professional assessment of your efforts and guidance about presenting your stories in the future. Also see the section on "Establishing media contacts" for help in establishing editorial relationships.

✔ **Aim for quality — not quantity.** Don't try to get publicity by papering the world with releases and don't write releases that are a single sentence longer than they need to be. Send releases only when you have news of interest to readers or viewers. Keep each release hype-free and to-the-point. Follow a standard news release format (see the following section), and get it right in terms of grammar and typing.

Writing news releases

The news release is the main tool used in the effort to generate publicity. Each news release summarizes the important points of a story appropriate for coverage in the editorial portion of news media. News releases are also called *press releases,* but with the ever-growing impact of broadcast and Internet news, the term *news release* provides a more appropriate and all-encompassing label.

All good news releases include a number of common features as described in the following list and illustrated in Figure 15-1:

✔ **Who to contact for more information:** At the top of your release, include the name of a knowledgeable person who can be contacted for more information, along with a telephone number (including area code) for reaching that person directly and without any cumbersome and time-consuming voice mail interfaces.

✔ **When the news can be released:** In rare cases, releases are sent with a line describing an "embargo," or an instruction not to release the news until a certain date or time. Unless you have a very strong reason otherwise, however, simply notify the media that the news is "For Immediate Release" by typing and underscoring those words right above the release headline.

✔ **A headline:** Every release needs a title, typed in capital letters, that is active (in other words, it should include a verb), succinct (it should fit on no more than two lines), and benefit-oriented (it should tell what's in the news for the media audience — not what's in it for you).

✔ **A dateline:** The meat of the news release begins with the name of the city and the abbreviation of the state from which the release was originated, followed by the date the release was sent.

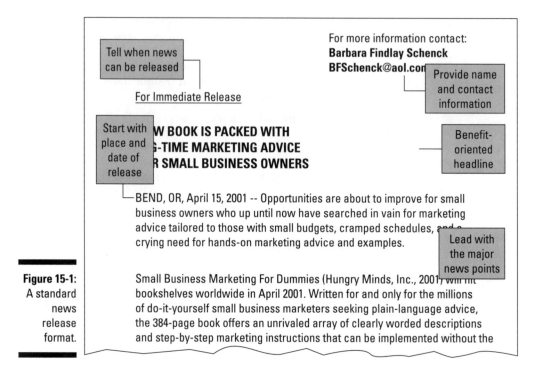

Tell when news can be released

For more information contact:
Barbara Findlay Schenck
BFSchenck@aol.com

Provide name and contact information

For Immediate Release

Start with place and date of release

W BOOK IS PACKED WITH
5-TIME MARKETING ADVICE
R SMALL BUSINESS OWNERS

Benefit-oriented headline

BEND, OR, April 15, 2001 -- Opportunities are about to improve for small business owners who up until now have searched in vain for marketing advice tailored to those with small budgets, cramped schedules, and a crying need for hands-on marketing advice and examples.

Lead with the major news points

Small Business Marketing For Dummies (Hungry Minds, Inc., 2001) will hit bookshelves worldwide in April 2001. Written for and only for the millions of do-it-yourself small business marketers seeking plain-language advice, the 384-page book offers an unrivaled array of clearly worded descriptions and step-by-step marketing instructions that can be implemented without the

Figure 15-1:
A standard
news
release
format.

📌 **Clear presentation of the facts:** Journalism 101 prevails in news release writing. Tell who, what, where, when, why, and how (known as the five *W*s plus how) in what is known as an *inverted pyramid* style. Here's what that means: Tell your news in your first sentence and pack the facts into the first paragraphs so that an editor can chop the entire end portion, if necessary to save space, and still retain the vital information.

📌 **One or several quotes:** Although editors alter all other portions of your release, your quotes will run verbatim if they run at all, so word them carefully to present meaningful comments from top management as well as from credible customers and industry sources. Always clearly identify the source of each quote.

📌 **Boilerplate information:** Every news release should end with a short paragraph, called a "boilerplate," that summarizes information about your company. The paragraph should tell your name, what your business does, a few points about how your business is unique, a line about your history (when your business was founded, your ownership, and other facts you believe are important to include when introducing your company), and anything you want to say about the size and scope of your business. For instance, releases from a fictional private high school might end with the following paragraph: "Amazing Preparatory School is a private academy graduating 100 college-bound students annually. Founded in 1975, the school is located on the grounds of the historic Smith Estate, where students from throughout the country live in dormitories or commute from throughout the surrounding metropolitan area. The school is a member of the Private Schools Association and the International Study Institute."

✔ **No more than three pages:** Print your news release on 8½-x-11-inch white paper. Use wide margins and one-and-a-half or double-spacing and try to fit it on a single page. If your release runs more than one page, don't print it on both sides of the same sheet, as editors frequently need to tear off and forward only the first part of the release for production. Type the word *more* at the bottom of the page if the release continues on, and start the next page by identifying the release in the top left-hand corner (for example, "Small Business Marketing For Dummies, Page 2"). Following the final sentence of your release, center three pound symbols (# # #) to indicate that the release has ended.

✔ **Supporting materials:** Instead of stretching your release onto extra pages, focus only on the news in your release. Attach separate fact sheets to detail price and availability information, lists of features, company background summaries, and frequently asked questions and answers. Don't go overboard. Attach only information that will assist the editorial staff in compiling a story.

✔ **Graphics:** Submit photos by enclosing a 5-x-7-inch or 8-x-10-inch glossy black-and-white photo print (or a 35mm slide for color publications). For illustrations, charts, or other artwork, submit camera-ready black-and-white reproductions (this means first-generation high-contrast reproductions on bright white paper). Accompany all graphics with clearly labeled captions.

As you write news releases test them against the information in Table 15-1.

Table 15-1	Spotting the Good and Bad in News Releases
Attributes of Releases That Get Results	**Attributes of Releases That Get Tossed Out**
Feature timely news about your products or services, your staff, recent legal or legislative actions, industry changes, or other items of interest to the public.	Contain promotional messages, recycled stories that have already been covered by competing news media, or self-serving puff pieces.
Are localized messages tailored to the audience of a specific news vehicle, often accompanied by a brief note written to an established editorial contact.	Are blanket mailings that relay the same exact news to competing media with no unique angle, no offer for interviews, or no other ways to customize the story.
Contain crisp, clear, accurate, and factual language.	Rely on superlatives (biggest, brightest, strongest, and so on), opinions, and hype.

(continued)

Table 15-1 *(continued)*

Attributes of Releases That Get Results	Attributes of Releases That Get Tossed Out
Describe benefits to the reader or viewer.	Emphasize product features rather than benefits and use insider terminology.
Make a clear point regarding why the news is important and how and when readers or viewers can take action.	Fail to answer the fundamental question, "Who cares?"
Use management quotes plus quotes from customers and industry leaders.	Fail to make a clear point about how the news impacts your industry, your business, or especially your market.
Are intriguing and believable.	Are boastful or stretch the bounds of credibility.

Getting your release into circulation

There are three main ways to get your news release to the media:

- ✔ **Distribute it yourself.** Mail or fax it to media outlets in distant locations and hand deliver it to local papers and broadcast stations, which have tighter deadlines.

- ✔ **Hire a public relations professional.** This person can distribute the release to select media and, if your news has broad-reaching market impact, to the Associated Press.

- ✔ **Use a news distribution service.** For example, Business Wire and PR Newswire both use electronic services to get time-sensitive material to newspapers, magazines, news bureaus, television and radio stations, online networks, and investment and research departments in the financial world.

Most small businesses focus their publicity efforts on local, regional, and industry-specific media, which are easy to target independently or with the help of a nearby professional publicist.

In addition to media distribution of your release, leverage its value by using it in the following ways:

- ✔ Post your release on your Web site.

- ✔ Distribute your release to an internal list that includes those of major influence to your business, including major clients and those in a position to refer business your way.

- ✔ Post it in your company. Employees should never have to learn their own company's news through the media.

Establishing media contacts

Create a list of the media that serve your geographic and industry area, including the following media outlets:

- **Your local daily newspaper:** In making contacts, keep in mind that general and "hot" news goes to the city or news desk. News that relates to certain sections of the paper — sports, home, business, entertainment, and so on — goes straight to the department editors. Study the paper. Certain reporters cover specific beats — education, small business, and technology, for instance. Call the person who covers your field to confirm whether you should deliver releases to the news desk or directly to the beat reporter.

- **Regional weekly and business papers:** Study back issues and media kits to familiarize yourself with the standing columns and upcoming special focus topics. Think about ways that you can contribute information, and about angles for stories that you can discuss with the editor. Then call to introduce yourself, find out the deadlines, and discuss ways that you can assist in providing information for news stories.

- **The radio and television stations that broadcast in your area:** Include those in distant cities whose signals come in via cable.

- **Your industry publications:** If you know your market (and if you don't, refer to Chapter 2), you know what publications your customers read. Make a list and then find out the names of the editors and reporters who cover the kind of news you generate and include them on your news release distribution list.

As you compile your media contact list, count on the resources of your local library. The reference desk should have copies of the *Bacon's Publicity Checker* and *Bacon's Radio/TV Directory,* which provide detailed information on editorial contacts at thousands of U.S., Canadian, Mexican, and Caribbean media outlets.

Maintaining media relationships

When you deliver your first news release, attach a note explaining that, along with your release, you're enclosing a kit of introductory information about your business, and that you stand by to answer any questions or to be a resource whenever you can be of assistance.

After that first contact, work to earn a reputation as a business that sends only newsworthy releases, passing on any item that isn't timely, doesn't announce a major milestone, or has no unique angle or hook.

Other advice: Be a good source and make yourself available to the media. Alert those who answer the phone to route media calls to you immediately. If you aren't the owner or president of your organization, do all that you can do to get the top person to be available as well. Nothing is worse that getting a reporter interested only to have the most powerful person in your company say "no comment" or refuse to be interviewed.

Promptly return media calls and be sensitive to deadlines. Don't call near deadline and don't take more time than you need. Offer to deliver or fax summaries of lengthy or complex material.

Finally, always assume that you're on the record. See the following section, "Managing media interviews," for more information on this topic.

Managing media interviews

When you finally hit the publicity jackpot and a reporter calls for an interview, be ready!

Before the interview

Get the details. In advance of the interview, confirm the publication or station name and the deadline, along with the interview topic, the angle of the story, and the type of questions you will be asked. Ask if others will be interviewed for the same story. This will give you an indication of the nature of the story angle and allow you to prepare your remarks accordingly.

Then take time to prepare yourself. If a reporter is on a deadline and wants to ask you questions on the spot, buy a couple of minutes' time by explaining that you need to wind up a meeting or project and return the call — and then do so, preferably within a half-hour. But before hanging up, ask whether the reporter has specific questions in mind so that you can have information available.

Once you know the scope of the interview, jot down the two or three most important ideas that you want to convey about the topic. Grab any appropriate reference materials so that you're organized and ready to make your points clearly. Consider negative issues that might arise and develop short responses, and think about what photos, charts, industry statistics, or other materials you'd like to offer to the reporter to enhance the coverage.

During the interview

Proceed with confidence — and caution — during media interviews. Answer questions clearly and then stop talking. If you try to fill time with additional comments you run the risk of saying something you don't want to see in print or hear on-air. Follow this list of advice and warnings:

- ✔ Do ask how much time the reporter has scheduled for the interview. Then watch your clock so that you make all the important points within the allotted time.

- ✔ Do admit that you don't know an answer rather than make a guess. And if you can't disclose information due to legal or regulatory reasons, tell the reporter that you have "no comment."

- ✔ Do speak slowly and in clear terms and take the time to explain your point if the reporter seems confused.

- ✔ Do make your most important points in the beginning and again at the end of the interview.

- ✔ Do keep your comments brief so that they make good quotes.

  Don't respond if you don't know the answer or if the answer should be provided by a qualified person, such as a tax, legal, or financial professional. Tell the reporter that someone else should answer the question, and then provide that person's name and number.

- ✔ Don't say anything you don't want to read or hear later. You can ask not to be quoted by saying a statement is "not for attribution," and you can say that a comment is "off the record." But there are no guarantees. The best idea is to bite your tongue before saying anything negative or potentially harmful or embarrassing.

- ✔ Don't take a jab at the competition.

- ✔ Don't pick a fight with the reporter.

- ✔ Don't stonewall. If a negative issue arises, provide a brief answer. If you avoid the issue, the reporter is apt to follow up by talking to someone who is far less apt to protect your position.

- ✔ Don't mention your advertising investment in the reporter's publication or station unless the point is relevant to the news story, which likely it isn't.

- ✔ Don't let your guard down or assume the slant of the story.

- ✔ Don't swear or make colorful comments unless you're prepared to see the words in a large quote accompanied by your name.

- ✔ Don't try to fill silences. You're most apt to get yourself in trouble when you start rambling. Answer the question and then wait for the next one, unless you choose to use the idle time to advance one of the major points you want to make in the interview.

Following the interview

Following the interview, thank the reporter and ask when the article will run or air. Don't demand prior review of the story, but do offer to be available to assist in confirming any facts or quotes.

Realize that sometimes even after interviews the stories get canceled or they don't run on the date you were told they would. Also realize that you may notice discrepancies between they way the story is worded and what you thought you said. Request corrections only for major errors, not for differences of opinion or approach. Instead, look for a positive aspect of the coverage and highlight that point in a thank-you note to the reporter. Good words will get you much, much further than nitpicking or criticizing.

Guidelines for broadcast interviews

In preparing for and conducting radio or television interviews, follow all the preceding interview advice and then add these items to your checklist:

- Ask whether the program will be live or taped. The good *and* bad news about live shows is that they can't be edited.

- Ask the name of the program and host and then watch the show to acquaint yourself with the style.

- Confirm the interview site and length. If the location is out-of-town, ask whether the studio pays transportation and lodging costs.

- Ask whether other guests will be part of the same show. If so, ask the producer who they are and what point of view they represent. The interviewer may be setting up a battleground — in which case you'll want to arrive at the interview with a bullet-proof strategy.

- Ask whether submitting a biography and list of possible discussion topics in advance would be helpful.

- Confirm the interview in writing.

- Try to visit with the host before tape rolls to relax a bit, but don't share your nervousness or give away your best talking points.

- For TV, avoid patterned clothes or jangly jewelry. Accept makeup assistance if it is offered.

- Acquaint yourself with the locations of the camera, microphones, and monitors, and, whenever you're in the studio, protect yourself by assuming that you're on-air.

- Think and speak in sound bites no longer than 20 seconds.

- On radio shows, use commercial breaks to learn from the host what topic you will discuss next.

- Avoid any effort to be cute, funny, or promotional and don't try to hog the microphone.

- Smile, show confidence, and be thoughtful with your answers.

- Don't take notes, don't answer if you don't know, and don't hesitate to build a bridge to a point you want to make by tagging a statement such as "by the way" onto an answer.

Watch your words

For the record, people pay a big price for attacking someone's reputation in the media. To stay out of trouble in media interviews, provide only facts and steer clear of opinions.

For the record, here are two terms you don't ever want to hear again:

✔ Libel: Printed statements that are untrue, defamatory, and harmful

✔ Slander: The verbal form of libel

Staging news conferences

Companies like the concept of news conferences a lot more than editors and reporters do. In fact, many media organizations, including many small-town newspapers and stations, simply won't attend ribbon-cutting and ground-breaking events, considering them promotional and easily described in simple news releases. Even the most newsworthy conference (in your view) can be eclipsed by late-breaking or seemingly more important news.

Stage a news conference only in the following cases:

✔ You have extremely time-sensitive announcements that need to be made simultaneously to all media.

✔ You have powerful news that is best told in person, backed by product displays, and followed by the chance for reporters to ask questions.

✔ You need to explain visual stories that are best understood if seen first-hand.

✔ You are presenting well-known speakers or celebrities.

If you do decide to host a news conference, schedule and announce the event well in advance. Send invitations in the form of brief letters or announcements that are formatted like news releases but with the words "Media Advisory" replacing the words "For Immediate Release." Here are some additional tips:

✔ Schedule the time with sensitivity to media deadlines. Most conferences start at 10:30 a.m. to best suit as many media schedules as possible.

✔ Start on time and hold speakers to their allotted schedules.

✔ Be sure that speakers can be seen and heard. If you plan far enough in advance, you're more likely to end up with a well-placed podium (situated with photo opportunities in mind), microphones, speakers, extension cords, and lights.

- Place a large company logo behind the speaker or on the front of the podium.

- Minimize speeches in favor of demonstrations that provide the basis for good photos and footage.

- Distribute news packets that feature a news release on the day's event, background company information, and the name and number of the spokesperson to contact for more information. Following the event, mail or deliver packets to major media not in attendance.

Dealing with bad news

Chalk it up to bad decisions or just plain bad luck, but like it or not, sometimes bad news happens. When it does, work fast to find out what went wrong and to fix the problem if possible.

Waste no time preparing a news release telling what happened and, if possible, what actions are being taken to see that it won't happen again. As much as you'd like to run and hide, don't. Almost certainly your company will fare better if you show a concerned face and release a truthful explanation. The last thing you want is for those who care a lot less about your reputation than you do to be speculating or spinning the story for you.

Public relations strategists have complete scenarios for use in what is called *crisis communications*. If your event is apt to have negative ramifications that continue for more than a few days and if the bad news seems likely to reach out farther than your local market area, call in a pro to help you manage the story. Look in the phone book under "Public Relations" or ask leading business colleagues in your area for references.

Part IV
Marketing Online

The 5th Wave   By Rich Tennant

"Right here...,crimeorg.com. It says the well run small criminal concern should have no more than nine goons, six henchmen and four stooges. Right now, I think we're goon heavy."

In this part . . .

The Internet has opened up a whole new world — a
world that can both baffle and bolster a small business. Although the Internet forces you to compete with
distant companies (who can speak to and sell to your
customers through their personal computers), it also puts
the benefits of a whole new competitive weapon at your
fingertips. In the never-ending marketing process, the
Internet can be an invaluable tool for product and competitive research, an integral new component in ad strategies,
and a priceless means of keeping in touch with prospects
and customers.

Part IV shows you how to put the advantages of the Internet
to work for your business, how to buffer yourself against
the competitive threats posed by the Internet, and how to
use the Internet to gain a big edge over your competitors.

Chapter 16

Putting the Internet to Work for Your Business

. . . .

In This Chapter

▶ Explaining Internet terminology

▶ Finding out who's online

▶ Recognizing the pluses and minuses of online marketing

▶ Determining whether your business is a candidate for online success

▶ Harnessing the Internet

. . . .

Small businesses experience fear of the unknown in epidemic proportions when the topic of the Internet arises. Many small companies feel threatened by the online world and even wonder whether they'll be in business in a few years as adoption of the Internet continues to increase. This chapter demystifies the topic and helps you sort through the pros and cons before diving into ideas for putting the Internet to work for your business.

The Language of Cyberspace

Everything about the online world is evolutionary, including the terminology. Even the technological experts tend to apply the labels interchangeably. But for the record, here are key terms and definitions. To fully immerse yourself in the topic of online marketing, go straight to *Marketing Online For Dummies* by Bud Smith and Frank Catalano (Hungry Minds, Inc.).

   ✔ **The Internet:** Referred to as the Net for short, the Internet is the huge network that links together networks from all over the world, therefore allowing any computer that has access to one network to have access to all the others as well. The Internet contains the World Wide Web and e-mail.

   ✔ **The World Wide Web:** The vast set of linked documents and computer files that includes corporate and product information, university course work, personal home pages, political campaign updates, and, yes, pornography.

✔ **E-mail:** Short for electronic mail, e-mail is a computer-to-computer communication system. Sending and receiving e-mail messages is the main reason that most people use the Internet. Estimates vary broadly, but the number of e-mail messages sent globally each year reaches into the trillions. (In comparison, the U.S. Post Office delivers fewer than 200 billion pieces of first-class — or "snail" — mail annually.)

✔ **Web page:** A computer file with its own address that is accessible through the World Wide Web. An example of a Web address is `www.dummies.com`. The "www" stands for World Wide Web. The next lineup of characters — "dummies" — is the domain name. The final part of the address — "com" — is the URL, or Uniform Resource Locator. Together they comprise a Web address, which is how your computer knows how to find the Web page when you request it.

✔ **Web site:** A group of related Web pages.

Who's Online and What Are They Doing There?

The Internet is really about communication — how people communicate with each other, how customers communicate with businesses, and how businesses communicate with each other.

Although it is widely accepted that e-mail is the most popular Internet application and the reason that most of your customers use the Internet, people log on for many other reasons, too:

✔ To look up information about products and services

✔ To shop for specific products, specifically for finding the best price

✔ To actually buy products

✔ To obtain customer support, training, or information

✔ For recreation and entertainment

And who exactly are the folks who are logging on? In April 2000, the Web ratings firm MediaMetrix, Inc., released a statistical profile of Web users. Surprise! The Internet's clientele is much more mainstream than the stereotypes would lead you to believe. Internet users are split 50/50 between men and women. Most users are between 18 and 54 years old, with the average user in the mid-40s. The fastest-growing user segment in the year 2000 consisted of women 55 and over.

Competing with the Internet

Competing with the Internet means competing with other companies that can reach your customers online *and* using the Internet as a competitive weapon as you grow your business.

Internet marketing advantages

- ✔ Your business can be open 24 hours a day, and your customers can shop any time they want.
- ✔ You can access customers outside your geographic region.
- ✔ You can get information to your customers without paying the cost of printing or postage.
- ✔ You can more easily and constantly update the marketing messages and information that you send to your customers.
- ✔ Especially for information-intensive businesses like newspapers, magazines, law firms, title companies, and travel agencies, the Web provides a means for delivering products directly to customers.

Internet marketing obstacles

- ✔ Online marketing is not free. You have to buy or rent software and hardware, invest in the creation and maintenance of your site, create and maintain your online distribution lists, and spend the time involved in creating, testing, and sending out information over e-mail. Here are some other obstacles to consider as you weigh the appropriateness of online marketing for your business:
- ✔ It is a cold hard fact that half of all households won't be shopping your business online. It is estimated that only one of two U.S. households was online in 2000. Although that number is certain to keep climbing, for now the number hovers at the half-way mark.
- ✔ Many customers use the Web only for information gathering. They prefer live interaction when they make their purchases.
- ✔ The Web has a reputation for frustrating customers who seek customer service. There's no nice way to candy-coat the fact that many online marketers lack customer service or inquiry response programs. As a result, many customers apply a poor-service stereotype to all online marketers.

✔ Many people are afraid to shop on the Web because they do not believe that it's a secure environment — they think that their credit card information may be stolen or that their information may be misused.

✔ Finding things on the Web takes time. With so many sites and so much information, customers get tired of searching and clicking.

✔ Ever-changing Web site information is often confusing. Customers visit a site, find something of interest, and then go back only to find that things have moved and they can't find what they want the second time around.

✔ Contrary to popular belief, moving your marketing to the Web is not always cheaper. You'll find a number of hidden costs (see Chapter 17), plus online customers expect a lot for free.

Mixed-bag attributes of the Internet

Because of the opportunities online, your business can cast farther for new business. But at the same time, customers located two doors away can search the world instead of dropping in to have their needs met by your business.

Comparison shopping takes on a whole new meaning because of the Net. Your customers can now directly access information from literally all over the world, and they can use the Web to find the best deals regardless of location.

The good news is that if your business offers considerable savings on price, or if you offer other unique product values, the Internet could offer a great business-building edge.

The bad news is that even if you offer a killer price, unless you're selling high-ticket items, customers may not be willing to spend the time searching the Web for the minor savings that your price differential would deliver.

Consider a product like a new car. If you could find a company willing to sell you a car for just $500 over invoice, compared to the usual $2,000, it would definitely make shopping online rewarding. Can your business offer that kind of a customer bonus? If so, the Web just may make the world your oyster.

Evaluating How Your Business May Fare Online

Closing up shop because another company is selling your products or services on the Web is not the answer! Nor is the solution to redirect every cent of your marketing budget into an online plunge.

Instead, review the preceding advantages and disadvantages to evaluate how they apply to your business. Then run through the following questions to see if you see a red, yellow, or green light when it comes to how your business will fare in the online world.

- ✔ Can you deliver your product economically and conveniently?

- ✔ Does your product appeal to a geographically broad market?

- ✔ Do you want to expand your business outside your geographic area?

- ✔ Will you realize economic benefits — including rent, labor, inventory, printing, and other savings — by marketing online?

- ✔ Does your customer want to be able to shop 24 hours a day?

- ✔ Is it easy for your customer to find competing products and services on the Web?

- ✔ Are you facing significant new competition from outside your region because of the Internet?

- ✔ Are you selling a unique product that is hard to get in other regions?

- ✔ Are you sending a growing number of direct mailings to customers who have asked you to keep them in the loop?

- ✔ Does your marketing information continuously change because you keep adding new products and services?

- ✔ Do you provide a service that is information-intensive — such as the offerings of law firms, travel agencies, and real estate agencies?

- ✔ Are you willing and able to spend the marketing time and money necessary to drive business to your Web site?

The more "yes" answers you rack up, the more apt your business is to gain from online marketing. You must have distinct product advantages, however, so that you fare well in an online shopping experience. It also helps if a behemoth, like Amazon.com or Drugstore.com, isn't already dominating your market.

Using the Internet in Your Marketing Program

Most businesses equate using the Internet with building a Web site. But here are some ways to reap benefits from the Internet even if you don't have a site:

- ✔ Use e-mail to communicate one-to-one with your customers.

- ✔ Use e-mail to communicate one-to-many, as you would do through traditional direct mail programs.

- ✔ Browse the Web to keep tabs on your competition.
- ✔ Connect with small business owners, consultants, and information resources to enhance management of your business.

Add a Web site, and your opportunities expand to enable you to

- ✔ Include the Web in your communications strategy, using it like an extended brochure that gives prospects more information.
- ✔ Use the Web as an advertising vehicle by posting on other sites or getting ranked in the search engines and directories.
- ✔ Use the Web to sell your products to current and new customers.

If you're thinking about selling informational content online — like newsletter subscriptions, for example — be cautious about your expectations for sales on the Web. Very few have been successful with this model.

Using e-mail in your marketing program

With cell phones, answering machines, and pagers, many small businesses question the need for e-mail, wondering just how many ways a customer needs to have access to a company. Think again.

E-mail has become part of 21st century life. Half of the people in North America say they use it regularly. It is a free way — and increasingly the preferred way — to communicate one-to-one or with many customers at the same time.

With e-mail comes an impressive list of advantages and at least one landmine for small businesses to avoid. See Chapter 6 for advice on how to manage the image that your business projects (or diffuses) through this increasingly vital communications medium. Remember that especially in small companies, every single act is a marketing act — including the look, tone, and content of every e-mail message.

One-to-one e-mail communications

Think about your customers who carry laptops and want to be in touch with you when they travel. Think about your customers who don't want to be interrupted with a phone call every time you want to let them know that their product has arrived. What if you have a law firm with lots of documents going back and forth and clients who don't want to spend time or money on deliveries? Or how about a travel agency that needs to communicate with customers who are frequently on the road? Or maybe a doctor's office that needs to confirm appointments?

To meet the needs of these customers, you won't require a Web site, just e-mail.

If you don't already have e-mail, first contact an Internet Service Provider (see Chapter 18) to arrange for Internet access and to set up an e-mail address. Then commit to using e-mail on a consistent and frequent basis. Many companies don't respond to e-mail. What does that say to their customers?

Establish a time at least daily to check your e-mail in-box. Set up a computer in a location that is easy to access and use — and almost impossible to overlook. Consider a cable modem so that you don't have to constantly dial in to gain access to the Internet.

One-to-many e-mail messages

Direct mail has long been a key component of small business marketing programs because it lets you sidestep broad-reaching and costly mass media and communicate directly with your target prospects and clients.

One-to-many e-mail messages are the online equivalent of direct mail — but without the costs of printing flyers and buying postage.

See Chapter 19 for advice on sending opt-in versus spam e-mail, which is the wired world's term for unsolicited junk e-mail.

Browsing the Web to keep tabs on your competition

To compete online, the first step is to figure out who and what you're up against. Go online and pretend that you're a customer searching for services or products like the ones you sell. Once you find competing sites, monitor them continuously, in the same way that you watch the activities of bricks-and-mortar competitors to evaluate how they might impact your business. Here are some suggestions:

✔ Search for products or services like yours in the directories or search engines. Try combinations of various words that your customers might use to define your offering to learn more about what they'll see when they shop on the Web.

✔ Look for Web site addresses in articles and ads in your industry's trade magazines to get a feel for which competitors are trying to reach your customers online.

✔ Go to the sites that provide specialized information to customers in your field. See whose Web sites are listed and whose advertisements appear.

✔ Sign up for the electronic newsletters offered on your competitors' sites. These publications help you to keep up with what they're doing and also give you new ideas that you can apply to your business.

✔ Buy products on the Web and rate your own purchasing and delivery experience.

As you browse the Internet, you need to know a couple terms that explain the passports to online travel:

✔ **Browser:** Software that lets you view Web pages. Netscape Navigator and Microsoft Internet Explorer are the two most commonly used browsers.

✔ **Search engines:** Search engines are like online automated card catalogs, but without the organization of the library Dewey Decimal System. Instead, search engines keep catalog entries on millions of Web sites. Then when an online user enters a keyword or keywords, the search engine scans for any Web sites that might contain the information, returning a list of sites in which the words were found. The most popular search engines are Webcrawler, Google (see Figure 16-1), Lycos, Excite, AltaVista, and Hotbot. Yahoo! is often referred to as a search engine, but it is really a giant directory like the printed Yellow Pages. For much more information on choosing and using search engines and their counterparts — directory sites — see Chapter 19.

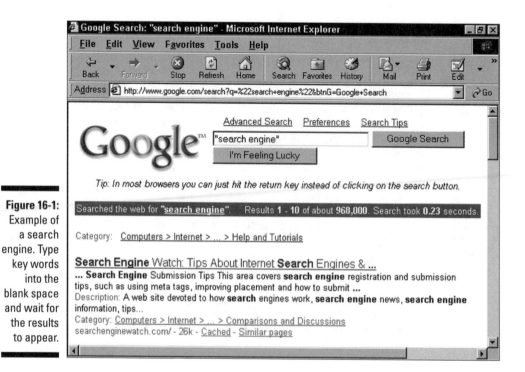

Figure 16-1:
Example of a search engine. Type key words into the blank space and wait for the results to appear.

Connecting with small business peers and advisers

The Web is rich with sites that can help you manage your business. Web sites offer information that can help you write business and marketing plans, discover products that will help your business, hire employees, get legal advice, and find research and information to aid in business and marketing decisions. Here are a couple great places to start:

- www.score.org: The Web site for SCORE, the Service Corps of Retired Executives
- www.sba.gov: The site for the U.S. Small Business Administration

Employing the Internet in your advertising and sales strategies

Check out Chapter 17 to assess whether you have a product that is apt to sell well online. Then see Chapter 19, which focuses on how to employ the Web as part of your advertising strategy and how to create buzz not only for your site but for your business and your brand as well.

Chapter 17

Answering the Web Question: To Make a Site or Not?

. . . .

In This Chapter

▶ Deciding whether a Web site makes sense for your business

▶ Determining the purposes of your site

▶ Selling online without your own site

▶ Calculating the costs of a Web site

. . . .

Deciding whether you need a Web site is no different than deciding to employ any other type of advertising tool or technique. It all comes down to two questions: Who are you trying to talk to, and how can you best reach those people?

The Internet is just one more tool in the communications bag that includes print and broadcast advertising, direct mail, publicity, and promotional events. But it happens to be the hottest and newest tool and the one that everyone is talking about. This chapter helps you sort through the issues involved as you determine whether the Internet is the right vehicle for bringing new prospects into your business or for providing new services and products to your customers.

Web Site Decision Factors

There are dozens of ways you can put the Internet to work for your business. But don't get trapped in the technology rush and decide that you need a Web site no matter what. Instead, follow these steps to decide whether a Web site makes sense for your business:

> ✔ **Define how you would use a site.** If you're considering online sales, determine whether you have a product that will fare well online. (See the section "E-commerce green light/yellow light indicators," later in this chapter.)

✔ **Figure out the cost of a Web site.** Include estimates of how much of your time will be involved and how much you will pay to build it, host it, and support it. Also consider what kinds of costs will be involved to drive demand to your site. (See "Figuring the Cost of a Web Site," later in this chapter.)

✔ **Evaluate your competition online.** Spend some time surfing for competitive products and services on the Web and see what's out there already. Use different search engines and try a variety of keywords. Flip through trade magazines for Web site addresses. Ask industry colleagues and media reps about sites that they think you should be aware of.

✔ **Think about how you will drive customers to your site.** Building a site is easy — like slapping up a sign that says, "Now open for business." The hard part is getting people through the door, or to the site. Chapter 19 is full of useful information on this topic.

✔ **Ask yourself: Is this the most effective use of time and resources?** You may very well decide that spending your marketing budget in other ways would bring in *more* business. Really think: How else would you use these funds and would the alternative provide a more effective way to grow your business?

If you don't already use the Web much, now is the time to get out and surf. To acquaint yourself with the opportunities of the cyber world:

✔ Take a basic Internet class and learn enough to navigate online.

✔ Find out who else is selling products and services like yours. If you aren't going to compete with them directly, give them a call and find out whether they've been successful with their site.

✔ See whether your local Internet Service Provider or Web design company can hook you up with companies that have situations similar to yours so you can discuss their online experiences.

✔ Look at Web sites for other businesses in your local area. Then call the business owners and ask who created their sites, what they cost, how much time they took to build, and whether they are effective.

Defining How Your Business Would Use a Web Site

Web sites can have a variety of purposes, but most small businesses use the Web in one or several of four ways:

✔ "Phone book" listing

✔ Online brochure

✔ E-commerce

✔ Customer support

Defining the purpose of a Web site is just like defining the purpose of any other advertisement or piece of sales literature. You need to know who you're trying to talk to, what people currently know or think about your business, what you *want* them to know or think, and, most of all, what action you want them to take after encountering this communication with your company.

See Chapter 8 for a list of the questions you should ask and answer before committing dollars to *any* marketing communications vehicle, including Web site creation.

"Phone book" listing sites

Yellow Pages or directory listing sites, such as the one shown in Figure 17-1, will become increasingly important as your customers shift from using the ever-weightier printed versions of phone books and instead start to seek listing information through search engines or online local directories. A simple "phone book" site is easy to build and a good way to provide online customers with a little information about your company.

Such a site helps people to locate and reach your business and provides a way to generate word-of-mouth leads by providing customers with an easy way to send information about your business to others.

Listing sites are easy and inexpensive to build. They include basic company information such as your business name, telephone number, open hours, e-mail address, and a brief description of who you are, what you do, the products and services you offer, and how to reach you online and at your physical location. Costs should be less than $1,000 even if you employ outside help to build your site, and maintenance of these sites is minimal because little should change about the basics of your business.

Online brochure sites

Good online brochures — just like good printed brochures — provide easy-to-understand company information in a form that skirts free of overkill or hype. (See Chapter 14 for tips on how to talk to your prospective customer rather than to yourself when you create brochures and other company materials.)

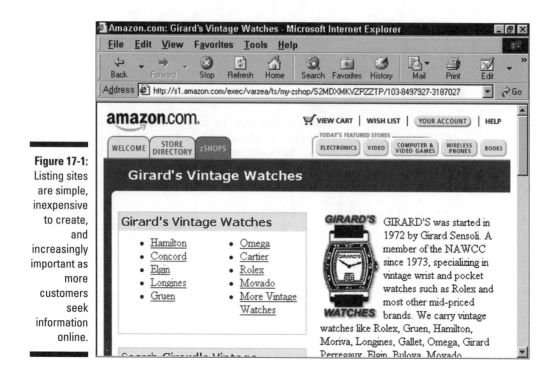

Figure 17-1:
Listing sites
are simple,
inexpensive
to create,
and
increasingly
important as
more
customers
seek
information
online.

Online brochures provide a means to educate prospects about your products and services in a way that convinces them either that they want to do business with your company or that they would like to receive more information about becoming a customer.

Online brochures are relatively easy to create and should cost somewhere between $1,000 and $5,000 — though the costs can climb higher (much higher) depending on the graphics, amount of text, and the complexity of the navigation system.

E-commerce sites

E-commerce sites allow you to actually sell products over the Web. Customers can look at your products, choose what they want, place orders, and submit payment.

E-commerce sites are complicated to build because they involve so many necessary features. Customers need to be able to learn about your products, pick the ones they want, pay in a secure way, and submit customer information. Standard software is making e-commerce site creation easier, but still it doesn't fall into the realm of the computer novice.

Price tags on e-commerce shops run the gamut, based on the technology and the complexity involved with each site. Even the most moderate foray into the e-commerce arena — doing the research involved to study the competition, assessing how well your product will fare online, producing the simplest possible site, and gearing up to serve an online market — costs a minimum of $5,000. Check out `www.wilsonweb.com` and `www.internetworld.com` for the latest technology.

E-commerce green light/yellow light indicators

For some small businesses, the opportunity to sell online unfolds a huge and exciting new business dimension. For others, it is a cost that doesn't quite pay off.

To decide whether e-commerce is for you and your business, consider the following questions. "Yes" answers are E-commerce green lights. "No" answers are flashing yellow lights — they don't mean that E-commerce isn't for you, but rather that you need to include some careful features in your online marketing to be sure you can overcome the obvious obstacles involved in selling your product over a distance.

- ✔ **Do you have a product or service that you can explain easily on the Web via written descriptions and photos?** Or do you have a "high-touch" product? High-touch items such as clothing sell online, but it is more difficult to communicate their descriptions in a way that ensures that customers really understand what they are buying.

- ✔ **Is your product easy and affordable to package and ship?** Perishable, fragile, or hard-to-ship products present special needs that you have to consider and plan around.

- ✔ **Does your product require only limited after-the-purchase support?** In other words, if assembly, installation, or usage training is required, can your customers handle the task on their own?

- ✔ **Is the risk relatively low if a customer makes an ordering mistake?** For example, if your customer meant 10 and typed 100 on an order of packaged goods, correcting the error involves only shipping costs. But if the mistake involves an order of custom-made windows, then you're talking about absorbing serious after-the-fact expense.

- ✔ **Is your product or service unique or difficult to find?** If it is readily available and easy to purchase in your prospect's local area, your online offer has to include competitive pricing or other enhancements to tip the decision in your favor.

- ✔ **Will your customer be willing to pay for shipping?** Or can you absorb the shipping cost and still come out ahead? Most online marketers require customers to pay shipping fees, but if your product is readily available locally, then you have to offer a better price or free shipping to win the business.

> ✔ **Are you ready for the administrative realities of marketing online?**
> Many software programs let you take credit cards online, but you need
> to institute new systems to allow customers to input data, select prod-
> ucts, make payments, and trigger shipping and billings — promptly, effi-
> ciently, without error, and, with luck, on a frequent and repeated basis.

Look before you leap online

Look closely at ways to protect yourself from fraud before you decide to
handle sales transactions on the Web. Many people think that customers are
the ones who should worry about fraud on the Web, but think again. The
Internet Fraud Prevention Advisory Council says that up to 40 percent of
transactions on the Web are fraudulent. In the United States, consumers pay
just the first $50 of fraudulent bank card charges. Merchants pick up the rest
of the tab. Go online to www.ifpac.org for information on fraud prevention
data, techniques, and software.

Support sites

Support sites provide online customer service and ongoing customer communication. They offer information about product installation, usage, and
troubleshooting; share industry trends and product update news; and help
customers put products to use. Sometimes support sites include e-commerce
components as well.

Support sites can be simple or complex depending on the types of features
included. Simple sites that feature straight information and graphics are much
easier to build than sites with interaction, with community features such as
discussion groups, and with the ability to verify the customer profile (that is,
verifying that the customer logging on is really a purchasing customer).

If you're thinking of including support and training as a purpose of your Web
site, begin by asking yourself the following questions:

> ✔ **Do your customers all seem to ask the same questions?** If so, a support
> site could provide this information. But if your customers need a wide
> range of information, you may need a more customized service
> approach.

> ✔ **Do you have a great number of customers?** If so, a support site is apt to
> pay off. But if you have only a few big customers, and therefore just a
> few major customer contacts, spending the time to build and maintain a
> support and training site may not make sense.

✔ **Will your customers go to a Web site?** Or will they continue to call you directly? Unless you believe they will embrace the Web site as their contact point, skip the cost of building support into your site.

✔ **Are you a reseller or a merchandiser of branded items?** If so, maybe you can simply send your customers to the manufacturers' Web sites for support, therefore avoiding the cost of building one of your own.

Selling Products without Building a Site

Even without your own Web site, you can sell your products online through storefronts and auction sites.

Storefronts

Storefronts are just like they sound. They are entryways to your business hosted by major "shopping malls" such as Amazon.com (see Figure 17-2) and Yahoo.com. These sites build your storefront, catalog your products or services, and allow you to sell your products and services online through their sites.

Figure 17-2: Online selling through an Amazon.com storefront.

Storefronts offer a couple benefits. You don't have to build a Web site and venture directly into the complexities of online administration and transaction processing. In addition, your online host will help you find customers.

On the flip side, you'll trade a few benefits when you opt for a storefront in lieu of your own Web site. With a storefront, your online presentation has to fit into an established format, so it's hard to project your unique brand or identity or to distinguish yourself from the other offerings of the site. Another drawback is that the "shopping mall" keeps a percentage of the take from all transactions made through their site. So you'll make less per sale — though possibly a greater number of sales — than you would have made selling the product through your own site.

Auction sites

An auction site allows you to auction a product just like you would in a regular live auction, only now it's online. Companies like Yahoo! and eBay have set up auctions to sell just about everything. They have been especially successful in selling merchandise such as surplus products, creative or unique products like art, used products, and products that are available only in a limited supply.

Most auction sites charge a transaction fee and some add a setup fee to cover costs involved with hosting the auction for you. The numbers vary, so check out auction sites for details.

Auction sites offer several benefits. You don't have to set up your own site. You don't have to figure out the price of your product (bidders do that for you). You don't even have to figure out how to process credit cards. Your role is to set the lowest acceptable price, write the marketing blurb on the site, upload a few pictures, and ship out the product. You don't do anything to find customers; you just wait for them to come to the auction site.

Participating in auctions even has a nice side benefit, in that you can include a link in your auction site to drive people to your own Web site.

What are the drawbacks of auction sites? You pay a commission to the auction site for finding your customer. And differentiating yourself against your competitors is hard on an auction site.

Following are the steps involved in selling products through online auctions:

1. **First, choose which online auction you want to sell through.**

   As a starting point, check out www.amazon.com and www.ebay.com.

2. **Post your product on the site, along with the lowest price you'll accept.**

A picture of your product greatly improves your chances of success, so you need a digital photo (which means that you need access to a digital camera).

3. **Watch as people bid on your item over a period of time.**

Obviously, you must know how to use a computer to manage the auction, upload pictures and descriptions, communicate with customers, and accept bids.

Many auction sites act as the collection agency to make sure that you get your money. This service is terrific because it greatly reduces your chance of being taken by someone who pays you with a bad check or credit line. Check out www.paypal.com for more information.

If You Build It, Will They Come?

Before building a Web site, consider whether those who deal with your business will want to find you online and, if so, for what reasons.

Chapter 2 helps you to create customer profiles, including where your customers live, who they are, and what their lives are like. It also tells you how to collect information about your customers. As you conduct formal and informal customer surveys, ask about computer usage. Do they use the Internet? Do they have e-mail addresses? Would they like to contact you online?

The only reason to create a Web site is that you have prospects, customers, and colleagues who want to access your business online. If they do, get with the program. If they don't, then decide whether you can appeal to a whole new group through an online presence, or whether you can entice your customers online because of the improved service and support available through your site.

To weigh your decision, take these steps:

1. **Create a list of the kinds of people who deal with your business.** Include descriptions of your various products along with a profile of the consumer who purchases each offering.

2. **Evaluate which of your consumer groups would visit a site if you had one.**

3. **List the key information you think customers would want to find on the site.**

4. **Prioritize what's really important to them and to you.**

Stickiness

Unlike in restaurants and most other traditional business establishments, in the online world, stickiness is a good thing. "Stickiness" is the ability to hold online visitors at your Web site and to keep them coming back again and again. If a site is not sticky, visitors drop in, and quickly click away to another site, often never returning again.

But whether stickiness is important to your site depends a lot on your site's purpose. A newspaper site like www.usatoday.com absolutely needs to be sticky because it wants you to visit, stay a while, and return every day to catch up on the news. But on the other hand, a site for a log home manufacturer may not require stickiness at all. Perhaps the purpose is simply to let customers know about the log home builder's offerings and quality, and inspire visitors to e-mail or pick up the phone and call for more information. The customer will buy only one log home, and the purchase will occur through a direct sales encounter and not through a Web site. So stickiness isn't an issue.

As a general rule, think about how you can develop features that 1) keep your visitors once they arrive and 2) bait them back after they leave.

A note of caution regarding stickiness: As you pour effort into bringing people back to your site, make sure that your features appeal to the right visitors so that return visits are more likely to result in additional sales.

A great starting point is to keep a log of the questions that you get from prospects and customers via the phone and in person today. Then ask yourself whether you think that those same prospects or customers would go online to seek the same information. This helps you prioritize the need for a site and what purposes you will want it to serve.

For example, a florist may decide to focus its Web site on the interests of brides shopping for wedding flowers — based on research indicating that brides shop and buy online. That same florist may also decide not to give as much online attention to people buying flowers for special occasions, because those purchases are usually made on impulse by people who want to deliver them in person, hardly the profile of an online shopper.

Figuring the Cost of a Web Site

As with any other construction project, don't start building a Web site until you have a feel for what it will cost and whether you have the funds to complete the project. Chapter 18 walks you through the process of requesting proposals from Web site creation companies, but before you even begin talking with outsiders, consider the costs involved:

✔ **The cost of an Internet Service Provider:** The ISP is the company that hosts your site — putting it on its machines and tracking who is coming to your site. You pay a monthly fee for this service. Refer to Chapter 18 for advice on making the ISP decision.

✔ **The cost of building your site:** The cost of a good site starts at a rock-bottom $500 and shoots all the way to seven figures depending on what you're trying to accomplish. Graphics, animations, and complex features, such as hosting online communities, increase costs. If you hire a Web design company, expect charges for the following:

- Building the navigational system, which determines how the user gets around the site.

- Building the individual graphics.

- Building each page on the site.

- Creating forms that site visitors complete and return via e-mail.

- Producing animations.

- Establishing a means for gathering and tracking information about site visitors. For example, if a customer provides a name, address, phone number, and e-mail address, you need a way to store, use, and update the information.

- Designing a means to accept, approve, and secure credit card transactions.

- Confirming transactions with the customer. Doing so may involve letting customers know that orders have been processed or confirming that they're signed up to receive your e-mail newsletter.

✔ **Buying a domain name:** See Chapter 18 for explanations of the "what," "why," and "how" of domain names, and go to www.internic.net for the current pricing in domain registration.

✔ **Registration and ranking costs:** If you want to register with search engines and directories, you'll pay for the visibility, plus you may want to pony up additional fees for higher rankings. (See Chapter 19 for tips on whether to register and how to get ranked.)

✔ **The cost of site testing:** A Web design company charges you for testing the site to make sure that the links work, that your site works with different Internet browsers, and that the customer can easily locate information on your site.

✔ **Gearing up to handle online inquiries:** Incorporate into your Web site a way for visitors to contact your business via e-mail. You also need to develop a system for checking e-mail at least daily and responding to messages on a prompt basis — which generally means within 24 hours.

✔ **Site updates:** Budget time and funds to keep your site current, accurate, and in perfect working order. But total "remodeling" isn't always a good thing in your customers' eyes, so before you budget for making frequent changes to your site, check out Chapter 18.

Chapter 18

Building Your Web Site

. . . .

. . . .

*I*f you're reading this chapter, then you're close to flipping on an Internet "open" sign for your business. Chances are good that you'll start with a pretty basic site and expand your online marketing effort as your marketing program proves capable of taking the next leap — possibly even into online sales.

This chapter covers the considerations to weigh and the steps to take before committing to a Web site. It wanders with you into the cyber traffic jam of domain names, helping you to choose and register a name. While you're reading this sentence, someone could be grabbing the name you want — on the slim chance that it's still available — so don't wait. If the idea of a Web site is in your near future, turn right now to the section "Choosing a Domain Name."

Another immediate step includes hooking up with an Internet Service Provider — which is a business field that makes shifting sand look permanent. The section "Hiring an Internet Service Provider" gives you tips on what to expect and how to compare and choose a good Internet access point.

Then this chapter is all about creating your site — on your own, with a design firm, or doing part yourself while outsourcing the rest. Either way, be prepared to apply your own marketing skills to achieve a site that contributes to the strength of your marketing program.

Attributes of a Good Site

Take a few hours to cruise the Internet looking for Web site examples to follow or avoid. Good sites have some common strengths:

- ✔ The purpose of the site is clear.
- ✔ You can tell who the company is and what it does.
- ✔ It's easy to find things on the site.
- ✔ You can figure out how to contact people at the company.
- ✔ The site comes up on your computer relatively quickly.
- ✔ The site is easy to read.
- ✔ The look of the site makes a good impression for the company.
- ✔ The site doesn't crash or give you error messages.
- ✔ The content is well written and limited to what you need to know.

As you evaluate sites, ask yourself the following questions:

- ✔ Do you feel lost on the site, or is it clear where to go for specific kinds of information?
- ✔ Once you leave the home page, or the main page, can you easily jump to another section? And then can you find your way back to the home page?
- ✔ Are there so many options and different ways to navigate that you find it just plain confusing?

 To test whether you are a good judge of Web sites, find a few sites that you think are easy to navigate, and then ask others whether they agree. Also, check out Jakob Nielson's site at www.useit.com, where you'll find lists of recommended site design books, an archive of columns on Web usability, and Web user statistics — including the fact that users lose attention if a Web page takes more than ten seconds to download.

Think about speed and ease of use as you rate various sites.

Site-Building Basics

You can turn to software programs and plenty of companies for help building your site. For that matter, you can use Web sites that create — and even host — your site. Here are the factors to consider as you work to build a site that is useful to those who deal with your business.

Creating content

"Content" is the term used to describe electronically delivered information. In the online world you don't hear words like "copy" or "information" or "manuscript." Instead, it's all about "content."

To build good content, you need someone with the following qualifications:

- ✔ Good communications skills
- ✔ Understanding of the products and services that you're offering
- ✔ A clear knowledge of the site's purpose
- ✔ A good understanding of the kinds of people who will be visiting the site, including prospective customers, actual customers, suppliers, media representatives, job applicants, or other groups of people that you think will want to find you online

If you aren't good at "getting things down on paper," rely on the talents of someone who works with you, or contract with a professional writer or editor. Use the following four guidelines as you write and review content:

- ✔ **Limit your words.** Know what you want to communicate, prioritize your objectives, and keep your message to the point.
- ✔ **Make it easy to skim.** Use short, bold headings at the beginnings of paragraphs. Or use bullets, lists, or other devices to make your pages easy to scan.
- ✔ **Talk directly to your customer.** Use short paragraphs and sentences.
- ✔ **Make it worthwhile.** From the very first moment users arrive at your site, you want to give them a reason to stay on your site. Use quotes, testimonials, headlines, graphics, or other quick-to-grasp methods to telegraph the message that "you'll find what you're looking for here."

Especially if you write your Web site material yourself, ask someone who is good at editing *and* unfamiliar with the technicalities of your business to review your Web site material when it is done. Doing so can help you to eliminate jargon and to keep your content focused.

Navigating the site

For all your hard work in content creation to pay off, be sure that visitors can navigate — or travel around — your site easily to find what they're looking for.

The simpler the site, the easier it is to use, so keep it pretty basic in the beginning. Concentrate on two main questions and create your site accordingly.

- ✔ Who will be visiting the site?
- ✔ What questions will they want answered?

Refer to Chapter 2 for help in defining your customer — or in this case your site visitor — and turn to Chapter 8 as you set the objective of your site and what it needs to accomplish.

As users go to various sections of your site, present them with clearly labeled selections. For example, labels such as "Technical Support," "Our Products," "Our Customers," and "Contact Us" tell people way more about what to expect than labels like "Features," "News," and "Information." Here are some tips to keep in mind when setting up your site:

- ✔ Start with a home page that tells visitors exactly what you want them to know about your company — clearly and immediately.
- ✔ Let visitors jump from section to section with ease.
- ✔ Provide links back to your home page from every page.
- ✔ Keep choices clear and to a minimum.

Online, image is everything

When people encounter your business for the first time online, you can't dazzle them with an in-person welcome, offer them fresh coffee, or impress them with the caliber of your business surroundings. You can't let them hold your product or watch it in use. All you can do is present yourself through the images on their computer screens. Your Web site *is* your business to the online visitor. Here are some ways to create a site that advances the right image for your company:

- ✔ **Keep your presentation clean, simple, and attractive — exactly as you would keep your physical location.**
- ✔ **Create a site that feels like an extension of the rest of your marketing materials.** If you worked with a graphics person to design your logo and printed brochures, ask that same person to help you with the graphic layout of your site — *if* that person is experienced in Web site design. Or at least provide whoever does help you create your site with a set of your image guidelines, as described in Chapter 7.

✔ **Use your site to reinforce your company's image and brand.** Chapter 7 is all about branding. Condensed to a single sentence, a *brand* is a name that, when heard, conveys a certain set of attributes that influence how people think and buy. Your brand is the set of characteristics that consumers associate with your name. Even if you don't mean to be creating a brand, you do so every single time you present your company in the marketplace — including through your Web site.

With one glance at your site, people interpret what they see as a reflection of your brand. If your site is slow to load, if it crashes, if it confuses, or if it just plain looks sloppy, they associate those same words with what your business stands for. Your brand isn't a symbol or a logo, but an overall perspective. And your Web site is the projection of your brand to online customers.

Building a site that works

What works on paper doesn't always work via electronic media, where machines crash, sites are slow, fatal errors pop up without warning, and getting lost takes on a whole new meaning.

Evaluate your site for the following three attributes:

✔ **Speed:** Your site must be quick. The time it takes for a site to load can be greatly impacted by something as basic as how the files are saved. Here's a general rule: Keep each page and its components under 20KB.

✔ **Graphics:** A picture's worth a thousand words only if it appears before the user tires of waiting for it to download. Reduce the dimensions of your graphics and use compression software to save time. You can also reduce the quality of the picture or change the file type.

✔ **Accessibility:** Hire someone who really knows computers to test your site, including how it works with all the major browsers.

Hiring an Internet Service Provider

The Internet Service Provider (ISP) world changes daily. Companies get bought, companies go under, companies merge. And it seems that everyone has a cousin who has hung up an ISP shingle.

If you currently get e-mail, then you are hooked up either with an ISP or with an online service, such as AOL. As you dive deeper into online marketing, though, you may want to associate with a different provider who can offer at least the following services.

✔ **Reliably handle e-mail.** Your ISP is the conduit to your e-mail box. The ISP receives your messages and routes them to you. You dial the ISP from your computer to collect and send your mail.

✔ **Provide access to the Internet via a local phone number.**

✔ **Host your Web site at a reasonable cost**, **making sure it stays up and running.** (ISPs charge varying rates for hosting your site, storing your content, and handling site visitors, so definitely shop around.)

✔ **Provide support.** Be sure that you get access when you're on the road, troubleshooting assistance, and, to the degree the ISP can, help fixing your site when something is not working.

You can easily work with an ISP that is not in your local area. Just make sure that you can dial in for access to the Internet and to your e-mail account by using a local number.

Comparison shop before you decide on an ISP. Figure 18-1 shows a page from the Zdnet.com Web site, where you can find ISP selection recommendations along with an interactive ISP search service.

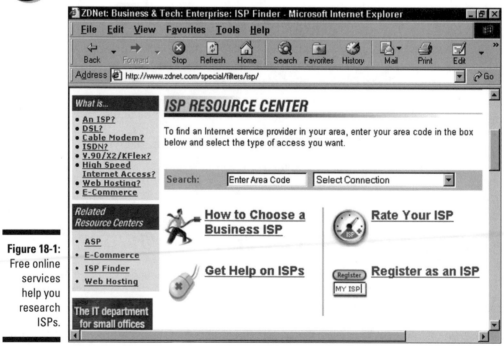

Figure 18-1:
Free online services help you research ISPs.

Choosing a Domain Name

A domain name is comprised of the string of characters that someone types in to get to your Web site. (It can also be used to locate you in e-mail and in other ways.) As an example, as you see on the back cover of this book, dummies.com is the domain name for the *For Dummies* books site.

You don't have to buy your own domain name, but think about it — would you rather have your customers have to type in www.yourname.com or www.chicagonet.com/~yourna/index.html?

Your cyberspace identity

The domain name is your online ID. It is composed of two parts: your name on the left and the "zone" on the right, separated by the now-famous "dot."

Different endings — which are also called top-level domains — have different meanings. For example, .com means that you're dealing with a company.

Here is a list of the three-letter zones and what they mean:

- .com: Commercial site or company
- .gov: U.S. government
- .org: Nonprofit organization
- .net: Network organization
- .mil: U.S. military
- .int: International organization
- .edu: Educational institution

Two-letter zones indicate country zones. For example

- .ca: Canada
- .us: United States
- .uk: United Kingdom

Your business only needs one domain name. If you are cookies.com, then you don't need to also go by cookies.org. The exception is that large global companies use names with various international codes to specify their international offices. For example, Microsoft.com/uk is the address for information about Microsoft products and services in the United Kingdom.

Choosing your domain name is an important step in online marketing for several reasons.

- You want something that's easy for your customer to remember.
- The right domain name can help you earn a higher ranking from search engines.
- Experienced users try guessing at your domain name by typing your company's name plus .com before they bother to try to find you by using search engines.

It's not yours until the registrar says so

The problem with domain names is that many good ones — in fact 98 percent of all words in the English dictionary — are already reserved. If the domain name you want for your business is already taken, you have a couple options.

- Get creative and come up with a different name that has something to do with your products and services and is easy for those who deal with your business to remember.
- Try to purchase your first-choice name from the existing owner.

This process is typically very expensive and usually takes some time.

To start your domain name search, go to the Web site of Network Solutions (www.networksolutions.com). This site (see Figure 18-2) can tell you

- Information about how domain names work and how to choose one.
- What domain names are already registered.
- How to buy or register your name. You can expect to pay around $70 to register an available domain name for a two-year period, which is the standard registration period.

  Be prepared to renew your registration several years down the road when the initial registration period is up. If you forget, then someone else can purchase your domain name.

Stay tuned for new top-level domain names such as .web and .shop. These names will open up a whole new domain name opportunity.

The Web Site Construction Blueprint

Okay, once you've decided to create a Web site, defined its purpose, hired an Internet Service Provider, and snagged a domain name, you're ready to start site construction.

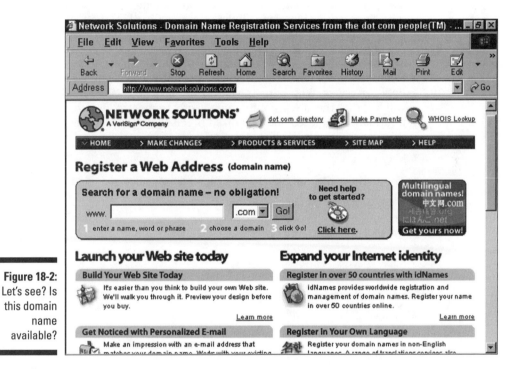

Figure 18-2:
Let's see? Is this domain name available?

Storyboarding your site

Storyboarding is the term used for creating the framework for your site.

1. **Define your customer.**

   This step is covered in Chapter 17. Who will use your site? What will users seek online? How do you prioritize their needs? The answers to these questions will guide your site development.

2. **Arrange your site.**

   The whole point is to help visitors quickly and easily find what they're looking for. Being redundant — or having the same information in several sections of your site — is perfectly okay and probably even necessary to make site visitors feel that your business is configured to meet their needs.

A Web site is composed of individual pages that can be linked to from any other place on the site. But don't make visitors jump around unnecessarily. If it makes sense to present the same information on three different pages because each page addresses a different visitor interest, so be it.

If you return to the florist business profiled in Chapter 17, it's clear that most site visitors are interested in buying — what else? — flowers. But some visitors are looking for wedding arrangements or special-occasion gifts. So instead of lumping all the offerings together, the florist should create two pages, one titled "Wedding Center" and one titled "Flower Arrangements." Each page can include some unique offerings and some offerings that are exactly the same as those on the other page. The redundancy is a customer bonus that eliminates a lot of back-and-forth between pages. Whether site visitors are brides or gift shoppers, they will feel that the site is configured exactly to meet their needs, with information targeted and organized precisely to their interests, rather than for the convenience of the florist.

3. **Map your site.**

The florist's site map would look like the map shown in Figure 18-3.

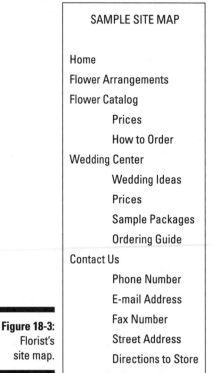

SAMPLE SITE MAP

Home
Flower Arrangements
Flower Catalog
      Prices
      How to Order
Wedding Center
      Wedding Ideas
      Prices
      Sample Packages
      Ordering Guide
Contact Us
      Phone Number
      E-mail Address
      Fax Number
      Street Address
      Directions to Store

Figure 18-3:
Florist's
site map.

Optimizing your site for search engines

You may decide that you're building your site exclusively for use by existing customers or for people whom you will direct to the site through personal presentations, advertisements, or sales literature. If so, then your existing marketing communications probably are sufficient to promote your site among its targeted clientele.

But if you want your site to be a point of introduction for your business — and a way to recruit entirely new prospects — then you'll probably want to be included in search engines. Chapter 19 is all about driving traffic to your site once it's up and running, and provides an overview of how search engines work and how you can use them to your advantage.

At the design phase, you'll want to plan your site to optimize how it ranks in the search engines. Lay the groundwork for inclusion in search engines by asking yourself what words and word combinations customers are going to use to find you online. Then write down all the thoughts that come to mind. Ask friends and customers to help by sharing the words and word combinations they think people might use when trying to find businesses like yours online.

Then prioritize and pick just 15 of those words or word combinations to incorporate into your text and programming code as you design your site. Then, when an Internet user puts those words into a search engine, the engine will be able to find your site. The way that you use the words — in text and in code — can help you optimize your site design for search engines. For more information, read the section on search engines in Chapter 19, and visit www.searchenginewatch.com for current information on registering and ranking online.

Deciding whether to collect customer data online

Another consideration that affects your site design is whether you request or require that site visitors provide you with personal information.

Many sites ask visitors to register before entering the site, and others require information before doing business. Usually these steps involve the collection of identifying information such as name, e-mail address, mailing address, and profiling information such as how the visitor arrived at the site, buying preferences, and desire for additional information.

Before deciding to collect visitor data, weigh these questions:

- ✔ **Will the request annoy visitors?** Many people refuse to register when visiting new sites. Will forcing them to provide information drive them away? If so, will the request cause them to lose interest in doing business with you?

- ✔ **Will you actually use the data?** Many companies go to great lengths to collect customer data that they never use again. If you decide to collect data, collect only what you know you will use. For example, if you send only e-mail communications, then you need only e-mail addresses, not street addresses.

- ✔ **How will you update the data?** Customer data changes frequently, and it's useful only if you keep it current.

- ✔ **What will it cost to collect and maintain the data?** Collecting customer information requires storage, which means development of a database, including setup, tracking, and updating.

The government is considering legislation and rules that regulate how consumer data is collected and used on Web sites. Protecting the privacy of the end consumer is a major concern. Make sure that you keep up with the laws. Sites like `www.wilsonweb.com` and `www.internetworld.com` both provide the most up-do-date developments on these issues.

Making the Do-It-Yourself or Outsourcing Decision

By now, you've done your storyboard. You've made preliminary decisions about how people will arrive at your site. And you've given thought to whether your site needs a mechanism for collecting visitor information.

Now it's time to actually start building.

That means it's time for a decision. Are you going to do this yourself or work with a professional designer? The steps involved are the same either way; the only difference is who will do the work and what level of expertise you will assign to the job.

In making this decision, ask yourself a few questions:

- ✔ Do you have time to create your own site?

- ✔ Is it worth your time to devote your effort to this task?

- ✔ Do you have at least basic computer and design skills?

By relying on the talents in your company, professional writing resources, and the "Creative Brief" sample and instructions in Chapter 8, developing your content is probably the easiest part to manage on your own.

The harder parts involve figuring out the site navigation, determining the look and feel of the site, making sure that the image reinforces your company brand, and actually building and testing the site to ensure that it works.

Hiring help

Web site development costs can range in price from $500 to millions of dollars. The hardest part about hiring a company to build your site is knowing what you're getting — and getting into.

Chapter 9 includes information about hiring marketing professionals, including requesting and evaluating proposals and defining contractual obligations. Much of the same information applies to your selection of a Web design firm.

The most important first step is to know what you're trying to achieve before you ask companies to offer you a proposed solution. With detailed specifications in hand, the Web companies do a better job of creating their bids, saving everyone time and effort. Plus, all design companies will be responding to the identical request, making the comparison of proposals an apples-to-apples proposition. Most of all, by defining what you want in advance, you'll eliminate many costly changes later.

Creating a request for proposal

The request for proposal should include the following:

- ✔ **Brief background information on your company.** Notice the word "brief." The design firms aren't trying to learn how to manage your company, only how to create a good Web site. Boil your information into a short statement that is just enough to help them understand your marketing objective — and no more.

- ✔ **A profile or description of the kinds of people you expect to visit your site.** Again, reduce it to a sentence, or a sentence for each visitor group.

- ✔ **Your site storyboard.** This can be a simple outline of how you think your site should work, as shown in the example in Figure 18-3.

- ✔ **How you plan to drive traffic to the site.** If you want to use the Web site as a way to bring new people into your business, then you'll probably want to be listed and ranked with search engines, and the designers need to know this in advance. They also need to know the key terms that you want the search engines to find.

✔ **The addresses of sites that are similar in look and complexity to the one that you would like to create.**

✔ **Copies of current marketing materials that represent your image guidelines.**

✔ **The level of site testing you expect from the design firm, and what you plan to do on your own.** (See "Testing your site," later in this chapter.)

✔ **The ways you plan to evaluate your site.** This will help the designers know what kinds of site traffic analyses and reports you will need, which will affect the overall site design. (See Chapter 19 for information on the ways that you can analyze your site effectiveness.)

Be organized as you solicit proposals and even more organized as you launch the project. Web design companies agree that the top two reasons that design costs run over the estimated budget are 1) unclear purpose and 2) content that wasn't ready when it was needed. Shave unnecessary expenditures off your Web design by being prepared, not changing your mind frequently, and having your content ready to hand off when it is needed.

Seeking responses from design companies

First, a reality check. If you're seeking a very simple, inexpensive site, don't ask a dozen firms to compete for the business. The scope of the project won't merit the bidding effort. Instead, interview a few firms, choose the one that instills the most confidence, and then ask that company for a cost estimate and design proposal.

On the other hand, if your site is complex, interview several firms and ask for bids from a short list of just two or three.

1. **Draw up a list of good Web site design firms.**

   You can find such firms by asking business associates for the names of good design companies. You can also look at the sites of local businesses. As you find sites you like, call and ask who created them.

2. **Narrow the list to those firms you want to consider.**

   Call each one and ask for general company information including a list of sites they have designed. Then take the time to view the sites. If you can't figure them out or don't like the look, take the company's name off your list. Focus on the companies that build sites that you like and that you think your customers will understand.

3. **Give your requirements to a select number of design companies.**

   Reach outside your local area if necessary to find the right talent, but do so realizing that communication over a distance is harder and more time-consuming. And in this arena, time *is* money.

Evaluating proposals

As you evaluate proposals, consider the following.

- ✔ Did the company respond to your request? Did it meet your requested proposal delivery date? Did it address the specific topics you outlined?

- ✔ Do you understand what the company says it will provide? If not, ask for clarification. Assume nothing.

- ✔ Call references. Ask whether the firm was easy to work with, if it stuck to the budget, if it produced quality work, and what happened when problems arose.

- ✔ Compare work samples.

- ✔ Clarify who will actually be doing the work, and decide whether you have confidence in the talents and working style of that person.

Signing a contract

Most Web design firms will have a contract for you to sign, but if they don't, make sure you have one created. The contract should cover the following:

- ✔ **An estimated cost of the site design:** This should include a breakdown of design time and outside costs involved.

- ✔ **What the estimate covers:** Has the firm based its estimate on the total number of hours it thinks will be involved? Has it provided a detailed breakdown of estimated costs involved with the delivery of such elements as graphics, navigation, testing, and other site-creation tasks so that you can go down the list and be sure that all necessary costs are covered in the estimate? Are time and costs for travel, if any, included? Is a round of changes included in the fee? Will additional changes lead to additional costs?

  Include a clause stating that the cost estimate cannot be exceeded without your prior written authorization. As you work with the designers to construct your site, you may make decisions that alter the scope and therefore the cost of the project. This clause assures that you understand how your requests will impact the price of creating your site — *before* you see the surprise on an invoice.

- ✔ **The payment due date:** Many Web design companies require a partial payment at the onset of the project. This payment schedule is standard, but make sure that you aren't required to pay the balance until the site is live, tested, and fully functioning. Put into writing the fact that final payment is based on your sign-off and acceptance of the site.

- ✔ **What happens if the site doesn't work:** Stipulate in the contract whether the design firm has to absorb the cost of alterations required to fix dead links and site crashes within a specified period.

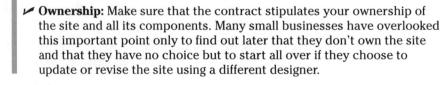

- ✔ **Penalties for non-performance:** These state that you will pay less if the firm doesn't meet the deadlines or the expectations.

- ✔ **Performance milestones:** Include a timeline that sets dates for major steps in the process, including your deadline for providing content (and in what format).

- ✔ **Ownership:** Make sure that the contract stipulates your ownership of the site and all its components. Many small businesses have overlooked this important point only to find out later that they don't own the site and that they have no choice but to start all over if they choose to update or revise the site using a different designer.

Handing off the content

Because you're the expert on your business, most likely you will build the content or at least oversee its development and provide it in a ready-to-go form to the design firm. Content includes the storyboard, the text for each page, the pictures, and any other graphics you are creating for the site. You'll make the process go smoother if you follow these suggestions:

- ✔ Create and provide the content in an electronic format that meets the agreed-upon specifications, so that you eliminate unnecessary costs and errors.

- ✔ The closer you can get your content to finished form, the less time (and therefore money) the designer will spend building your site.

- ✔ Be concise and clear with your instructions regarding how you want the content to appear.

- ✔ Be thorough with your preparations. Don't send your content in dibs and dabs.

- ✔ Review your content carefully before you hand it off. Complete all your editing *before* the designers begin working on the site — not after, when changes cost time and money.

If you do it yourself

To create your own site, you can rely on the resources provided by a Web creation site, or you can use software tools to start from scratch on your own. See *Creating Web Pages For Dummies*, 5th Edition, by Bud Smith and Arthur Bebak (Hungry Minds, Inc.), for details on how to publish your own Web page.

Using a Web page creation site

Web page creation sites walk you through the process of building a site.

✔ **Advantages:** Web creation sites make it easy for you to build and maintain your own site. You don't have to buy software tools or hire a Web design company. Many sites are free, and some will also host your site, eliminating the need for an Internet Service Provider.

✔ **Disadvantages:** Web creation sites limit your design options and the features that you can incorporate into your site.

Examples of Web creation sites include:

✔ Bigstep.com, shown in Figure 18-4, is a great free service full of example sites and case histories, a free "test drive" through the site creation process, and a range of free support and add-on fee services.

✔ Geocities.com is the free Yahoo! Web construction site, also offering business domain name registration and Web site hosting services.

✔ Angelfire.com is the Lycos construction site, with free online building tools and tips, personalized URLs, and lots of Web site samples.

Figure 18-4:
Bigstep.com
provides a
gallery of
sample sites
to guide
your
construction
plans.

If you plan to use a Web creation site, you need at least basic computer skills and should be comfortable using a word processor or publishing software. You also need to be certain that the time spent saving money on site design isn't time that you could better spend managing and marketing your business. This comes back to the questions asked earlier: Do you have the time, and is it worth your time to take on this task?

Using software tools

If you want more design flexibility and a wider range of site features, consider buying software tools and building the site yourself. You need at least intermediate computer skills, expertise using word processing or publishing software, and a comfortable knowledge of your operating system. You'll have to buy software tools such as Adobe Page Mill and Go Live, Microsoft Front Page/Express, and Netscape Communicator. Keep in mind that tools change frequently. Software resellers can help you decide what's best, as well as help you to determine the best way to learn and use the software.

You also need an eye for design, but not actual design skills. Most of these tools include design templates to let you build a good Web site without bringing your own artistic and Web layout background to the task.

Using HTML to build your site

HTML stands for Hypertext Markup Language, the code that underlies most Web pages and the common language of the Web. HTML codes tell your browser what's what in a Web page — what's a heading, where a picture goes, and everything else that you see on your screen.

Part of the appeal of the software tools mentioned in the previous section is that they eliminate the need to learn HTML altogether by building the code for you. But if you do decide to use HTML as a programming language, you'll find plenty of tutorials and books available to simplify the task. On top of that, to build a Web site all you really need is an understanding of part of the programming language — kind of like learning a phrase book instead of taking a full language course.

Testing your site

Self-evident as it sounds, test your site before you launch it.

An embarrassing number of businesses learn that their brand-new sites don't work only when their customers call to say that the sites aren't usable. Take the following steps to spare yourself trouble later:

✔ Ask friends, family, and employees who have never seen your site to perform tasks that your typical customer will be trying to accomplish. Does the wording on the site make sense to them? Do they find the information that they are looking for? Do they encounter obstacles or problems?

Get feedback from at least five people before you change your site. Be sure the problem you hear isn't unique to one user.

✔ Measure how fast your site comes up on your screen. Realize that most people access the Internet with a 56K or slower modem. Any wait time of over ten seconds is completely unacceptable to most users.

✔ Check out your site by using different browsers. Try it on AOL, Netscape Navigator, and Microsoft's Internet Explorer to measure how fast your site comes up on the screen and to see whether the formatting meets your expectations.

✔ Check each link to make sure that it works. Links are places that you can click to get to another page. Wherever your site offers a link, test it. Be sure that it goes where you expect it to go.

Planning Changes to Your Site

Most small companies feel compelled to constantly change their Web sites. This costs time and money, often with a negative return on investment, because too often the changes only confuse the customer. Instead of undertaking ongoing site changes, schedule changes on regular intervals, say once a quarter. Or time all your changes to coincide with the addition of new products or services to the site. You can make an exception if your site has major errors that are frustrating to the customer, in which case you need to make changes now!

When and why to update your Web site

Before you face the obstacle of site updates, think about whether you really need to change your site constantly. If you expect to have the same customer returning to your site often and frequently, then you'll have to have changing content to make each visit worthwhile. But if you're using your site solely to generate leads, which you then handle directly or via the phone, then you don't need to update your site, because the same people likely won't return twice.

The following examples describe two fictional businesses — one that benefits from a Web site capable of conveying changing information and the other that benefits from a Web site with a reliable, constant message:

Think Snow is a fictional retailer selling ski gear, ski wax, and clothing. A typical customer visits the store and makes purchases two or three times a year. The owner would like to use a Web site as a way 1) to gain business from customers who do not live in the area but who usually shop when they're in town on ski vacations and 2) to increase sales by enhancing relationships with local shoppers. A good way for the owner to accomplish both objectives is to use the site as the pulse point for local ski activity — by posting ski race schedules and results, upcoming mountain events, local ski conditions, daily wax recommendations, and in-store specials and promotions.

Obviously such a site needs to be designed for continuous update to constantly re-attract the same customers.

Jim Smith is a lawyer who specializes in divorces. He uses his site to let people know about his business, his credentials, his reputation, and why people want to do business with him. Most people need a divorce lawyer only once (hopefully). When that single time comes, Jim wants them to call him.

It doesn't make sense for Jim's site to constantly change. Customers will visit the site only once. They don't need changing information, and in fact should they return a second time, they would probably be comforted by the fact that Jim is still presenting the same reliable, consistent image.

When changing a site is a bad thing

Imagine if you walked into your favorite grocery store and the location of everything had been reorganized. The aisle where you found eggs the last time is now where you find shampoo. Milk is where vegetables used to be. And *this* week they no longer carry your favorite ice cream. How long would your favorite store remain your favorite store? Is change always a good thing for the customer? Of course not.

Sites like www.usatoday.com are constantly updated, but other than a change in the news, nothing alters the customer experience on the site.

As you consider how to provide changing content on your site, consider the following points:

- ✔ Change your content but don't constantly change the experience of the customer. For more information on the importance of establishing and maintaining a consistent look and image, see Chapter 7.
- ✔ If you're going to alter your site, save up your changes, make them all at once and only once in a while, and alert your visitors to expect changes. Explain the new features as *benefits* to those who visit your site.

✔ Repairing your site isn't the same as changing your site. If something isn't right, don't think twice — fix it immediately. Dead links or other site mishaps are interpreted by site visitors as a lack of customer concern. Do everything you can to avoid them.

Site Design Checklist

As you review your site design for final approval, run through the list presented in Table 18-1 for advice to follow and mistakes to avoid.

Table 18-1	Site Design Considerations
DO	**DON'T**
Do consider that your online customer may need personal assistance when you aren't available to offer it. Include e-mail on your site and promise customers your prompt reply.	Don't assume that customers who need personal assistance will be satisfied to simply call you back if you're not available when they first try to contact you.
Do treat your Web site like all other marketing materials. Launch it when it is ready and not a second before.	Don't allow a partial launch, with parts of your site labeled "Under Construction." You wouldn't hand out brochures with parts headlined, "Sorry, this part wasn't done when the presses rolled." Use the same judgment online.
Do protect ownership of your site. Include a copyright notice followed by the year at the bottom of your home page, for example, © 2001, Your Business Name.	Don't make assumptions about your site ownership. Follow the formal steps to protect your copyright. Visit the U.S. Copyright Office Web site at: http://lcweb.loc.gov/copyright/.
Do be moderate with your use of graphics. Design it so that someone on a modem connection can download your site within just a few seconds.	Don't overlook the reality that three things slow the download: the size of your site and its graphics, the computer that your site is hosted on, and the speed of the connection the host has to the rest of the Internet.
Do check out the latest in site design research on www.useit.com where you can keep up with evolving Web design principles, technologies, and online features.	Don't steal content or graphics from other sites. Seek permission from the site owner or author before using material you see online.
Do keep your site clean and professional and keep your site navigation easy.	Don't create one of the many sites that suffer from too much flash and too little focus on why the customer came there in the first place.

Chapter 19

Driving Traffic to Your Web Site

· ·

In This Chapter

▶ Finding ways to promote your site

▶ Getting ranked by search engines and directories

▶ Marketing your site through electronic newsletters, Web rings, discussion groups, and affiliation programs

▶ Understanding banner advertising terms, costs, and swapping programs

▶ Discovering the best traffic-building methods for your site

▶ Measuring the effectiveness of your Web site

· ·

*T*he big Web myth is that millions upon millions of people are cruising the Net looking to find your business online. The truth boils down to something more like this: Opening a Web site isn't all that different from getting a toll-free phone number. It is a huge customer convenience *once you tell people about it.*

Driving people to your site is what this chapter is all about.

It presents information on how people find businesses online, ways to match your site marketing with your customer profile and site objectives, and — finally — how to measure the effectiveness of your online marketing effort.

Promoting Your Web Site

Having a Web address is the litmus test for "cool" in business today. Everyone wants a site because everyone else seems to have a site. But having a site helps your business to expand only if you succeed in promoting it effectively and before the right audiences.

With the exception of pure listing sites, the launch of your Web site should begin an intensive effort to integrate your site address into all your other marketing efforts.

Start by "coattailing" on all the communications that your business currently sends into the marketplace. Use this checklist as you look for appropriate places to include your site address.

✔ **Add your site address to your stationery products.** Look beyond letterhead to order forms, invoices, fax cover sheets, envelopes, and especially business cards.

✔ **Check your signage.** Add the site address to your company sign and to promotional signs used at special events and trade shows — but only if people can easily read the address. Otherwise don't bother.

✔ **Use news releases to get your address in circulation.** Start by sending a release announcing your site address to media in your local community, in the areas where you have offices or do significant business, and to the publications that serve your industry. Then on an ongoing basis, include the site address in the closing paragraph of all news releases that you send. (See Chapter 15 for more on news releases.)

✔ **Include your site address in the signature of your e-mail messages.** Instead of just signing your name at the end of your messages, include your site address. To automate the process, go to the help section of your e-mail program for instructions on setting up a signature file that allows e-mail recipients to click on your address to go directly to your Web site. (For more information on e-mail messages and automatic signatures, including the value of including a company tag line, refer to Chapter 6.)

✔ **Feature your site address on ads, in brochures, and on other sales literature.** If your marketing includes an emphasis on television and radio advertising, try to choose a Web site address that is easy to hear, understand, and remember. Otherwise you may be wasting valuable airtime to spell out an address that few can recall afterwards. As you consider addresses, test them on friends. As an example, think about the difference in recall for these two: www.cookiesncream.com and www.cookies.com. One is obviously faster to spell out on air and far easier to recall correctly later.

✔ **Look beyond your marketing program for other existing communication opportunities.** Include your site address on product documentation, on packaging, and certainly on instruction materials — especially if your site features customer support. Use the telephone to market your Web site by including the address in your voice mail message. Also, be sure that everyone in your business who might answer the phone knows your site address and is able to share it with callers.

How People Find Businesses Online

Millions of shoppers are "just looking" online, but with more than a *billion* Web pages to visit, the chance of randomly landing at your address is remote at best.

People need to be led to your site, usually through one of the following ways:

✔ Through your letterhead, business cards, brochures, and ads

✔ Via personal contact with someone from your business

✔ Reading an electronic newsletter that you send out

✔ Reading an educational article that you write for another site

✔ Entering a keyword in a search engine or directory

✔ Clicking on a banner advertisement

✔ Finding your address included on another site or in another electronic newsletter

✔ Receiving a "tell a friend" message from someone who visited your site

✔ Through an affiliate program

Using Search Engines and Directories

Search engines such as Lycos (www.lycos.com) and directories such as Yahoo! (www.yahoo.com) are sites where customers go to find what they're looking for online. The difference between a search engine and a directory is the way that information is cataloged.

✔ **Search engines** collect information automatically, using a program called a "spider" that "crawls" around the Web reading and indexing Web sites and sending the keywords of sites back to the search engine index. Then when someone asks the engine to perform a search, it goes to its database to find the sites with words that match the request. The most important search engines that robotically "spider" or index your site include AltaVista (see Figure 19-1), Excite, Google, HotBot, Lycos, Northern Light, and WebCrawler. You can find them at the following addresses

- AltaVista: www.altavista.com

- Excite: www.excite.com

- Google: www.google.com

- HotBot: www.hotbot.com

- Lycos: www.lycos.com

- Northern Light: www.northernlight.com

- WebCrawler: www.webcrawler.com

✔ **Directories** are site listings categorized by people who read the sites and index the information. The most recognized directory is Yahoo! (www.yahoo.com) (see Figure 19-2), followed by many industry-specific directories.

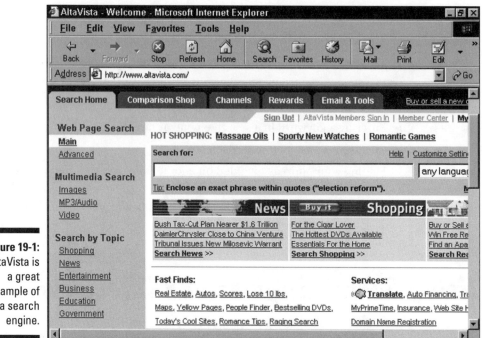

Figure 19-1:
AltaVista is
a great
example of
a search
engine.

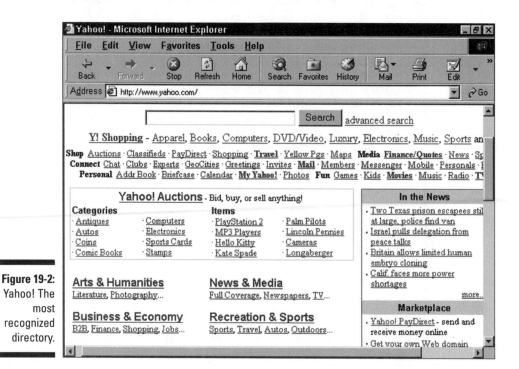

Figure 19-2:
Yahoo! The
most
recognized
directory.

How search engines and directories work

Search engines use various approaches for accessing and cataloging site information, and the rules change constantly to improve the service provided to online customers.

Directories such as Yahoo! are more static simply because real people read and categorize the information, and doing that takes longer and therefore the information can't be updated as often.

But regardless of whether you're being listed by a search engine or a directory, some elements of your site affect how easily people can find it.

✔ **The text on your Web site:** The good news is that the content on your site triggers how search engines find you. The bad news is that each search engine has its own way to catalog text, with no universal formula that you can write to.

Most (though not all) search engines look for *keywords,* which are key descriptors in your text. Some search engines scan the entire site, and others just go through the first 300 or so words. To be safe, include your keywords not only often but also early in your site. Be aware that some search engines hunt only for single words, while others can search two-word descriptors. Have at least some of both.

Don't leave it up to your site designer to choose your keywords. You know better than anyone else the words people will use when they look for your products, so make the selections and direct the designers accordingly.

As an example, consider a company selling bicycle parts online. Getting ranked in search engines is key to its success, but it also needs to limit the amount of time and money spent building its site around different words. Getting listed under "bikes" or "bike parts" might be one approach, but if customers type either of these words into a search engine or directory, they will get back thousands of responses and, unless the online retailer can get ranked in the top 10, which is highly unlikely, it won't benefit from much traffic.

The business could build its site around words such as "brakes" or "wheelsets," but searches for those words will cross over into nonbiking industries — and again it is unlikely that the site will come up in the top ten.

A good approach is for the company to study the products that sell well on the site, and then to build the site around those names, which are specific to the bike industry and of prime interest to the target market.

✔ **The commands in the HTML programming code on your Web site:** These are called <META> tags, and you can't see them on your site. They're hidden so that the search engines can more easily scan your content. Some search engines index only the words that appear in <META> tags, so definitely direct your designer to include codes for the keywords and descriptions that will optimize your ability to be found by search engines.

- ✓ **The number of other sites that include links referring people to your site:** Here's where marketing comes to the rescue. You need to make alliances, write articles, and undertake the many activities described over the rest of this chapter to get your site address in other sites to increase its recognition by search engines.

- ✓ **The number of times people click on your site:** Traffic builds traffic. Advertise your site and give people a reason to visit it. As visitors increase, so does your recognition by search engines.

- ✓ **Whether you register your site with search engines and directories, and whether you pay additional fee-based services to promote your site on the search engines:** This step is explained in the following section.

Be aware that even the search engine with the widest coverage keeps track of only 16 percent of the Web's pages, and the top 11 search tools combined index only a minor portion of the Web. These percentages will decline even further as more people go online with Web sites. The search engines and directories simply can't keep up!

Before counting on search engines and directories to direct customers to your site, ask yourself the following questions:

- ✓ Is my product unique or hard to find?

- ✓ Am I offering products or services on a national basis?

- ✓ Do I have a minimal competition on the Web?

- ✓ Do people already know that they need or want my product?

- ✓ Are there specific words that people will consistently use to find my product?

If you answer yes to all five of these questions, then focusing your efforts to get listed in search engines and directories will be well worth your while. But if you answer no to even one of these questions — in other words if your product is widely available, if competition is stiff, if the need for your product still needs to be developed, or if people all explain your offering using different words — then the major effort involved to list and be ranked with search engines may not deliver returns for your business.

Getting listed and ranked in search engines

Search engines and directories are constantly updating the way that they categorize sites for searches. A good place to find the latest information is Search Engine Watch (www.searchenginewatch.com). This site is packed with lists of search engines including site addresses, reviews, and advice and information on how to get ranked on each site, along with registration directions (see Figure 19-3).

Registering your site

To register with most search engines, all you have to do is go to the site, enter your Web address, and provide your e-mail address. The search engine takes it from there, sending out its spider to index your site and add the findings to the search engine's data bank for use when someone is looking for the kinds of things you offer.

For information on site registration, go to Submit It (www.submit-it.com), where you'll find details on how to register and promote your site with search engines, along with a registration service that enters you into a package of search engines for free, with additional services available at various fees. Be aware that you don't need to contact the search engines when you make changes to your site. The spiders go out every few weeks and automatically notice your revisions.

Search engines can lose registrations. Also, your site can be dropped from the index if the search engine performs several routine rechecks and your site is unavailable. Every six months, at least, scan the line-up of search engines to be sure your site appears and also to watch for new search engines on which you should register your site.

Ranking online

The process of registering your site is the easy part of online marketing. It is the steps preceding the moment of registration that affect your success. To rank well in search engines and directories, you must design your site to feature the words and word combinations that people are going to use most often when they try to find you — or someone who offers products like yours — online. (For more information, see Chapter 18.)

Getting ranked online is like getting your news release printed in newspapers and magazines. There are no guarantees that your efforts will result in your desired outcome every time, but you have to try anyway. Create the best site you can, gear it toward your target market, use the words they use, and register with crossed fingers. Then study your results and be ready to adjust your site based on search engine and customer response.

Generating Business via E-Mail

The Internet has opened a whole new opportunity for direct contact with prospects and customers. Because of the ease, efficiency, and popularity of e-mail, marketers can send promotional messages exactly as they used to send direct mail, but without the printing, handling, postage, and time lapses involved in the postal process.

Especially if customers request the e-mail — if they *opt in* by asking for information on relative topics — e-mail is a highly effective marketing vehicle. But just like with traditional direct mail, electronic e-mail includes a lot of unsolicited and annoying mass junk mail, called spam in the online world.

Sending unsolicited e-mail is just plain not an effective way to market to individuals. At the least, you'll alienate a good number of the recipients, and at the most, you'll run head into the justice system, as many states are considering laws against the electronic distribution of spam.

Spam — *Is it or isn't it?*

Spam is the term for e-mail that is sent to a large number of e-mail addresses — none of whom requested the information, and most of whom feel invaded when they find the message in their in-box. Spam is the polar opposite of "opt-in mailings" and something to avoid at all costs.

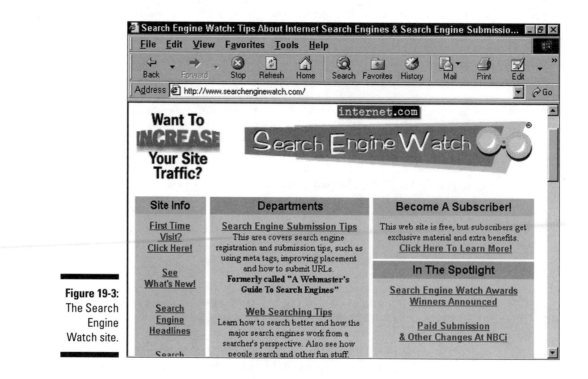

Figure 19-3:
The Search Engine Watch site.

If you can answer yes to at least one of the following questions, you're probably not spamming anyone:

- ✔ Did the recipient ask you to provide information?

- ✔ Do you know this recipient? Is the recipient a friend, a colleague, a supplier, a customer, or a prospect who previously requested related information from your business?

- ✔ Are you confident that this person is interested in your message because an associate asked you to send the information? As an example, if you're promoting a 10K race by using an e-mail list provided by the local running group, you can be pretty sure that your message will be welcomed. Still, to be safe, include a line in your message associating your business with the referring source — just as you would if you were making a telephone cold call based upon a referral from a mutual friend.

 To avoid becoming an innocent accomplice to spam mailers, don't publish lists of e-mail addresses on your site. You've probably seen company sites that include customer contact lists, event sites that post participant lists, or athletic event sites that post finish results, including names and e-mail addresses. Opportunistic spam mailers, many pornographic in nature, cruise the Net looking for lists like these to add to their mailing lists. Protect your customers by hiding their addresses.

Opt-in electronic newsletters

Effective e-mail marketing begins with a request for information from a prospect or customer. This is called "opting in."

One of the most successful ways to invite people to opt in is by offering to e-mail them a free newsletter full of information on good deals, useful tips, and advice.

Here are some questions to ask before you dash out to start creating newsletters:

- ✔ **What is the purpose of your newsletter?** How will it be worth the reader's time? Will it announce specials and events? Will it provide product tips? Will readers be the first to know of new product arrivals?

- ✔ **How often will customers want to hear from you?** An office supplies distributor may determine that customers want to receive special offers and order reminders weekly. Meanwhile, customers of a resort hotel may want a reminder only four times a year — once before each season. Let market interest, market cycles, and common sense guide your schedule.

✔ **Do you have the time and skills to produce a newsletter?** Newsletters require the talent of someone who is good at marketing and someone who is capable of writing both well and at the interest level of the audience. You can do it yourself, assign the task within your company, or invest in outside talent. But no matter what, commit to the project for the long haul, because the value of opt-in newsletters is the opportunity they provide to build lasting customer relationships.

✔ **How will you create, update, and use your customer e-mail list?** You'll find shelves of software to help you build and keep your mailing list. Check with your software dealer and do research on the Internet at sites such as InternetWorld.com (www.internetworld.com).

Newsletter writing etiquette

Because the Web provides a one-to-one medium, people have come to expect online messages that speak to them in a one-to-one voice.

As you write your newsletter, write like you talk — as long as when you talk, you speak clearly, use good grammar, and get to the point quickly! Here are a couple of tips to keep in mind:

✔ Be chatty, but not overly informal.

✔ Be relaxed but still businesslike.

Think of the difference between boardroom and Friday-casual office attire. One is relaxed, and the other is buttoned-down, but both are still appropriate to the business environment. Hold the content of your electronic newsletter to the same standard.

Publishing electronic newsletters

Here are some do's and don'ts when publishing newsletters online:

✔ Know the purpose and frequency of your newsletter and stick to what you promise to provide.

✔ Include an easy way for people to remove themselves from your distribution list.

✔ Keep your content short and to the point. Your customer can handle only a couple of screens before tuning out. To hold attention, be sure the newsletter contains information of interest and importance to the customer.

✔ Have a detail-oriented person edit and proofread your newsletter before it goes out.

✔ Save the newsletter as a text file — and not as a word processing file — before sending it out. (Check your word processor for instructions.)

✔ Include a link to your Web site. If you are highlighting a specific part of your site, for example, the page for a new product, then link directly to that page.

✔ Expect people to keep the newsletters. If you present a limited-time offer, be clear about the valid dates. And if you provide links to your site, be sure that those links will work well into the future. (If they don't, a customer trying to link to your site a year from now may think that you've gone out of business.)

✔ Test the newsletter by e-mailing it to a couple test e-mail accounts before sending the full distribution. Use the test to check the formatting and to be sure the links all work.

✔ Send the newsletter in batches if your distribution list is large. By sending a portion of the list each day over, say, a week-long period, you can better manage the responding e-mails and phone calls.

✔ Don't reveal the names on your distribution list in your newsletter. Your software should allow you to send out an e-mail so the receivers can't see who else you sent it to.

✔ Don't give or sell your newsletter list to another group or business. People who have requested your newsletter have entered a trust relationship with your business. By sharing their names, you risk breaking that trust.

✔ Don't send unsolicited newsletters. Tempting as it may be to just add names to your list, don't. Instead, take the time to let people know about your newsletter and invite them to become free subscribers. Otherwise you risk frustrating them by invading their in-boxes with your mailing.

Publishing Articles Online

To publish online, start by referring to the section on generating publicity in Chapter15. Then create a list of Web sites that you think your prospective customers might frequent, and where you might be able to place in-depth, newsy articles.

For example, a florist might write an article for a bridal Web site, advising readers about the latest flower colors, explaining how wedding planners are matching flowers to gowns, and giving ideas for flowers that go further and cost less. Brides-to-be would likely read the article at the same time that they are considering forming a relationship with a florist. The article would aim to establish trust and provide a link to the florist's Web site. To get it published, the florist needs to follow these steps:

✔ Contact the Web site to obtain the name of the editor of the online newsletter or site where you hope your article will be reproduced.

✔ Send an e-mail query:

- Provide a backgrounder on your expertise and a list of topics that you believe would be relevant to site readers — and why.

- Offer to write and submit an article for free in exchange for a link to your site.

- Set a timeline for response. Let the editor know that you would like to be contacted by a certain date and that you will hold the time open to write the article.

Writing articles takes time and effort. If your market area is limited to your local area, writing an article that reaches a national or international audience may deliver very little return for your business — unless your goal is purely to enhance your reputation.

If you have unique expertise and writing ability, you may even get paid to write for other sites. When they purchase articles, sites usually pay between five and ten cents a word for content.

Using Banner Ads

Banner ads are narrow strips — usually 1½ inches high and 4 inches wide — that can be purchased on Web sites to present advertising messages. When viewers click on the banner, they go directly to the advertiser's site.

Here are some factors that influence the effectiveness of a banner ad:

✔ **Creative design:** Animation, questions that invite interaction, free offers, and good use of colors increase ad response.

✔ **Targeted placement:** A shop selling snow goggles is wise to place banner ads on the sites for ski resorts; a regional realtor is likely to get results by advertising on the site for the local newspaper. In other words, place your ads where your prospects are likely to be visiting.

✔ **Frequency:** Get in front of your prospect frequently and be consistent with your message. Many of the top banner ad specialists advocate that you create a number of ads all with similar messages. Try them all out and then quickly — within a day or two — watch what's working and yank the bad ones. You can track your success by watching how many people click on your ad for more information, known in the Web world as a "clickthrough."

Costs and considerations

Companies normally pay for banner ads based either upon the number of people who view the ad *or* the number of people who click on the ad. Following are explanations for the terms that influence online advertising costs.

- **Banner or page views:** This term indicates the number of times the Web page and banner ad are seen by viewers. If the same person views the page five times, that counts as five views. ("Impressions" are the same as banner or page views.)

- **CPM (cost per thousand page views):** The current average CPM is $35, which means that an advertiser pays $35 for every 1,000 people who see its banner ad. This does not mean that the viewers click on the ad, just that they *see* it. Be aware that the CPM price point for banner advertising is highly contended and negotiable. Some sites promise a thousand viewers for as low as $1, while other sites charge up to $200 for access to what they consider a highly exclusive 1,000 viewers.

- **CTR (clickthrough rate):** When advertisers pay based on CTR, they are paying only for the number of times people *click* on the banner ad. Only a few years ago the average CTR was 2 percent (in other words, two out of every 100 viewers clicked on the ad). The CTR has dropped substantially, though, as customers have gotten more accustomed to seeing and avoiding banner ads. Current clickthrough is less than a half percent. The cost for clickthroughs varies by site.

Sites that host banner ads provide a rate card stating pricing and contract terms. When you study the rate card, be aware that it indicates the starting price — and usually the price from which you can negotiate downward.

In selecting sites for your banner ads, your first consideration should be whether the site is likely to attract viewers who match your customer profile. After you feel that a site is a good match, take the following steps:

- Ask for a summary of the demographic profile of the site visitor to confirm that it matches the profile of your target prospect or customer.

- Ask how many times the site is viewed on a typical day, and how many pages a typical person visits during a site visit.

- Verify that the site's software allows you to rotate through a number of different banner ads.

- Avoid contracts that commit your business to extensive advertising on a single site.

- Monitor whether the clickthroughs result in actual purchases of your product or services, or in registrations that allow your business to begin building new customer relationships.

Web Rings

Web rings join related sites into directories that users can go to when they're seeking particular kinds of information (see Figure 19-4). To be effective, Web rings have to remain limited to specific interest areas. For example, a Web ring that revolves around the topic of wolves might feature sites that promote anything from the protection of wolves to artwork featuring wolves. But as long as the site deals with wolves in one way or another, it is a good candidate for inclusion in the ring.

The Web ring is marketed as a single online destination. After visitors arrive, they can go through the directory to access any site in the ring.

For information on Web rings, how to join an existing ring, or how to start a new ring, visit Yahoo! WebRing (www.webring.org).

Discussion Groups

The Internet has changed the way that people purchase products by providing a whole new level of opinion sharing. Through online discussion groups, prospects can talk to current customers, to disgruntled customers, and to customers of competing products before making buying decisions. Even product suppliers are getting in on the act, participating in the discussions to offer product usage advice, to clarify warranty and production information, and to offer opinions on the pros and cons of buying one product over another. To use discussion groups to your business advantage, follow these tips and warnings:

- ✔ Search the Internet for discussion groups that focus on the kinds of products and services you sell.

- ✔ Visit the groups to find out what people are saying and to collect customer feedback.

- ✔ Participate if you have information to add, and share your Web site address when appropriate. But don't post blatant advertising.

   For example, in a discussion group for people with arthritis, the participants probably will react negatively to a drug representative who touts a new drug. But they will be accepting if the same person asks questions and participates in the forum discussion, leaving his or her Web address as the closer.

- ✔ Don't misread the length of participant comments as an indicator of the power of the discussion group. Most people log onto a discussion group just to read, never posting a comment of their own. Be aware though, that each comment — positive or negative — is seen by many people who never make their presence known.

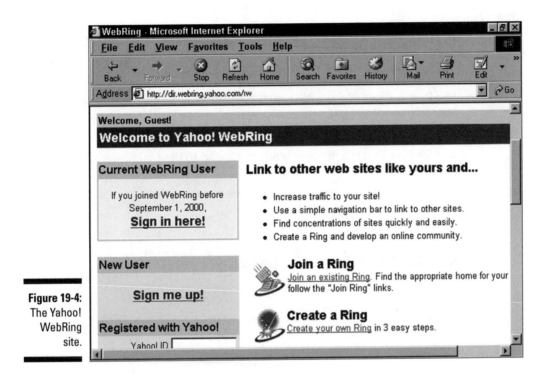

Figure 19-4:
The Yahoo!
WebRing
site.

Online Referrals

Referrals are the way that marketers warm up cold calls. A referral allows you to contact the friend of a friend instead of contacting a stranger. The Internet is rich with opportunities for cultivating various types of referrals online:

- ✔ **Manufacturer referrals:** If you're a retailer, ask manufacturers of the products that you carry to include links to your business on their Web sites.

- ✔ **Professional referrals:** If you belong to a professional organization with a Web site, ask that a link to your Web address be included in the membership roster.

- ✔ **Associate referrals:** If you receive frequent leads from other businesses or organizations, consider swapping links so that a visitor to your site can link to your associate business or organization, and vice versa.

Adding "tell a friend" features to your site

An easy way to increase referrals to your site is to have your Web site designer add a button that allows visitors to send a Web page from your site to a friend. When visitors click on the button, a box appears that allows for insertion of a name and online address. When adding this feature, keep these tips in mind:

- ✔ Be sure that the process sends the friend to the exact location on the site, not just to the home page.

- ✔ Include a feature that allows visitors to write brief notes telling friends why they are receiving the message.

Gaining referrals through affiliate programs

Affiliate programs were the brainchild of Amazon.com, where they were created as a way to entice publishers and other businesses to promote their offerings on the Amazon site.

An affiliate program includes two key players:

- ✔ **The fulfillment company:** This company has products or services to sell. Becoming a fulfillment company takes computer savvy and retailing expertise. It also requires software to track who visits the site, which merchant referred the visitor to the site, and what the person purchased on arrival. The fulfillment company also needs to recruit, manage, and pay commissions to the reseller companies.

- ✔ **The merchant, or reseller company:** This company finds the customers and directs them to the fulfillment site in return for a commission on all resulting sales.

In the case of online booksellers, Amazon.com is the merchant or reseller, and a self-publisher who gains referrals through Amazon.com is the fulfillment company.

If you represent affiliate companies on your site by promoting their products and then linking your visitors to the affiliate site to make the purchase, your e-commerce site is the merchant, and those you link to are the fulfillment companies.

For information on affiliate and referral programs, go to Refer-it.com (www. refer-it.com), where you'll find a long list of affiliate categories across the industries. The site also provides a tutorial in building affiliate programs, along with tools to help you establish and manage your affiliate program.

Prioritizing Your Traffic-Building Opportunities

Use Table 19-1 to match traffic-building methods with your marketing objectives, your budget, your product, and even the time and expertise that you bring to the task.

Table 19-1		Web-Site Traffic Builders		
Traffic-Building Vehicle	**Cost Considerations**	**Computer Expertise**	**Time Commitment**	**Complexity of Product**
Opt-in newsletters	You need list management software; you may need to contract for writing/editing.	Required	You need time to manage lists, create the newsletter, and respond to e-mail and phone calls.	Newsletters work well for explaining complex products or detailed product lists.
Publishing articles online	Minimal costs	Not required	You need time to research and contact sites and to write articles.	Articles on complex issues/products have higher online demand.
Search engines and directories	Site maintenance and optimization can run up to $500 per month.	Required	Time required to monitor online traffic reports and search engine rankings and to adjust your site accordingly.	If you have a distinct product category and clear keywords, then product complexity doesn't matter.
Banner ads	Costs range from $.01 per clickthrough to $35 per 1,000 people who view your ad; costs also are involved to create and update ads.	Not required	Minimal time required.	Product complexity isn't a factor.

(continued)

Table 19-1 *(continued)*

Traffic-Building Vehicle	Cost Considerations	Computer Expertise	Time Commitment	Complexity of Product
Banner ad-swapping programs	Ad placement costs are covered by trade agreements, but you'll incur costs to have ads created.	Not required	Minimal time required.	Product complexity isn't a factor.
Web rings	No expenditures required.	Not required	Minimal time required to register with Web rings.	Web ring visitors discuss products and services, so more complex offerings are more appropriate.
"Tell-a-friend" features	The only costs are incurred at the time of site design.	Not required once the function is added to your site	No time required.	Product complexity isn't a factor.
Referrals from other sites	No expenditures required.	Not required	Time is required to locate good referral sites and to negotiate postings.	Product complexity isn't a factor.
Affiliate programs	Costs are involved to set up the program, and then you'll pay a percentage of revenue from resulting sales.	Yes	Time is required to recruit affiliates, manage them, and make sure they get paid.	Product complexity isn't a factor.

To evaluate which traffic-building efforts are and aren't working, consider setting up what is called a *redirect*. This is a page where referrals will land before being redirected to the appropriate page on your site. By creating a redirect, you can measure traffic coming to your site from each link. You can also use your redirect to measure traffic generated by your opt-in newsletters.

Use redirects only if people are clicking on a link to reach your site. If people have to type in your address, forget about redirecting them because your address will become too long. For example, if you are sending customers to www.mycompany.com, don't make them type in www.mycompany.com/ redirect.html. You may lose them, thereby defeating the purpose of measurement altogether.

Evaluating the Effectiveness of Your Site

A Web site is a big investment. It deserves careful evaluation to measure whether it is delivering the level of visibility, traffic counts, and sales that you projected.

So much data, so little time: Measuring what's important

For a small monthly fee or at no charge at all, most ISPs and hosting companies provide tracking reports for your Web site. These reports include statistics on how many people have visited your site, when they visited, where on your site they traveled, how they arrived, what words they used to find you in search engines, and all kinds of related information.

Your search engine and directory rankings

If you rely on search engines and directories for site traffic, your rankings are key to your success. Your standing will change on a daily basis, so watch your numbers carefully by following the answers to these two questions:

- ✔ **Where do you rank at each search engine?** If you're not making the top 20, don't expect to get many leads.

- ✔ **What words are people using to find you?** If you see that one search engine is successful finding you with certain keywords, you may want to consider focusing on these keywords with other search engines as well.

Watch to see whether certain word combinations — such as your hometown *and* the nature of your business — prove more powerful in drawing qualified prospects.

Your site traffic analysis

Your traffic reports will show whether customers arrived at your site via a search engine or via another site, or because they had saved your address as a bookmark. This information will help you monitor the success you're having with various links and marketing efforts.

To correlate your site traffic with your marketing efforts, use a separate calendar to keep track of all marketing communications that include your site address. Then when you receive your traffic reports, match traffic patterns with marketing efforts to determine which tactics are most effectively driving users to your site.Study your reports with these thoughts in mind:

✔ Various Web tracking software programs vary hugely in the way they track and report data, so don't try to compare reports generated by one kind of software with those from another.

✔ As you study your reports for the geographic origin of visitors, don't get tricked into thinking you have a huge market of willing customers in the state of Virginia. Many of the millions of AOL subscribers are funneled through the AOL hub in Virginia, and show up on tracking reports as if they live in that state.

How people navigate your site

Your reports tell you the links that people clicked while on your site and, therefore, the parts of your site they visited. To learn about how people navigate your site, watch for the following indicators:

✔ Study the areas that prospects are viewing and which areas they never seem to visit. Maybe they're getting lost or confused. If nobody is clicking on a particular portion of your site, step back and study whether the name of that particular area makes sense or whether the information offered is simply not relevant to your customers or prospects.

✔ If you find that most of your site visitors land on your home page but then leave before venturing deeper into your site, consider that you may be marketing your site to people who are uninterested or unqualified to be prospects for your business. The exception is if your home page is designed to answer the majority of a prospect's questions, including information on how to contact your business by phone, mail, or a personal visit.

More stuff to measure

Finally, take time to study how your customers react to your site. Compile and review answers to the following questions:

✔ **What questions do you receive via e-mail?** Your site should include a way for visitors to send e-mail messages to your company. Track the questions that you receive, and see whether you can incorporate the answers the next time that you revise your site.

✔ **How many sales result from visits to your Web site?** When a customer buys a product or service from your bricks-and-mortar establishment, ask how the customer found you in the first place. See how often your Web site comes up as the point of introduction.

✔ **How do customers arrive at and travel through your site?** You can ask your ISP or search the Internet for commercial and free software that lets you track customers through your site, step by step. You can track the version of the browser each customer uses when arriving at your site. You can also track the types of computers that visitors come through.

The true question is: Are you actually going to make business decisions based upon this information? If nothing changes in your business as a result of your data review, then stop spending the time to look at it. But if you will use the information to guide and build your online business, then treasure it, study it, track it, and respond to it. Doing so is how online success stories happen.

Part V
The Part of Tens

The 5th Wave   By Rich Tennant

"Okay, so maybe the Internet wasn't the best place to advertise a product that helped computer illiterate people."

In this part . . .

*I*f you need a shorthand guide to customer service and
satisfaction, or if you want to know the ten top thoughts
to consider before choosing a business or product name,
you've come to the right place in Part V. If you need to
know how to write a marketing plan (in a hurry!), or if you
want to know where to turn to for more information as
you implement your marketing plans, you'll find the
answers here.

The marketing world operates on a fast clock. Part V gives
you rapid-fire advice and ten-step solutions for the most
frequent challenges that you're likely to face as a small
business marketer. Here's to your marketing solutions —
and to your marketing success!

Chapter 20

Ten Questions to Ask Before You Choose a Name

• •

In This Chapter

▶ Looking at a name from every angle

▶ Determining whether the name you want is available

• •

*T*he name of your business is the key to your brand image in your customer's mind. Chosen well, your name will unlock an image that is unique, memorable, appropriate, likeable, and capable of advancing a promise for your business. Here are ten questions to ask before committing to a name for a new business or changing the name of an existing business.

What Kind of Name Do You Want?

Most business names fit into one of the following categories:

✔ **The owner's name:** If Jim Smith is opening an accounting company, he can name it Jim Smith Accounting. The name is easy to choose, easy to register, and sure to put forth the promise that Jim Smith is proud of this business and willing to give it his own name. On the downside, the name is hard to pass along if Jim decides he wants to sell his practice.

✔ **A geographic name:** If a new financial institution calls itself Central Coast Bank, the name has local market appeal but it restricts the institution from expanding outside the Central Coast area.

✔ **An alphabet name:** With a name like ABC Paving, you can assure yourself first place in the Yellow Pages — if the name is available. Be aware, however, that the name is generic and doesn't advance a personality or promise.

✔ **A descriptive name:** This type of name tells what you do and how you do it. A consulting firm specializing in business turnarounds might call itself U-Turn Strategies to convey its business offerings and customer promise.

✔ **A borrowed interest name:** This type of name bears no direct relationship to the company or product. Borrowed interest names require an advertising commitment to link the name to a business image. Done right, though, they can work marketing magic, as proven by Apple, Nike, or Infinity.

✔ **A fabricated name:** You can create a name from an acronym, from words or syllables linked to form a new word, or from a letter combination that results in a word with a pleasant sound but no dictionary meaning. A fabricated name is likely to be available and protectable, and because the word doesn't yet exist, the domain name is also likely to be available.

What Do You Want the Name to Convey?

Choose a name that depicts or supports your desired business image and position (see Chapter 7). Attributes you may want your name to convey include service, speed, quality, skill, expertise, convenience, efficiency, creativity, professionalism, and unique knowledge.

Your name should stake a believable claim that you can live up to, but try to avoid words like *quality, creative,* or *premier.* Fair or not, there's an inverse relationship between companies that claim that they're the best and consumers who believe that they are.

Is the Name You Want Available?

The law will stop you from using a name that is too close to an existing business name or trademark. Before you allow yourself to fall in love with a name, see whether it's available. If it is, move quickly to protect it for your use.

✔ **Screen the name.** The Patent and Trademark Depository Libraries (PTDL) have directories of federally registered trademarks and an online database of registered and pending registrations of trademarks. Go to www.uspto.gov to conduct an online search.

✔ **See whether the name is available as a domain name.** Enter the name in the search field of at least three major search engines to see whether the name is already part of a domain name. Or go to www.networksolutions.com and follow the instructions for registering a Web address.

✔ **Protect the name if it's available.** Begin at the business registry division of your secretary of state's office to gain use of the name in your home state. If you also want to trademark the name, contact an attorney who specializes in trademark protection. If you choose to tackle the task yourself, visit the Web site of the U.S. Patent and Trademark Office at www.uspto.gov.

Is It Easy to Spell?

The best names have four to eight letters, look good in writing, and are spelled just like they sound.

Avoid spaces, hyphens, or symbols, aiming instead for straightforward presentations that consumers are almost certain to spell correctly based on guesswork alone. Be aware that names that begin with "The" or "A" are confusing to find in the Yellow Pages. And try to steer clear of clever alternate spellings (for example, "Compleat" for "Complete") unless you have the ad dollars to teach the market how you spell the name.

Is It Easy to Say?

If you show your name to people and ask them to read it, will they pronounce it correctly? Is it phonetically pleasing? Is it a name that works well in normal business conversation?

Imagine a receptionist answering the phone using the name. ("Good morning, this is Greatname Consulting. May I help you?") Be sure that the name is easy to say and sounds good when it is said aloud.

Is It Original?

Look up the name in your local phone book and in the phone book for the biggest city in your state to see how many other companies have sound-alike names. Aim for an original name that stands apart from the pack.

Avoid names tied to local geography, as they tend to get lost in a line-up of similarly named businesses. For example, in a mountainous area, you find names like Mountain View, Mountain Comfort, Mountain Country, Mountain Cycle, Mountain Pine, Mountain Shadow, and dozens of other similar and easy-to-confuse names.

Is It Universal?

The Internet has given every company access to a worldwide market, so think globally as you settle on a business name. Look for a name that has a positive connotation in a range of major languages — and especially in the languages of those you feel may represent future markets for your business.

Is It Memorable?

Look for a name that reflects a distinct aspect of your company.

Businesses named after their founders are easy to remember because they link to the face of the owner, which triggers recollection of the name. Similarly, businesses named after a physical characteristic (Pebble Beach, for example) are memorable because the unique attribute creates such a strong impression. Strong logos that reinforce the name also add to consumer recall of names.

Can You Live and Grow with This Name?

You're going to live with this name a long time, so the most important question of all may be "do you like it?" Ponder this question alone. Names are like ads in that they don't get better as they undergo consideration by a committee. It's your business. Be sure that you like the name, you're comfortable saying it, and you'll be proud repeating it countless times over years to come. And that leads to the next most important question: Will the name adapt to your future? Be careful about names that tie you to a specific geographic area or product offering, and especially be careful about names that include faddish buzzwords that can get stuck in time.

Are You Ready to Commit to the Name?

Once you've settled on a name and determined that people can spell it, say it, remember it, and relate well to it (even in other cultures), you're ready to take these steps:

1. **Register the name in your state, file for a trademark if you choose to, and secure the domain name if you can.**

2. **Create a professional logo to serve as the face of your name.**

3. **Make a list of every place that your name and logo will appear (see the Impression Inventory in Chapter 6) to use as you plan your name introduction.**

4. **Look for new ways to advance your name — on uniforms, golf shirts, vehicle signage, notecards, and other items that increase name awareness.**

If you're changing your name, don't be "two-faced" by trying to use up your old materials while also introducing the new ones. Make a clean break.

Chapter 21

Nine Truths and Ten Tips about Customer Service

In This Chapter

▶ Keeping customers from walking out the door

▶ Finding golden opportunities in customers' complaints

*E*ven in the smallest businesses, customers get lost in the workload shuffle. They are overlooked, treated like intrusions, asked to wait too long, and confronted with rules that send them right out the door. That shouldn't happen — and it *won't* if you understand and apply the basics of customer service outlined in this chapter.

"Services" and "service" are not the same thing

Services are what you provide to customers as part of your product. *Service* is how well you do what you do — how well you deliver what you're providing to the customer. If you have a great refund policy, free shipping, and impeccably clean restrooms, then you have good services. But if the person who explains those services is snapping gum and rolling his eyes, then you have lousy service. Companies renowned for their customer satisfaction levels have great services *and* great service.

Service leads to customer loyalty

Products lead to sales, but service leads to loyalty. Service hooks clients for life. To improve your service, consider the following:

✔ **Create a service guarantee.** Assure customers that promises will be met or exceeded. Make the guarantee straightforward and liberal (no small print), relevant and substantial (worth the effort it takes to request it), available immediately (no management approvals required), and easy to collect.

✔ **Listen for hints of dissatisfaction.** Compensate customers on the spot by offering upgrades, discounts, or premiums when something goes wrong. Don't wait for a complaint. Most people never register dissatisfaction verbally. Instead, they quietly slip out the door once and for all, perhaps politely saying "thanks" as they exit your business for the final time.

✔ **Spend time every quarter brainstorming how to enhance service.** Aim to create a service level that amazes customers and baffles competitors.

Loyal customers are the best customers

Loyal customers are the lowest-cost and highest-volume customers you'll ever find. They reduce the cost side of your profit and loss statement. According to the U.S. Consumer Affairs Department, it costs five times more to get a new customer than it does to retain a customer who is already part of your business. Loyal customers benefit the revenue side of your statement. Customers spend more each year that they deal with your business. They begin by carefully weighing their purchase decisions and then, as they become familiar with your offerings, your services, and — most important — your staff and service, they relax, increase their trust, and buy more.

Are you still looking for reasons to coddle your existing customers? Here's one last carrot: Loyal customers are new business ambassadors, spreading your message and serving as in-person ads for your business.

Indifference sends customers away

In study after study, customers admit that they quit doing business with a company when they become dissatisfied with the way they are treated. When questioned further, they admit that their decision to "fire" a business didn't result from a poor-quality product, high pricing, or blatantly bad service. Rather they felt they were treated with *indifference* that led them to feel that they were unimportant to the business. Fight indifference with an obsession for customer care and service.

Complaints are springboards to customer satisfaction

Use customer complaints to lead your business to service improvements and satisfied customers. Follow these tips:

✔ **Talk with customers.** Listen for direct and indirect complaints along with suggestions for how you can improve your service.

✔ **Encourage complaints.** A complaint handled well leads to loyalty.

✔ **When you receive a complaint, first fix the customer, then fix the problem.** Let the person talk, hear the full story, listen to the degree of disappointment and the level of anger, and then make amends — quickly. Don't make excuses or blame others, and don't simply complete a complaint form. Resolve the issue with a refund, an alternate product, or whatever feels like a fair trade for the customer's inconvenience. Then once the customer is calmed down and out the door, take actions to see that the problem doesn't happen again.

✔ **Treat returned products as nonverbal forms of customer complaint.** If products are coming back, either they're faulty, or your communication was unclear and the product was misrepresented. Similarly, watch what's backlogged as an indicator of unmet consumer demand.

✔ **Encourage customer pickiness.** Businesses that win customers for life create discerning and demanding customers with expectations so high that no other business can rise to the occasion.

Ask and your customers will tell you

Invite customer comments and study them well:

✔ Talk with current customers to learn their opinions, their ideas, and how you could better serve them.

✔ Talk with past customers to learn why they left, where they took their business, and what differences they were seeking.

✔ Ask your employees what kinds of complaints they hear from customers and what kinds of customer needs are not being addressed.

✔ Talk frequently. Create a dialog rather than a one-time survey.

✔ Respond to input promptly.

✔ Show your appreciation. If input leads to change, tell the customer and offer thanks for leading you to important customer service decisions.

There's no such thing as bad customers

There are good customers and non-customers. And among the good customers are transaction customers and relationship customers. *Transaction customers* are interested only in price. They represent sales and generate word-of-mouth for your business, but they'll leave you for a deeper discount in a split, so gauge your efforts accordingly. *Relationship customers* value loyalty and commitment. Recognize them, remember them, do them favors, offer them gifts, bend your rules, anticipate their needs, and win their trust, and they'll become loyal customers for life.

Bad news travels faster than good news

Someone who thinks highly of your company is likely to tell 5 other people, while someone who things poorly of your company is likely to tell 20 other people. Stack the odds in your favor by handling every customer exchange with a view as to how that person will describe the encounter to a friend. Show care, competence, and concern; anticipate and exceed expectations; provide great service; and send each customer away from your business with only good words to share with others.

It takes a great company to make a great customer

If you want satisfied customers, make customer satisfaction a core value of your company. Insist on customer respect and courtesy. Don't air laundry about customer disagreements. Don't bad-mouth your employees, your competition, or your customers — ever. Empower employees to do the right thing for customers. Give rewards to great employees and to great customers. Treat employees and customers like VIPs.

Ten ways to ensure customer satisfaction

If you want satisfied customers, here are some surefire tips:

- ✔ Get to know your customers, recognize them as individuals, and treat them like friends, insiders, and valued partners.
- ✔ Create a team of great service people within your business.
- ✔ Anticipate customer needs.
- ✔ Communicate often.
- ✔ Thank customers for their business.
- ✔ Encourage customer requests and respond with tailor-made solutions.
- ✔ Bend your rules to keep loyal customers happy.
- ✔ Provide extra services and favors to high-volume and long-time customers.
- ✔ Make dealing with your business a highlight of your customer's day.
- ✔ Teach your customers to expect your company's service and keep your standard so high that no other business can rise to the level you set.

Chapter 22

Ten Steps to a Marketing Plan

In This Chapter

▶ Tailoring a plan for a small business

▶ Using the plan to reach your goals

F or some reason, small-business managers think that marketing plans are
for the "big guys." They hear the term "marketing plan," and immediately
they envision a dust-covered tome weighting down a polished bookshelf in a
high-rise corner office. In reality, however, in as few as a handful of pages you
can write a marketing plan for your small business that turns your marketing
into a planned investment rather than a hopeful risk. The following ten steps
tell you how.

Step 1: Stating your business purpose

Start with a one-sentence summary of your business purpose. For example,
the purpose statement for *Small Business Marketing For Dummies* could be
"To empower small businesses and entrepreneurs by providing big-time
marketing advice scaled to fit the clocks, calendars, budgets, and all the
other pressing realities of the small business world."

Step 2: Defining your market situation

In a paragraph or a page, describe the changes, problems, and opportunities
that you will face over the coming marketing plan period. In analyzing your
situation, consider the following factors:

✔ **Your customers:** Are they undergoing changes that will affect their
buying decisions? (See Chapter 2 for help defining your customers and
their needs.)

✔ **Your competition:** Are new businesses competing for your customers'
buying decisions? Are competing companies making new moves that will
make them more threatening to your business? (See Chapter 4 for help
assessing your competitive situation.)

✔ **The market environment:** Do you anticipate economic changes that will affect your business? What about physical changes such as a building renovation that will affect buying patterns, or roadwork that will alter access to your business? If your business is weather-reliant, are forecasts in your favor? Factor these conditions into your situation analysis.

Step 3: Setting goals and objectives

Your marketing plan details the program you will follow to reach your business goal and objectives, so obviously your plan must state your goal and objectives right up front. Your *goal* defines *what* you want your marketing plan to achieve. An example of a goal is "to increase sales by 5 percent to $250,000." Your *objectives* define *how* you will achieve your goal. An example of an objective is "to increase sales by introducing a new product."

Turn to Chapter 5 for help. Once you've set your goal and objectives, plan to stick with them for the duration of the market plan period. Each time that a marketing opportunity arises, ask yourself, "Will this opportunity help us meet our goal? Does this opportunity support one or more of our objectives?" If the answer to either question is "no," quickly pass on the opportunity.

Step 4: Defining your market

Define your target consumer so that you can do the following:

✔ Select marketing tactics that appeal to your prospects.

✔ Make wise media decisions to reach your prospects.

✔ Create advertising messages that appeal to the unique interests and emotions of your prospects.

See Chapter 2 for information on how to collect and use customer information. After you define your market geographically, demographically, and psychographically, you have all the information you need to accept media opportunities with confidence *or* to reject them quickly as inappropriate to your plan.

Step 5: Advancing your position, brand, and creative strategy

Your marketing plan should state your company's position and brand statements, along with the creative strategy you will follow, so that all marketing efforts implemented over the marketing plan period will advance a single, unified image for your company. Here are some definitions to help you with this step:

✔ Your *brand* is the set of characteristics, attributes, and implied promises that people remember and trust to be true about your business.

✔ Your *position* is the available, meaningful niche that your business — and *only* your business — can fill in your target consumer's mind.

✔ Your *creative strategy* is the formula you will follow to uphold your brand and position in all your marketing communications.

See Chapter 7 for information, examples, and step-by-step advice for creating your brand, positioning, and creative strategy statements.

Step 6: Setting your marketing strategies

The next component in your marketing plan details the strategies you will follow, including the following:

✔ **Product strategies:** Will you be introducing new products or revising existing products over the marketing period? See Chapter 3 for information on analyzing your product line, enhancing the appeal of existing products, and developing new products.

✔ **Distribution strategies:** Will you be altering the means by which you get your product to your customer? Chapter 2 includes a section on how to analyze sales by distribution channel, along with advice on how to respond if a distribution channel begins to taper off in volume.

✔ **Pricing strategies:** Are you considering new payment options, a new frequent buyer pricing schedule, quantity discounts, rebates, or other pricing offers? Chapter 3 includes pricing facts to consider, along with advice for building a pricing strategy capable of bringing in new business rather than simply cutting prices on purchases by existing customers — and eroding your bottom line as a result.

✔ **Promotion strategies:** This part of your marketing plan describes how you will support your marketing strategies through advertising and promotions. For example, if your product strategy calls for a new product introduction, your promotion strategy needs to reflect that effort through a new product promotion campaign.

Once your strategies are set, you can spend time implementing an orchestrated and well-planned marketing program rather than frantically reacting to far-flung ideas all year long.

Step 7: Outlining your tactics

The next section of your marketing plan outlines the tactics you will employ to implement your strategies. For example, if one of your strategies is to introduce a new product, the sequence of tactics may look like this:

✔ Review and select an ad agency; develop ad concepts.

✔ Develop direct mailer concept and list.

✔ Develop and price a product brochure.

✔ Develop a publicity plan.

✔ Develop a Web page.

✔ Place ads in industry magazines.

✔ Print and send direct mailer.

✔ Generate industry and local-market publicity.

✔ Train staff.

✔ Unveil product at a special event.

Part III of this book details the marketing tools that you can use in your tactical plan, and Part IV helps you make decisions about whether you need a Web site and online sales capability.

Step 8: Establishing your budget

Next, your plan needs to detail what your marketing program will cost.

Avoid simply pulling out last year's budget and adding 5 percent for inflation. Opt instead for what is called a zero-based budget, which means starting with nothing and adding in all the costs involved to fund your plan. Include costs for ad production, media placements, direct mail costs, Web site design, trade shows fees, display costs, and line items to cover any other tactics included in your plan.

If you think you will need the professional assistance of freelancers or an agency, or if you will require additional staffing to implement your plan, now is the time to incorporate those costs into your budget request. Then add a contingency of up to 10 percent to cover unanticipated costs.

No one ever built a successful business by marketing with leftover dollars. Plan your marketing budget as an integral part of your marketing plan, get it approved as part of the plan, and invest the money wisely.

Step 9: Blueprinting your action plan

This part of your plan brings all of your strategies and tactics together into a single action plan. One easy way to make your blueprint is to prepare an action agenda in calendar form for each month of the year. Simply describe in four columns the action, the budget for that action, the deadline, and the responsible party for each step along the way.

Step 10: Thinking long term

In the final section of your marketing plan, include a targeted list of the market development opportunities you will research over the coming year for possible action in future marketing plan periods. Your expansion analyses might focus on the development of one or several of the following areas:

- ✔ New or expanded business locations to serve more consumers
- ✔ New geographic market areas outside you current market area
- ✔ New customers different than those represented by your current customer profile
- ✔ New products or product packages that will inspire additional purchases
- ✔ New pricing strategies
- ✔ New distribution channels
- ✔ New customer service programs

Choose only one to three opportunities to explore each year and commit to producing an analysis before you develop next year's marketing plan.

One final step: Using your plan

This step is the easiest and the most important. *Use your plan.* Share it with key associates. Use it to provide background to your ad agency. And use it to keep yourself on track as you manage your business to marketing success.

Appendix A

Where to Find More Information

The resources for marketers are infinite. To simplify your search, start with these information-rich Web sites, periodicals, and books.

Small business Web sites

American Express Small Business Exchange: www.americanexpress.com/small business. This site is rich with business advice and information including an area titled "How to write a business plan" that includes detailed market planning information.

Bizadvantage: www.bizadvantage.com. Full of financial and credit data from Dun & Bradstreet along with thousands of powerful business information sources, this site also serves as a great starting point for an initial trademark search.

SCORE: www.score.org. The Web site of the Service Corps of Retired Executives includes an area titled Business Resources where you'll find links to everything from associations to zip codes.

Small Business Administration: www.sba.gov. Visit the SBA's site and click on Marketing for advice and information including links to dozens of useful sites.

SmartBiz: www.smartbiz.com. This aptly and self-proclaimed "supersite" offers free how-to resources and tips. Click on Marketing for surveys and statistics, associations, and links to marketing vendors and suppliers.

Advertising and marketing Web sites

Advertising Media Internet Center: www.amic.com. The site's Ad Talk area includes answers to questions on marketing and media issues. Click on Media Guru for media and Web marketing terms and an explanation of the media planning process.

Advertising World: http://advertising.utexas.edu/world. This University of Texas site features a superb collection of advertising-related links. Find your interest area and access a world of related resources.

The Idea Café: www.ideacafe.com. A site full of ideas for small businesses. Click on Running Your Business to reach an area crammed with tools and tips.

Internet marketing Web sites

Internet World Online: www.internetworld.com. A site full of information and insights for business leaders weighing online marketing decisions.

Microsoft bCentral: www.bcentral.com. Full of tools for small businesses and online marketers, including a banner ad exchange, a search engine submission area, and promotion tools and resources.

Network Solutions: www.networksolutions.com. This site features Web site building advice, e-business resources, and a no-obligation domain name search function.

Search Engine Watch: www.searchenginewatch.com. Visit this site for name submission and Web searching tips, search engine reviews, and online marketing resources.

Wilson Internet Services: www.wilsonweb.com. This site offers online marketing news, an Internet marketing forum, and a Web Marketing Information Center.

The newsstand

American Demographics: www.marketingtools.com. A magazine devoted to tracking consumer trends. The Web site includes a searchable archive and links to data sources.

Business 2.0: www.business2.com. Insights and advice for trekking today's business landscape. For an archive of articles, visit the Web site's marketing channel.

Entrepreneur: www.entrepreneur.com. With business advice for growing companies in print or online.

Fast Company: www.fastcompany.com. Information on recruiting, managing, and fueling your career, with a Web site offering access to the *Fast Company* archives.

Inc.: www.inc.com. "The magazine for growing companies" offers its wealth of information at the newsstand and online.

The Wall Street Journal: http://public.wsj.com. Breaking news, financial news, and marketing news with a Web site, providing links to free resource sites.

Advertising periodicals

Advertising Age: www.adage.com. A weekly magazine covering advertising and industry trends, news, and insights.

AdWeek: www.adweek.com. Weekly news on the advertising community. The Web site includes an article archive and announcements of marketing seminars.

Communication Arts: www.commarts.com. A highly regarded creative resource with top-quality reproductions of advertising and marketing materials.

...For Dummies books

Creating Web Pages For Dummies: Advice for those with no page-building experience, including tips for getting your page online. By Bud Smith and Arthur Bebak. (Hungry Minds, Inc.)

Customer Service For Dummies: This book holds the keys to quality service and success. By Karen Leland and Keith Bailey. (Hungry Minds, Inc.)

Marketing For Dummies: A guide for creating marketing plans for new products and for revitalizing existing plans to address competitive challenges. By Alexander Hiam. (Hungry Minds, Inc.)

Marketing Online For Dummies: Advice for getting domain names, creating Web sites, and competing online. By Bud Smith and Frank Catalano. (Hungry Minds, Inc.)

Sales Closing For Dummies: This book offers hands-on tools to execute the critical part of the sales negotiation — the close. By Tom Hopkins. (Hungry Minds, Inc.)

Sales Prospecting For Dummies: Full of insights about prospecting — the first step of a successful sales effort. By Tom Hopkins. (Hungry Minds, Inc.)

Ten more marketing classics

Guerilla Marketing: Secrets for making big profits from your small business. By Jay Conrad Levinson. (Houghton Mifflin Co.)

How to Win Customers and Keep Them for Life: An action-ready blueprint for achieving the winner's edge. By Michael LeBoeuf. (Berkley Pub Group)

Maxi-Marketing: The new direction in advertising, promotion, and marketing strategy. By Stan Rapp and Tom Collins. (McGraw-Hill, Inc.)

Ogilvy on Advertising: Insights and advice from one of the advertising industry's greatest leaders. By David Ogilvy. (Random House)

Positioning, The Battle for Your Mind: How to be seen and heard in the overcrowded marketplace. By Al Ries and Jack Trout. (McGraw-Hill, Inc.)

Selling the Dream: How to promote your product, company, or ideas — and make a difference — using everyday evangelism. By Guy Kawasaki. (HarperCollins)

Selling the Invisible: A field guide to modern marketing. By Harry Beckwith. (Warner Books, Inc.)

The One-to-One Future: Building relationships one customer at a time. By Don Peppers and Martha Rogers, Ph.D. (Doubleday)

The 22 Immutable Laws of Branding: How to build a product or service into a world-class brand. By Al Ries and Laura Ries. (HarperCollins)

Why We Buy: The science of shopping. By Paco Underhill. (Simon & Schuster)

The library reference area

Bacon's Directories: The *Newspaper/Magazine Directory* lists media descriptions and editorial contacts at American and Canadian newspapers, magazines, newsletters, and news services. The *Radio/TV/Cable Directory* lists U.S. stations.

CACI Market System Group Sourcebooks: Find consumer characteristics in the *Sourcebook of ZIP Code Demographics* and the *Sourcebook of County Demographics.*

Standard Rate and Data Service (SRDS) Sourcebooks: SRDS publishes a *Business Publication Advertising Source, Consumer and Magazine Advertising Source, Newspaper Advertising Source, Out-of-Home Advertising Source, Direct Mail Source, TV and Cable Source, Radio Advertising Source,* and books on interactive and international media. Each features media circulation facts, editorial and advertising contact names, advertising material specifications, and rate information.

SRDS Lifestyle Market Analyst: Demographic and lifestyle data organized by geographic market area, lifestyle preferences, and consumer profiles.

Appendix B

Glossary of Marketing Terms

*F*ollowing is a list of marketing terms used throughout *Small Business Marketing For Dummies.*

advertising: How businesses, organizations, and individuals inform and persuade potential and current customers by using paid announcements carried by such mass media as newspapers, magazines, television and radio stations, and Internet Web sites.

advertising frequency: The number of times that an average person is exposed to an ad.

advertising reach: The number of individuals or homes exposed to an ad.

banner ads: Narrow strips — usually 1—1/2 inches high and 4 inches wide — that can be purchased on Web sites to present advertising messages.

barter: The exchange of merchandise or services rather than monetary payment for advertising time.

brand: What people remember and trust to be true about the values and personality of a business.

broadcast media: Television and radio stations.

collateral: The term for brochures, fliers, sales folders, posters, and other printed items that carry your logo, message, and reputation into the marketplace.

competition: The contest between businesses for customers and sales. The opposite of competition is a *monopoly,* where a single company has complete control of an industry or service offering.

coupon: An offer that a customer can redeem at the time of purchase.

database marketing: Compiling detailed information about customers and prospective customers and then using that information to create and send marketing messages focused on the specific needs of unique consumer groups.

direct mail: A primary means of direct marketing communication that involves sending print ads — in the form of letters, postcards, or packages — directly to targeted prospects.

direct marketing: Communication that is designed to generate a direct exchange between a seller and a buyer without involvement by retailers, agents, or other intermediaries. Direct mail, direct-response advertising, direct sales, database marketing, and telemarketing are all means of direct marketing communication.

direct-response advertising: Ads that invite consumers to take an immediate action — either to make a purchase or to become more involved by requesting additional information.

direct sales: A sales transaction that occurs over distance and directly between the buyer and seller. Mail-order and e-commerce are primary means of direct sales.

display advertising: Print ads that use a combination of space, art, headline, copy, visual elements, and the advertiser's logo in a unique design that aims to draw reader attention and to communicate quickly and clearly.

distribution: The means by which a business gets its product to the end user.

e-commerce site: Online selling using a Web site that allows customers to look at your products, choose what they want, place orders, and submit payment.

e-mail: Short for electronic mail, e-mail is a computer-to-computer communication system.

market saturation: When a business captures the sales of close to a majority of the potential customers within the target market. Usually that figure is pegged at about 40 percent.

market segmentation: Grouping customers into segments that share distinct similarities. Marketers segment by *geographics* (segmenting customers by regions, counties, states, countries, zip code areas, and census tracts), *demographics* (segmenting customers by age, sex, race, religion, education, marital status, income, and household size), and *psychographics* (segmenting customers by lifestyle characteristics).

market share: Your slice of the market pie; your portion of all the sales of products like yours that are taking place in your market area.

marketing: The process through which a business creates — and keeps — customers.

marketing goal: The overall sales or professional target that a marketing program seeks to achieve.

marketing mix: The combination of marketing actions that businesses employ to meet their goals and objectives. The mix includes strategic use of the four marketing functions of product, place, price, and promotion.

marketing objectives: The measurable results that will be necessary to achieve a marketing goal.

marketing strategies: The plan of action for achieving marketing objectives.

marketing's Four Ps: The four marketing functions of product, price, promotion, and place (or distribution).

mass media: Communication vehicles that reach many people simultaneously, including print media (newspapers, magazines, and directories), broadcast media (television and radio), outdoor media (billboards, transit signs, building murals, and signage), and New Media (Internet banner ads, Web casts, Web pages, and interactive media).

new media: Internet banner ads, Web casts, Web pages, and interactive media.

news release: The main tool used in the effort to generate publicity; a document that summarizes the important points of a story appropriate for coverage in the editorial portion of news media. Also called *press release.*

out-of-home ads: Billboards, transit displays, waiting bench signs, wall murals, sports and recreational facility signs, vehicle signage, movie theatre ads, and even flyover signs.

positioning: Figuring out what meaningful and available niche in the market a business is designed to fill and then filling it and performing so well that customers have no reason to allow anyone else into the market position.

print media: Newspapers, magazines, and directories.

promotion: A marketing activity that aims to increase sales over a short period of time by offering an incentive that prompts consumers to take immediate action.

prospect or prospective customer: A person who wants or needs the kinds of products or services you offer, who can easily access your business via a personal visit, phone call, mail contact, or Web site visit, and who is able to make the purchase from you by reason of financial ability or ability to meet any qualifications required to buy or own your product.

public relations: Doing the right thing and then talking about it — using publicity and other nonpaid communication opportunities to inform those whose positive opinions favorably impact your business.

publicity: Unpaid editorial mentions about a business in the mass media.

rebate: An offer that a customer can redeem following the purchase, usually by filling out and sending in a rebate form.

sales: One way that a business communicates its marketing message; the point at which the product is offered, the case is made, the purchasing decision occurs, and the business-to-customer exchange takes place.

specialty media: Items imprinted with an advertiser's name and message.

spot: A broadcast ad term that means 1) the time slot in which an ad runs, 2) the broadcast ad itself, or 3) the television time purchased on specific stations rather than on an entire network.

tag line: The phrase that helps consumers link a business name to a brand message.

target market: The portion of the market that is within the sphere of a business's influence. The *target market* is a portion of the *total* market, which includes all those who might purchase a product like yours in the entire nation or world.

telemarketing: Communicating with prospects and customers over the telephone, either via inbound calls made by consumers to toll-free numbers they see in ads or sales materials or via outbound calls made by a business to the homes or offices of target prospects.

unique selling proposition or **USP:** The compelling proposition that consumers associate only with your business; what draws people to you and distinguishes you from your competition.

Web page: A computer file with its own "address" that is accessible through the World Wide Web.

Web site: A group of related Web pages.

World Wide Web: The vast set of linked documents and computer files including corporate and product information, university course work, personal home pages, political campaign updates, and other online material. The Internet is part of the World Wide Web.

Index

• C •

Notes

WWW.DUMMIES.COM

YOUR ONLINE RESOURCE

Discover Dummies Online!

The Dummies Web Site is your fun and friendly online resource for the latest information about *For Dummies* books and your favorite topics. The Web site is the place to communicate with us, exchange ideas with other *For Dummies* readers, chat with authors, and have fun!

Ten Fun and Useful Things You Can Do at www.dummies.com

1. Win free *For Dummies* books and more!

2. Register your book and be entered in a prize drawing.

3. Meet your favorite authors through the Hungry Minds Author Chat Series.

4. Exchange helpful information with other *For Dummies* readers.

5. Discover other great *For Dummies* books you must have!

6. Purchase Dummieswear exclusively from our Web site.

7. Buy *For Dummies* books online.

8. Talk to us. Make comments, ask questions, get answers!

9. Download free software.

10. Find additional useful resources from authors.

Link directly to these ten fun and useful things at **www.dummies.com/10useful**

For other technology titles from Hungry Minds, go to
www.hungryminds.com

Not on the Web yet? It's easy to get started with *Dummies 101: The Internet For Windows 98* or *The Internet For Dummies* at local retailers everywhere.

Find other *For Dummies* books on these topics:
Business • Career • Databases • Food & Beverage • Games • Gardening
Graphics • Hardware • Health & Fitness • Internet and the World Wide Web
Networking • Office Suites • Operating Systems • Personal Finance • Pets
Programming • Recreation • Sports • Spreadsheets • Teacher Resources
Test Prep • Word Processing

Hungry Minds™

FOR DUMMIES
BOOK REGISTRATION

Register This Book and Win!

We want to hear from you!

Visit **dummies.com** to register this book and tell us how you liked it!

- ✔ Get entered in our monthly prize giveaway.

- ✔ Give us feedback about this book — tell us what you like best, what you like least, or maybe what you'd like to ask the author and us to change!

- ✔ Let us know any other *For Dummies* topics that interest you.

Your feedback helps us determine what books to publish, tells us what coverage to add as we revise our books, and lets us know whether we're meeting your needs as a *For Dummies* reader. You're our most valuable resource, and what you have to say is important to us!

Not on the Web yet? It's easy to get started with *Dummies 101: The Internet For Windows 98* or *The Internet For Dummies* at local retailers everywhere.

Or let us know what you think by sending us a letter at the following address:

For Dummies Book Registration
Dummies Press
10475 Crosspoint Blvd.
Indianapolis, IN 46256

™

BESTSELLING BOOK SERIES

Small Business Marketing For Dummies®

Cheat Sheet

The rules of marketing in 2 minutes flat (continued)

On online marketing: Build a Web site if your prospects, customers, and colleagues want to reach your business online, if you believe that you can appeal to new prospects through an online presence, or if you can provide current customers with improved service and support through the Internet. *(Chapter 17)*

On Web sites: Your Web site is the projection of your brand to online customers. If it is slow to load, if it crashes, if it confuses, or if it looks sloppy, customers will associate those same words with your business. *(Chapter 18)*

On generating online traffic: With more than a billion Web pages online, the chance of a prospect randomly landing at your Internet address is remote at best. You need to lead people to your site. *(Chapter 19)*

On business names: Your name is the key to your brand image in your customer's mind. *(Chapter 20)*

On customer service: *Services* (plural) are what you provide to customers as part of your product. *Service* is how well you do what you do, how well you deliver what you're providing to the customer. *(Chapter 21)*

On marketing plans: The single biggest mistake that small business marketers can make is to market without a plan. *(Chapter 22)*

10 steps to a marketing plan outline

1. State your business purpose. *(Chapter 5)*
2. Summarize your market situation, focusing on issues that will affect your customers (Chapter 2), your product (Chapter 3), and your competition. *(Chapter 4)*
3. Define your goal and objectives. *(Chapter 5)*
4. Define your target markets and customer profile. *(Chapter 2)*
5. Define your position, brand, and creative strategy. *(Chapter 7)*
6. Detail your marketing strategies. *(Chapter 5)*
7. Outline your communication tactics. *(Parts 3 and 4)*
8. State your budget. *(Chapter 1)*
9. Detail your action plan. *(Chapter 22)*
10. Define opportunities for long-term market development. (Chapter 22)

Hungry Minds™

For Dummies™: Bestselling Book Series for Beginners

Small Business Marketing For Dummies®

Cheat Sheet

The rules of marketing in 2 minutes flat

On marketing: Selling is not a substitute for marketing. *(Chapter 1)*

On customers: Customers vote with their billfolds, and the cash register is their ballot box. *(Chapter 2)*

On products: People don't buy *products*. They buy the promises, the hopes, and the satisfactions that they believe the products will deliver. *(Chapter 3)*

On competition: No matter what a business is selling it faces one common competitor with all other businesses — the customer's ability to choose to do or buy nothing. *(Chapter 4)*

On commitment: Dedicate time or money — or both — if you want to market your business from where it is to where you want it to be. *(Chapter 5)*

On communications: If you want people to call your business, help them to understand what you offer, make your phone number legible, and give them a reason to dial it. *(Chapter 6)*

On branding: Consistency builds brands, and brands build business. *(Chapter 7)*

On ad effectiveness: Four out of five consumers read only the headline in a print ad. They absorb no more than seven words from a billboard, and they remember one idea from a broadcast ad. *(Chapters 8 and 11)*

On features vs. benefits: When an ad describes a *feature* of a product or service, the advertiser is talking to himself. When the ad describes a *benefit* that the product or service delivers, the advertiser is talking to the prospect. *(Chapter 8)*

On hiring professionals: "Getting professional help" is an indication of marketing success. It means that a business is willing to invest in the image and message it projects into the marketplace. *(Chapter 9)*

On targeting your message: It doesn't matter how many *people* a business reaches with its advertising; what matters is how many *qualified prospects* receive the message. *(Chapter 10)*

On copywriting: The word "you" is the most magnetic word in advertising. *(Chapter 11)*

On ad scheduling: In creating an advertising schedule remember that it takes *reach* to achieve awareness, but it takes *frequency* to change minds. *(Chapter 12)*

On direct mail: A great direct mail list can outperform a mediocre list many times over, and the definition of a great list is one that reaches genuine prospects for the product or service. *(Chapter 13)*

On sales literature: A brochure is a marketing tool designed to compel prospects to take the next step in the buying process. *(Chapter 14)*

On public relations: If you wait to launch a public relations program until you face an image problem, you have waited too long. Use public relations and publicity to enhance a strong image, not to right a wrong or fix an image disaster. *(Chapter 15)*

On the impact of the Internet: Comparison shopping takes on a whole new meaning because of the Internet. Customers can use advanced tools on the Web to find the best deals regardless of location. *(Chapter 16)*

(continued)

For Dummies™: Bestselling Book Series for Beginners